Medieval Literature on Display

Medieval Literature on Display

Heritage and Culture in Modern Germany

Alexandra Sterling-Hellenbrand

BLOOMSBURY ACADEMIC
LONDON • NEW YORK • OXFORD • NEW DELHI • SYDNEY

BLOOMSBURY ACADEMIC
Bloomsbury Publishing Plc
50 Bedford Square, London, WC1B 3DP, UK
1385 Broadway, New York, NY 10018, USA
29 Earlsfort Terrace, Dublin 2, Ireland

BLOOMSBURY, BLOOMSBURY ACADEMIC and the Diana logo are trademarks of Bloomsbury Publishing Plc

First published in Great Britain 2020
Paperback edition published 2021

Copyright © Alexandra Sterling-Hellenbrand, 2020

Alexandra Sterling-Hellenbrand has asserted her right under the Copyright, Designs and Patents Act, 1988, to be identified as Author of this work.

For legal purposes the Acknowledgments on p. xiii constitute an extension of this copyright page.

Cover design: Terry Woodley
Cover image © Nibelung Museum in Worms. Window in the Hörturm looking toward the cathedral. Photograph by Alexandra Sterling-Hellenbrand.

All rights reserved. No part of this publication may be reproduced or transmitted in any form or by any means, electronic or mechanical, including photocopying, recording, or any information storage or retrieval system, without prior permission in writing from the publishers.

Bloomsbury Publishing Plc does not have any control over, or responsibility for, any third-party websites referred to or in this book. All internet addresses given in this book were correct at the time of going to press. The author and publisher regret any inconvenience caused if addresses have changed or sites have ceased to exist, but can accept no responsibility for any such changes.

A catalogue record for this book is available from the British Library.

ISBN: HB: 978-1-7883-1689-7
 PB: 978-1-3502-4672-0
 ePDF: 978-1-7867-3633-8
 eBook: 978-1-7867-2627-8

Typeset by Integra Software Services Pvt. Ltd.

To find out more about our authors and books visit www.bloomsbury.com and sign up for our newsletters.

Contents

List of Figures	vi
Preface	vii
Acknowledgments	xiii
Introduction Wolframs-Eschenbach: A Statue and a Story	xv
1 Medievalism and Memory	1
2 Adapting Medieval Narratives	33
3 A Knight at the Museum: Medieval Literature and/as Local Heritage at the Museum Wolfram von Eschenbach	67
4 The Machinery of Myth: The Nibelung Museum and the Interrogation of Cultural Memory	103
5 Presencing the Narrative Past: Old Structures, New Stories?	135
6 The Future of the Past: Medieval Literature on Display	157
Notes	173
Bibliography	208
Index	223

Figures

1. The town of Wolframs-Eschenbach, *author's own* — ix
2. Museum Wolfram von Eschenbach Room 1 display "Kann man Literatur Ausstellen?," *author's own* — x
3. The Wolfram Monument in the Central Square of Wolframs-Eschenbach, *author's own* — xvi
4. Nibelung Museum window in the *Hörturm*, *author's own* — 5
5. Images of Ywain at Rodenegg, South Tyrol, *Wikicommons* — 38
6. Museum Wolfram von Eschenbach exterior entrance, *author's own* — 68
7. Museum Wolfram von Eschenbach diagram of museum interior from museum guide, *Museum Wolfram von Eschenbach* — 72
8. Museum Wolfram von Eschenbach Room III: A forest of lances, *author's own* — 81
9. Museum Wolfram von Eschenbach Room VIII: The battlefield of Willehalm, *author's own* — 93
10. Nibelung Museum exterior, *Book of the Anonymous Poet*, pg. 23 — 106
11. Nibelung Museum Sehturm, *Book of the Anonymous Poet*, pg. 24 — 112
12. Nibelung Museum Sehturm collage, *author's own* — 115
13. Nibelung Museum Sehturm collage, *author's own* — 121
14. Nibelung: The thrones of the Hörturm, *author's own* — 126
15. Museum Wolfram von Eschenbach Museum sign visible from the town's central square, *author's own* — 171

Preface

Kann man Literatur ausstellen? [1]

(Museum Wolfram von Eschenbach)

Memory takes root in the concrete, in spaces, gestures, images, and objects ... [2]

(Pierre Nora, "Between Memory and History")

This book started almost thirty years ago with a class field trip and a question. In November of 1992, I was a student at the University of Cologne, participating in a seminar on the reception of Wolfram von Eschenbach's *Parzival* from the Middle Ages to the present. The class was a unique experience in many ways, not least because it involved a weekend excursion by bus to the small Franconian town of Wolframs-Eschenbach. At that time, I had not heard of the town; it was a place I had not yet encountered either in my studies of medieval literature or in my travels through Germany. I remember eagerly anticipating this excursion—to a town named for one of my favorite medieval poets, to his alleged birthplace, to a place where he may have lived and written—it felt like an opportunity for pilgrimage much like the trip to the city of Worms later that year, where I excitedly stood on the steps of the cathedral's north portal and mentally recreated the dramatic quarrel of the queens from the fourteenth adventure of the *Nibelungenlied*. I recall the quaint charm of the area, the immaculately well-kept buildings, the narrow streets, the unusually well-preserved double wall encircling the center of town. Around every corner, one could see how the town paid homage to its (Germany's) medieval literary heritage. We slept on mats in the school gymnasium in the part of town that had Lamper streets named for Hartmann von Aue and Heinrich von Morungen, German medieval poets and contemporaries of Wolfram von Eschenbach. We enjoyed a few glasses of a fine *Minne-Pils* from the now-closed Gentner brewery. As an American student of German medieval literature, I felt exhilarated by the living connections to the Middle Ages, from the actual medieval remnants of the still-extant thirteenth-century city wall to the kitsch of the tall wheat beer glass decorated with a copy of Wolfram's portrait from the Manesse manuscript.

Our seminar instructor had also arranged this visit in Wolframs-Eschenbach for an exciting reason, the more so because it was so unusual: we were there to learn about the town's new museum dedicated to the works of the town's namesake, Wolfram von Eschenbach. We heard from the museum planners about their project, even receiving a brief tour of the work in progress. I have to confess that, even in 1992, I was completely fascinated by the museum's concept: transform the second floor of the old city hall ("Altes Rathaus") into an homage to the works of Wolfram von Eschenbach, display medieval literature as local culture, dedicate a town museum ("Heimatmuseum") to ideas instead of objects, ask a daring question ("Kann man Literatur ausstellen?"), and show the emphatically affirmative response. The plan struck me then as intellectually adventurous and outrageously innovative, not to mention unusual and eccentric, particularly for a small rural town in upper Franconia (Oberfranken). The idea of the museum captivated our imaginations; this was an experience of what our class was calling "Mittelalterrezeption" in action and it sounded, frankly, really cool. Most of us, however, probably left wondering what on earth the result would look like. I certainly did, and the desire to see the final result actually never completely subsided. Unfortunately, the busy minutiae of daily life and career conspired to delay my eventual return for another decade and a half.

From that first visit, I recall that the town of Wolframs-Eschenbach blended beautifully, with its monument and its planned museum, into its natural and cultural landscape. It still does, as my subsequent visits have confirmed (**Figure 1**). The region around Wolframs-Eschenbach, known for tourism and agriculture, literally and figuratively cultivates its history and its land; indeed, a number of local museums throughout the area celebrate various aspects of the collective regional history. In the words of Eric Hansen, an American journalist and enthusiastic admirer of the German Middle Ages, the museum's nine rooms had resurrected Wolfram's mind ("In nur neun Räumen hatte man Wolframs Gehirn auferstehen lassen").[3] It was not until 2008 that I had the opportunity to return again to see how the museum's theoretical concept had taken concrete form; another decade later still, the museum remains as Hansen's idiosyncratic description presents it: nine rooms in which Wolfram seems to live again in the verses and ideas depicted in each. The museum itself will be the subject of Chapter 3.

It was the central question of the museum (Can literature be displayed?) and its creative answer that took root to become the starting point for *Medieval Literature on Display*. The question is perhaps not unique; there are other museums in Germany (and not only there) that attempt to display literature and the literary. We will have occasion to visit several of these in more detail in Chapter 2. Nevertheless, an anomaly awaits in the museum behind the half-timbered walls of the old city hall in Wolframs-Eschenbach. And it is the nature

Figure 1 The town of Wolframs-Eschenbach, *author's own*.

of this anomaly that *Medieval Literature on Display* takes as its focus. In essence, the central concern of the book is the resounding "yes" that the Museum Wolfram von Eschenbach answers to the question it poses: Can literature be displayed? (**Figure 2**). Of course, it can. The ways in which medieval literature is put on display, I will argue in this book, reveal the role of medievalism in the practice of cultural memory, the creation of heritage, and the exploration of community identity. The book focuses on two case studies from the turn of the twentieth century in the time immediately following the reunification of Germany in 1990. Both case studies involve the design and construction of German museums dedicated to medieval literature: the first is the already-mentioned Museum Wolfram von Eschenbach in Wolframs-Eschenbach (1995); the second is the Nibelung Museum in Worms (2001). Largely unknown to wider audiences outside of their geographic regions, these museums deserve greater attention. They reveal how memory, through the lens of the Middle Ages, creatively shapes modern cultural identity and heritage. In the absence of historical or archaeological artifacts, the museums visualize and interpret literature in exhibits that emerge from a complicated nexus of accumulated intertexts. As they reconstruct and transform medieval narratives for the

Figure 2 Museum Wolfram von Eschenbach Room 1 display "Kann man Literatur Ausstellen?," *author's own*.

contemporary audience, the museums offer a thought-provoking response to the question of how literature—regardless of national origin and period—can assert its relevance for modern communities.

Not only did the communities make considerable investments of time and effort and capital to build the museums. A look at their current tourist information reveals how both the communities of Worms and Wolframs-Eschenbach continue to promote the museums as integral parts of their cultural landscape, as part of their local history, as an expression of the past that they wish to remember and represent—for visitors and for themselves. In their display and interpretation of medieval literature for modern audiences, the museums offer unique examples of ways in which the older narratives have shaped memory, which, in its turn through the lens of the Middle Ages, shapes contemporary cultural identity and local history. The museums show, in the words of Pierre Nora, how memory "takes root in the concrete" through unique images and newly designed spaces; despite a lack of objects, the museums strive to make literature and ideas concrete, attempting to situate themselves with respect to the "temporal continuities" and "progressions" characteristic of history.[4] Indeed, the museums become a new link in the relations between literature and history, between the Middle Ages and the present, between each community and its visitors. They have become part of what Macdonald has described as the "memorylands" of Europe, where "land- and city-scapes have filled up with the products of collective memory work" such as heritage sites, museums, plaques, and art installations "designed to remind us of histories that might otherwise be lost" and "recuperate fading or near-forgotten pasts."[5] The work of memory has only increased since 1989 and the dramatic changes in Europe since the reunification of Germany and the collapse of the former Soviet Union. The museums in *Medieval Literature on Display* position medieval literature at vibrant intersections of memory, heritage, and history for their respective communities, making the past continually present and relevant.

This book also sits at what I hope is an equally vibrant intersection. Before we go any further, however, I must confess that I realize it is probably much easier to describe what this book is not. It is not a book on museum studies, though it does focus on two museums, nor on literary museums, per se—though the two museums at the book's center put literature on display. It is not a book on heritage studies, though it does examine these museums as examples of heritage-making in two German communities. It is not quite a book on reception history of medieval German literature, though reception plays a key role in how the literature is adapted over time. It is not quite a book on medieval studies, not at least as I learned the tools of what I might consider the traditional discipline in the 1990s. This book does occupy an interface where it draws from all of these areas in order to examine two German museums that express the aspirations of their respective municipalities in the display of medieval texts with particular significance for each community. Each museum is unique, as is each community. The museums are similar, however, in their display of medieval literature as part of the communal past that shapes the present toward the future. This book is about giving literature and ideas tangible form, about making the past present, about connecting the medieval to the contemporary.

Like the museums it explores, this book is, I believe, an example of medievalism at work.

Acknowledgments

The preface tells the story of how this book got started. The museums I discuss here captured my imagination because of the way they configure medieval narratives for the contemporary audience. They offer a response to the question of how enduring stories assert their relevance for modern communities. I believe that this is the mission of literature, language, and the humanities; it is my mission, too. And it is a mission that one does not accomplish single-handed.

Time and funding are essential to a project like this, especially one that needed to be managed around sundry administrative duties. Several University Research Council grants from Appalachian State University in 2008 and 2016, as well as two sabbatical leaves in 2011 and 2018, supported the research for *Medieval Literature on Display*. As the lone German medievalist at Appalachian, I value my interactions with colleagues in medieval German studies, whether yearly at the ICMS in Kalamazoo or at other conference venues. My fellow Germanists from both sides of the Atlantic have patiently listened to various presentations on this research and have given insightful yet gracious feedback, though I am sure everyone will be happy to hear me talk about something else at the next conference. I owe Ann Marie Rasmussen a particular debt of thanks for a conversation in 2015 that changed the course of the project, as she prompted me to extricate the topic of heritage and culture from an otherwise sprawling text. The debt I owe to Frank Gentry is even more evident now that the project has reached completion; when I was a young grad student in Madison, I could not imagine how much of my own work would intersect with his in the ways that the following pages clearly show. It is to him I owe the experience of that long-ago Madison concert by Eberhard Kummer that I have never forgotten and that struck (pun intended) such a deep resonant chord in my medievalist consciousness. Without Frank's belief in my abilities, I would not have ended up at Appalachian, a place where I have enjoyed many opportunities to continue doing what I love.

This project has taken a winding road to completion, benefiting from many conversations with colleagues, students, and family members; a single "thank-you" is only the proverbial tip of the iceberg. I do, however, wish to express my gratitude to those without whom I absolutely could not have reached this point. The staff and editors at I.B. Tauris and Bloomsbury have been patient, helpful, and supportive throughout the publication process. I greatly appreciate the insights of the anonymous reviewers, whose thoughtful questions and comments challenged me to make the manuscript stronger and the book, I hope, even better. When this project first began to take shape, I was a young assistant professor of German at Goshen College. In the eight years that we worked together, Judith M. Davis was my department chair and colleague in French. Judith modeled for me how to cultivate scholarship and an intellectual life as a medievalist while managing the hectic daily schedule of a career in teaching and administration. I am grateful for her wise and generous mentoring over the years since she hired me in my first position at Goshen College, and I am beyond grateful for the gift of our friendship. My family has anchored my work. Sons Ryan and Matthew patiently endured, sometimes motivated by extra Gummibärchen or the promise of an ice cream cone, many visits to odd little museums in small towns that were not on the standard travel itinerary of any of the other kids in their class. And Jack—patient listener, meticulous editor, finder of chronically misplaced books—has lived with this project ever since we took that seminar in Cologne together over thirty years ago. Thank you for being my adventure partner on our version of a hobbit's journey, ever going there and back again … again and again. This book is for you.

Introduction Wolframs-Eschenbach: A Statue and a Story

There he stood, Wolfram, crowned with laurels, at his side a sheathed sword and at his feet swans spewing water. Oh, how the Romantics loved their poets![1]
(Eric Hansen, Die Nibelungenreise)

Ghosts, monuments, and old furniture are some of the many means by which the past may inhabit the present—and the future—or perhaps that a continuous past may embrace present and future.[2]
(Sharon Macdonald, Memorylands)

Wir sind es, die einen Anlaß, einen Ort, einen Zeitpunkt, nötig haben, um Lebenszeichen zu geben—nicht nur solche, der Gewohnheit und angeblichen Tradition, sondern der Festlichkeit und unserer Befähigung zum Gedächtnis an das ganz Andere, an uns selbst.[3]
(Adolf Muschg, Rede für Wolframs-Eschenbach)

In 1917, the Franconian town of Obereschenbach received permission from Ludwig III of Bavaria to call itself "Wolframs-Eschenbach." The new name refers proudly to the town's alleged native son, the early-thirteenth-century Minnesänger Wolfram von Eschenbach, who is memorialized by a statue of the poet erected in 1861 in the town's main square. In the final chapter of his *Nibelungenreise*, Eric Hansen describes his first impressions of Wolframs-Eschenbach upon his arrival there:

> My first impression of Wolfram's hometown: quite a long way from the highway.
> I drove on endless winding country roads, passing by neatly kept fields and lonely farms with old sunken roofs. On the horizon there was a green patch: the dark, eerie Mönchswald. Finally, the street narrowed to one lane and ducked under a medieval city gate.
> A cobblestone street led beyond the gate rising on a slight incline, going by ordinary two-story houses that were painted yellow, green, orange and brown, and opened onto a square in the middle of the little town.
> There he stood, Wolfram, crowned with laurels, at his side a sheathed sword and at his feet swans spewing water. Oh, how the Romantics loved their poets!

Colorful banners fluttered in the sunshine. All of the important city buildings faced toward the monument, as though paying homage: the old city hall, the new city hall, the old governor's residence, the church, the café, the hairdresser[4] (**Figure 3**).

Figure 3 The Wolfram Monument in the Central Square of Wolframs-Eschenbach, *author's own.*

Time seems to have stood still. When one enters the town from the south gate, one can literally still see exactly what Hansen describes, following the cobblestone street through the gate up the slight incline and coming to the small square to stop in front of the monument. Over the years, shops may come and go. On one of my visits, the hair salon had disappeared or at least changed locations; the banners remain, and the Café Parzival invites visitors to linger over afternoon coffee and cake. Like the café, the other "important city buildings" still frame the square with the monument at its center; flanked by brightly colored banners that show the German and Bavarian flags as well as the city's own logo in green and white,[5] the statue of Wolfram faces both the new city hall as well as the old city hall. The latter has housed the Museum Wolfram von Eschenbach since 1995. Behind the two city halls, we find the church of Our Lady (the "Liebfrauenmünster"), the supposed location of Wolfram's tomb.

The modern town of Wolframs-Eschenbach proudly capitalizes on its name today, identifying itself in promotional materials as *Stadt des Parzivaldichters* ("city of the Parzival poet").[6] At the end of the 1980s, the city of Wolframs-Eschenbach wanted to upgrade the city museum in the old city hall building. The city had a chance to consider who it was—how it wanted to present itself to the public, to the region, to visitors. What did it want to show the world? A statue of Wolfram von Eschenbach stands directly across from the Rathaus. It was logical to consider a connection of the new city museum to the town's most famous son. What could one do? In fact, a team was assembled (supported by funds from the city and the state) to take up this very question. The museum could have resembled more traditional museums of local history and culture, the type known in German as a "Heimatmuseum"; however, the leadership in Wolframs-Eschenbach took another path entirely. Rejecting more traditional approaches, the Museum Wolfram von Eschenbach attempts to engage its visitors with a twofold question: Can one exhibit not just literature in general but the literature of the Middle Ages (represented by the town's namesake Wolfram von Eschenbach)? In its response to this question, the museum in Wolframs-Eschenbach offers a sophisticated presentation of literature and history that effectively integrates the town itself into its display. Opening in 1995, the museum envisions the thirteenth-century Wolfram von Eschenbach and his texts as part of the modern narrative of Wolframs-Eschenbach on the cusp of the twenty-first century.

The community of Wolframs-Eschenbach, as we will see with the community of Worms in our second case study, uses medievalism now in the contemporary task of making the past present through their displays of German medieval literature as heritage. The case studies show the museums as creative attempts to make the Middle Ages relevant, even profitable, for local municipalities. By way of a methodological introduction, I want to return briefly to the Wolfram monument in Hansen's effusive description quoted earlier. I would like to use the statue and the monument as a model to demonstrate how *Medieval Literature on Display* will treat medievalism. The monument is, first of all, an elegant piece of nineteenth-century neo-medieval sculpture. As it depicts the town's native son, the poet Wolfram von Eschenbach, the statue makes a clear statement about the town's past and its pride in that past. The statue also encapsulates the central argument of *Medieval Literature on Display*: in the words of Sharon Macdonald, the monument shows how the past of this small town inhabits its present in addition to providing a kind of bridge to connect with a "continuous" past that may hopefully "embrace present and future."[7] In this way the monument offers a good starting point for the discussion of medieval literature on display that the museums will continue in greater detail. The statue represents the poet Wolfram von Eschenbach, evidence of whose life can be found only in his thirteenth-century works, portrayed in yet another fictional incarnation as the troubadour knight, extracted from those narratives to be made physically permanent in the square of the town that would later take his name as its own. Wolfram, cast in stone, steps out of his thirteenth-century stories through nineteenth-century Romantic memory into the town's present, becoming a tangible object and a real focus, around which the town can create itself. I will situate the monument historically as well as in the landscape of the town and the region. Then, we will focus on the Wolfram monument as an intertextual palimpsest, whose layers reveal dynamic intersections of literature and history and heritage. A reading of the monument as palimpsest illuminates not only the history of Wolframs-Eschenbach but also the perception the town has of its literary past. Finally, the monument demonstrates the way in which the town shapes that literary past as heritage and then further molds that literary past to create and promote its local and regional identity in the present.

The monument

Geographically, Wolframs-Eschenbach lies just north of what is known as the Franconian lake district ("Fränkisches Seenland"), where a number of artificial lakes offer excellent venues for outdoor recreation. About fifteen kilometers to the northwest is the county seat of Ansbach; approximately forty kilometers to the north and east, one finds Nuremberg; if one drives thirty kilometers to the west, one finds oneself, at least in the summer, among the thousands of tourists from all over the world who have flocked to Rothenburg ob der Tauber. The countryside offers an idyllic landscape, consisting of gently rolling farmland, punctuated by church steeples rising from walled medieval towns and crisscrossed by bicycle paths; the darker clusters of trees, which Hansen describes as eerie, are offset now at intervals by newer clusters of wind turbines. The town of Wolframs-Eschenbach, still encircled by its imposing double wall, is filled with picturesque half-timbered and brightly painted houses, decorated with flower boxes of red and pink geraniums; the buildings, many of which date back to the fifteenth and sixteenth centuries, have been immaculately and beautifully maintained. The church's steeple is its landmark, displaying vividly colored mosaic with the city's emblems: a harp, a jug, the headpiece from Wolfram's portrait in the fourteenth-century Manesse manuscript.

Designed by Eduard von Riedel, the later architect of Neuschwanstein, the monument is a fountain in a neo-Romanesque style; out of the basin rises a square pedestal upon which a likeness of the town's native son stands. This is the Wolfram of Hansen's description, standing triumphant in his poet's glory. His right hand rests on his harp as it leans against his knee, his left hand on the hilt of his sheathed sword; crowned with a laurel wreath, the poet is elegantly yet simply robed, depicted just as the nineteenth-century sculptor imagined him as victor in the song contest at the Wartburg Castle. This would have been the song contest perhaps best known to the audience of the monument.[8] The four swans still perch at his feet, one on each corner of the pedestal.

From his elevated vantage point, the poet surveys his domain, the central square of Wolframs-Eschenbach, his gaze directed toward the church and the town hall, both the old and the new. The side of the pedestal that faces the church displays this quotation from Wolfram's *Parzival*:

> Vom Wasser kommt der Bäume Saft,
> Befruchtend gibt das Wasser Kraft
> Aller Creatur der Welt.
> Vom Wasser wird das Aug' erhellt.
> Wasser wäscht manche Seele rein,
> Daß kein Engel mag lichter sein. (aus *Parzival*)[9]

The text is positioned on the side of the pedestal corresponding to the direction the statue faces. A laurel wreath is centered above the text, and beneath the text, we find the date of completion and the name of the patron, Bavarian king Maximilian II. The text appears as we see it, indicating where the verses come from, namely *Parzival*, but with no other identifying information.[10] The finished monument was dedicated and celebrated with great pomp on May 1, 1861. It remains unchanged today, though it did undergo renovation in the late 1980s to replace the two swan figures that had disappeared during the Second World War. The monument itself, its story, and its role in the town's history are all important for understanding how medievalism works in this book. We have to understand the significance of the monument in context. That is why we will take a short detour for a moment to look briefly at the history of Wolframs-Eschenbach and at the town's relationship with the poet Wolfram von Eschenbach. The history of the town and the story of its native son converge in the monument at a time in the nineteenth century when the reputations of both, town and poet, become matters of regional pride. The monument sits at a busy intersection of cultural, literary, and political associations—drawing them together into a purposeful statement of identity, rich in history, resonant with heritage.

The town

Erwin Seitz, son of former mayor Anton Seitz, and town historian Oskar Geidner recount the town's story in *Wolframs-Eschenbach. Der Deutsche Orden baut eine Stadt*.[11] Earliest sources, dating from around 800, show the establishment of several monasteries in the area, notably in Ansbach, a town currently located approximately ten kilometers from Wolframs-Eschenbach. Evidence suggests that Eschenbach was one of the stations on the well-trafficked trade route between Strasbourg and Nuremberg in the High Middle Ages. The Teutonic Order (*Deutscher Orden*) also began to establish a foothold in Eschenbach in the early thirteenth century around 1220, when the local count, Boppo of Wertheim, handed over the patronage of church in Eschenbach to the Order. Eschenbach also had a desirable physical location on a hill, as well as a favorable commercial situation on the trade route from Nuremberg to Dinkelsbühl. By 1332, the Order was able to establish its administrative authority more permanently, as it sought and received from Emperor Ludwig IV a city charter for Eschenbach. The new city of Eschenbach subsequently became a kind of showpiece ("Prestigeobjekt") for the Order in Franconia; the Order had an opportunity to show what it was capable of. Indeed, the city's imposing double wall indicates its prominence and its importance as a fortification. As long as the Order thrived, the city thrived as well, at least relatively speaking. After the wars with Napoleon, Eschenbach and the rest of Franconia were ceded to the kingdom of Bavaria. The citizens of Eschenbach swore their oaths of loyalty to the king of Bavaria in July 1806, and Bavaria subsequently secularized the Order. The act of secularization seems to have directly contributed to its decline, and then three years later, Napoleon dissolved the Teutonic Order entirely. Eschenbach faded into relative obscurity as a result. In a short span of time, the town of Eschenbach went from being a proud Franconian *Ordensstadt* to just another one of many charming little Bavarian provincial towns.[12]

The town's poet

Perhaps most significantly for our purposes, Eschenbach became known over time as Wolfram's self-identified home. Like many of his medieval contemporaries, Wolfram was not named in any extraliterary sources, such as chronicles or histories or deeds. Any surviving details of his life come, in circular fashion, from autobiographical references in his own texts; even the dates we can establish for Wolfram, that he was active between 1200 and 1220, come only from his narratives. The scope of his reputation can be gleaned from the mention made by his contemporaries of his work, whether meant in praise or in criticism, like Gottfried von Strassburg's disparaging remarks about Wolfram's seemingly haphazard narrative style, which seems to dart like a hare across a field. We will return to the hare metaphor, and address Wolfram's self-referential autobiography in more detail in Chapter 3, since the museum dedicates an entire room/exhibit to the latter.

The lack of Wolfram's actual verifiable biography did not prevent the town, however, from capitalizing on it, either in the statue or in the name of the town. Despite the fact that Wolfram's birthplace was (and remains) disputed, and despite Wolfram's own insistence on his place of origin, the residents of the area held firmly to the belief that Wolfram had lived and was buried in Eschenbach.[13] In fact, local pride seems to have driven the competition of several towns in the early nineteenth century to claim the name of Eschenbach.[14] In the nineteenth century, it was Maximilian II who ultimately decided in favor of the Eschenbach near Ansbach; he decreed that the city of Obereschenbach should be able to call itself Wolfram's home. The town later acquired its present name on the basis of persuasive arguments offered by local scholar Johann Kurz, who presented a dissertation to the University of Erlangen in 1916 on Wolfram's home and family entitled "Heimat und Geschlecht Wolframs von Eschenbach."[15] On the basis of Kurz's research, the town received permission in 1917 from Ludwig III of Bavaria to call itself "Wolframs-Eschenbach."

We are coming back around to the monument again. While his works demonstrated steady popularity throughout the Middle Ages and the early modern era, Wolfram von Eschenbach was not a poet with local or regional reputation until the late eighteenth century. The process to become the official city of Wolfram von Eschenbach began, according to Seitz and Geidner, with the general rediscovery and subsequent new appreciation of German medieval texts after 1750. The turn of the nineteenth century saw the rise of philology, an increasing interest in older German literature, which in turn strengthened emerging German national sentiments.[16] Enthusiasm for older literature combined with nascent national sentiment to feed a developing consciousness of a German literary history that provides a firm foundation for a new nation. In the case of Wolfram, a number of local and regional initiatives sought to elevate Wolfram's standing as a poet of national importance for German literature.[17] An early essay in 1837 by one Andreas Schmöller seemed to offer definitive arguments for establishing Eschenbach as Wolfram's birthplace and home.[18] Twenty years later, Maximilian II of Bavaria participated in the dedication of the Goethe-Schiller monument at the national theater in Weimar in 1857. In the same year, Maximilian II also authorized a commission that would begin the process leading to the eventual construction of a Wolfram monument in Eschenbach. His commission of the Wolfram monument seems to reflect a desire to raise the profile of the medieval poet to the level of Goethe and Schiller on the national scene.[19] Regional literary politics undoubtedly also play a role here; the Wolfram commission was done in tandem with one for the Walther statue in Würzburg in a commission from 1857. As Franconia had recently come to Bavaria, the Bavarian court would logically seek further legitimation in Franconia through a strategy of literary politics, as it were, by honoring "local" poets. Celebrating Walther von der Vogelweide and Wolfram von Eschenbach, for example, would perhaps demonstrate the medieval roots of the long-established literary tradition in Franconia in contrast to the comparatively much more recent Goethe and Schiller, icons though they were. As Seitz and Geidner observe, Maximilian II achieved two goals with the dedication. First, Eschenbach gained overnight fame as a city with literary-cultural significance (a city of poets/"eine Dichterstadt"). Second, the festivities supported Bavarian regional unity, as the state of Bavaria could claim as its own the patriotism of the Franconian natives shown for their hometown poet.[20] The statue gave shape to the proud memory of a distant medieval past fueled by a nineteenth-century patriotic nostalgia that led to the celebration of that past in the present. Wolfram's growing reputation supported the hopes of a town that had been watching its once-high profile diminish.

Tangled narratives

As it honors the town's alleged native son, the Wolfram monument resonates with entangled narratives while also asserting posterity's claims through Wolfram von Eschenbach to "his" town. Located at a temporal as well as a spatial intersection, it is an object, in the words of Mikhail Bakhtin, that is "overlain with qualifications" and "charged with value" by multiple intersecting narratives over time.[21] They have become "entangled" with resonances of cultural memory. Over time, narratives participate in complex interrelationships that shape not only discourse but memory, leaving, as Bakhtin writes, a trace in narrative layers or complicating and enhancing its expression. These resonances accumulate to form multilayered palimpsests over time, as Linda Hutcheon describes the process of adaptation in *A Theory of Adaptation*.[22] Audiences experience adaptations as palimpsests, whose layers of text are perceptible through the memory of other works that resonate through repetition and variation. The text on the monument's base addresses two of those narratives generally: the narrative of Wolfram's *Parzival* and the narrative of the nineteenth-century German Romantic fascination with medieval literature. The palimpsest consists of multiple layers, however. We can see here how it works on at least two levels. Level one involves the nineteenth-century vision of Wolfram with harp and sword. This Wolfram has emerged victorious from the famous song contest (*Sängerkrieg*) that allegedly took place at the Wartburg castle, where Wolfram competed with Heinrich von Ofterdingen and Walther von der Vogelweide before the Landgrave of Thuringia. The story of the song contest captivated the imaginations of German Romantic writers and composers in the nineteenth century: works by authors such E.T.A. Hoffmann (*Der Krieg der Sänger*, 1818) and Friedrich de la Motte Fouqué (*Der Krieg der Sänger auf der Wartburg*, 1828); Richard Wagner's opera *Tannhäuser* (first version 1845) and the mural of Moritz von Schwind at the Wartburg Castle itself (1855). Indeed, the statue of Wolfram appears perhaps ready to step onto the stage of Wagner's *Tannhäuser*, and perhaps we hear the first gentle chords of the baritone aria "An den Abendstern" ("To the Evening Star") from the opera's third act, sung by that Wolfram as he expresses his unrequited love for Elisabeth. In addition, to stretch the musical metaphor a bit further, the Wagnerian overtones also include visual echoes of *Lohengrin*. The four swans found at the monument's corners allude to Parzival's son Lohengrin, the swan knight of Wagner's opera whose story is briefly told at the conclusion of Wolfram's poem.[23] If the first level of the palimpsest layers involves the intertextuality of nineteenth-century imagery, the second level brings us back to the written word. The lines of verse on the base of the statue point to yet another layer of intertexts, connecting the figure explicitly not only with the written word but also with Wolfram's own words, albeit in modern German translation. The passage comes, in fact, from book XVI of Wolfram's *Parzival*:

> von wazzer boume sint gesaft.
> wazzer fruht al die geschaft,
> der man für creatiure giht.
> mit dem wazzer man gesiht.
> wazzer gît manege sêle schîn,
> daz die engl niht lihter dorsten sîn.[24] (817, 25–30)

These are the words of the priest to Parzival's speckled heathen brother Feirefiz near the end of the narrative. Feirefiz and Parzival have dueled, recognized one another, and reconciled. Shortly thereafter, Feirefiz agrees to be baptized because of his intense love for, and desire to be married to, Parzival's aunt Repanse de Schoye, the Grail bearer. In Wolfram's narrative, then, the water that nourishes Creation ("saps trees" and "fruits all creatures") is the water that saves the soul of the heathen, so that he too may "have sight" as well as a soul with "such sheen that angels need be no brighter." The salvific effects of this water should extend also to the onlookers at the monument's dedication in 1861. For them, centuries removed from the events of Wolfram's tale, the water is not only that of the fountain, sapping trees and quenching human thirst, or that of Feirefiz's baptism, giving spiritual sight; it is also the literary water that figuratively nourishes their cultural (German) soul at the alleged source of Wolfram's own being. The modern German translation of Middle High German verse further recalls the nineteenth-century rediscovery and critical study of older German texts that made essential contributions to the development of disciplines such as linguistics and medieval studies through the editorial work of Karl Lachmann, Karl Simrock, and others. Finally, the statue's gaze is turned toward the Altes Rathaus containing the museum that opened there in 1995. Resonating with entangled narratives from the thirteenth through the twentieth centuries, the monument offers an excellent example of palimpsestic intertextuality.

Presencing the literary past (or literature as artifact)

The multiple intertexts, which coexist palimpsest-like, draw the literary past into the present of the onlooker. Swiss author Adolf Muschg hints at the shape of the analysis we need to do it. Author of the 1993 novel *Der rote Ritter* (*The Red Knight*), an expansive adaptation of Wolfram's *Parzival*, Muschg was invited to speak at the opening of the Museum Wolfram von Eschenbach in January 1995. While Muschg concentrates on the museum in his remarks, his words apply in microcosm to the monument as well when he addresses the need for memory and commemoration. Muschg begins by giving the audience a central role, emphasizing the inclusive "we" to show that he is part of that audience as well: of visitors to the museum and other tourists but also of town residents. He could be speaking for a broader audience as well; his "we" potentially resonates on a spectrum from the local to the global. It is we, he says, who experience a communal need; we seek, we require, a reason or a focal point to remember together. We need an occasion, says Muschg, but we also need a place and a time to recall these signs of life. We want to see these signs of life—from the past, so that we feel the past alive in front of us and within us perhaps. We live as descendants of that past, whose relics or remnants or mementos we see before us. Muschg exhorts us, however, not only to look back on when we have these commemorative occasions, not only to look back to custom or to what we believe is tradition. We should also look forward, heeding the signs of life that we crave and that also give us cause for celebration and serve as a memory aid. These signs bring us to new knowledge of the "Other" (that which is entirely different, in the formulation that Muschg uses) and by extension bringing us once again to ourselves—renewed, anew.

Muschg speaks about the museum, and we will return to his comments in more detail shortly. In the Wolfram monument, too, we find that the historical past and the literary past merge into a story that, celebrated as communal memory, is eventually immortalized as heritage in the Wolfram monument. In this context, I draw heavily on the work of British anthropologist and museum scholar Sharon Macdonald. Macdonald's research focuses on what she describes as the European memory complex, a topic she adroitly explicates in her 2013 monograph *Memorylands: Heritage and Identity in Europe Today*: the wide spectrum of ways in which that memory complex manifests itself in the contemporary cultural landscape: seeing, telling, feeling, showing the past. Macdonald coins the term "past presencing" to describe an "on-going process in which the past is continually reconfigured in a changing present."[25] In her work on memory and commemorative practice in modern Europe, Macdonald uses the term "past presencing" to describe the "ways in which people variously draw on, experience, negotiate, reconstruct, and perform the past in their ongoing lives." Not only do people "grasp and articulate the past" in various ways; these "multiple forms" of articulation also enable us to recall various pasts "selectively," to use those pasts "within the present" where they are variously "performed and lived." This process includes the present and the future as well as "questions of temporality more widely"— all are "almost invariably bound up in the presencing of the past."[26] In her work, Macdonald deals primarily with the memorialization and musealization of Europe's twentieth-century past. As she makes clear, however, the past materializes and is made to materialize variously in buildings, places, people, and things at any given time. Thus, the Wolfram monument firmly anchors the literary past in pavement of the town square; the imagined and revered poet Wolfram becomes a fixture of the contemporary landscape. The monument to Wolfram von Eschenbach, positioned in the central square of a small but proud Franconian town across the street from a museum that celebrates medieval literature, demonstrates how the intertexts that intersect in this statue form a kind of arc over time. The monument firmly and literally locates viewers/visitors in a concrete space with the actual objects and real images that are needed to anchor reflection in experience.

Muschg addresses this need in his speech as well, when he talks about how visitors to, and residents of, Wolframs-Eschenbach ("we") seek a reason, a place, and a time for the living to celebrate, to remember, to reflect. Muschg posits that it is a matter of our continued existence, our understanding of ourselves, that motivates us to create real and imaginative spaces for remembering our own selves and for remembering the other ("das ganz Andere"). The town of Wolframs-Eschenbach must necessarily have a different relationship to the poet it wishes to celebrate from, for example, the town of Weimar to Goethe or the town of Bayreuth to Richard Wagner. Places like Goethe's residence on the Frauenplan or Wagner's Wahnfried, says Muschg, serve as treasuries of memory that store traces of their famous inhabitants; indeed, sometimes these places appear carefully and self-consciously constructed around the lives of their famous occupants and are subsequently inherited by later generations as a kind of text. The town of Wolframs-Eschenbach can never pinpoint Wolfram's birthplace or his residence. The museum, for example, has no medieval artifacts—no objects or manuscripts—to exhibit. Volker Gallé, chair of the Nibelungen-Gesellschaft in Worms, makes a similar comment about the Nibelung Museum almost twenty years later.

Just as the town of Wolframs-Eschenbach claimed the works and ideas of Wolfram von Eschenbach as its cultural heritage, the city of Worms made a similar claim with respect to the *Nibelungenlied*. The *Nibelungenlied* itself also gives this process a place. In typical epic fashion, the narrative anchors its story in a familiar geography

> Ze Wormeze bî dem Rine si wonten mit ir kraft.
> in diente von ir landen vil stolziu ritterschaft
> mit lobelichen êren unz an ir endes zît.
> si ersturben sît jæmerliche von zweier edelen frouwen nît. (v. 4)

> They resided with their armies in Worms by the Rhine. Many proud knights from their lands served them with honor and renown until their end came. They afterwards died wretchedly because of two noble ladies' enmity.[27]

The Nibelung legend, of course, has its roots in various historical circumstances that play out in this geographic area. The city provides a geographical anchor for the events of the narrative, at least in the first part.[28] Worms becomes a fixed point not only as the center of the Burgundian kingdom, the home of Kriemhild's family, the place from which people leave and to which they return but also as Siegfried's last resting place (C also makes mention of the founding of the monastery at Lorsch) and as the final still undisclosed location of the almost unimaginably huge Nibelung treasure. The treasure lies in the depths of the Rhine river, put there by Hagen, who tried to protect his kings from a potential threat from their sister Kriemhild. Hagen never retrieves his material reward; he loses his head as Kriemhild's final victim in her quest to avenge the loss of Siegfried and of the treasure.[29]

The city of Worms and the narrative remain inextricably intertwined. Indeed, the modern city of Worms seems to have been as obsessed with the *Nibelungenlied* as Kriemhild eventually was with the treasure, with a passion that might threaten to overshadow other aspects of the city's rich heritage. Chapter 4 will treat this more fully; however, a slight digression here will reinforce the broader connection to Wolframs-Eschenbach. From street and place names to public art or advertising for the yearly summer festival (the *Nibelungen Festspiele*) that takes place outdoors on a stage near the cathedral, the Nibelungs are omnipresent in contemporary Worms; we can see the city has created a tangible presence for the Nibelungs that belies the relative absence of historical artifacts. Indeed, when a community's cultural heritage is a story like the *Nibelungenlied* or the legend of the Nibelungs, Volker Gallé suggests that story must be displayed or performed: when the monument that sets a city apart is a cultural artifacts and not a building but a narrative, then it becomes necessary to give the text a stage.[30] The story represents a particular kind of monument, and the performance requires a place and a stage. For the communities of Worms and Wolframs-Eschenbach, the well-known medieval narratives of the past offer an opportunity for each city to provide just such a place, just such a stage. The museums offer tangible landmarks to communities in need of them as they seek more than just, in Muschg's words, the familiar air of utopia ("die Heimatluft einer Utopie"). They seek more also than the connection evoked by mere mention of a title (*Nibelungenlied*) or name (Wolfram). Muschg wants his audience to consider the name Wolfram as an opportunity: "the name for an opportunity, where once there was a lot going on and, when we recall that opportunity, a lot can happen now, can happen in the future."[31] The Museum Wolfram von Eschenbach takes the opportunity suggested by the name and by the monument and transforms thought into possibility for action—at the very least in the act of entering into the museum and its display of Wolfram's works. Indeed, as it invites us in, the act of display facilitates the process of "past-presencing" through German medieval literature, creating a new discursive space. Literature and art evoke "a profound desire" for solidarity, for belonging, and for community, says cultural theorist Homi Bhabha, particularly when the "house of fiction" provides a stage on which we may perform or work through the "ambiguities" of the world in which we live.[32] The desire for belonging may encourage or affirm our aspirations, ease our uncertainties, resolve our ambiguities—the process of navigating that desire describes, for Bhabha, one of the primary functions of art or literature in an increasingly fragmented modern world. I will revisit this idea more fully at the conclusion of the next chapter. For now, it will suffice to say that we can also thus describe the function of making the past present in the creative display of medieval literature. When we visit Wolframs-Eschenbach or Worms now, as we will in Chapters 3 and 4 of *Medieval Literature on Display*, we will find an imaginatively supple place for memory and for newly meaningful encounters with older (hi)stories. Emerging from a nexus of intertexts and interfigures framing explorations of medieval literature, adapted narratives, cultural memory, and local history, the museums turn spaces, images, narrative, and text into vehicles for memory and subsequently identity for audiences—this is the process of past presencing at work. It is also the process of heritage-making in a place (Wolframs-Eschenbach, Worms) that wants very much to remain significant to its surrounding communities (Franconia or Germany), a place that wishes to capitalize on its capacity to tap into the "affective resonance of history presented as heritage"[33] for present and future visitors.

In sum, we can see in the Wolfram monument an example of the complex intersections that combine in the embrace of literature as heritage. The monument stands as an intertextual palimpsest that encapsulates the book's argument about medievalism, memory, and history: a town (Eschenbach) seeking to recover its more illustrious past catches the eye of a monarch (Maximilian II) also seeking to assert his realm's (Bavaria) cultural authority based on medieval literary credentials opposed to growing Prussian influence in the mid-nineteenth century[34] and erects a statue to honor an alleged native son real poet (Wolfram) in an entirely fictional pose (the troubadour of the Wartburg song contest). The monument gave shape to the proud memory of a distant medieval past fueled by a nineteenth-century patriotic nostalgia that led to the celebration of that past in the present. In its depiction of Wolfram and in its display of Wolfram's verses, the monument continues to show how the engagement with medieval literature displayed for a public audience in a public space can accommodate a community's need to remember, negotiate, experience, and perform its past. On a larger and more complex scale, the two museums at the center of this study demonstrate this engagement in their display of medieval literature. The town clearly intends to use what is perceived as medieval to constitute its identity as a community. The intertextual resonances become even more intricate in the museums both in Wolframs-Eschenbach and in Worms. The medievalism of the museums is related also to the cultural and historical intersections of the late-twentieth century that led to their design.

To understand these intersections, it will be fruitful both to define the terms we will need in order to examine them as well as to know the texts on which they are based. That is the task of the next chapter, Chapter 1, entitled "Medievalism and Memory." This chapter will identify, clarify, and briefly define several interlocking terms needed to place the museums and their work in the context of current scholarship; these terms will be framed with Macdonald's concept of past presencing. These terms include not only medievalism and memory but also nostalgia and heritage. The overarching concept of medievalism is the *process* of presencing the medieval past in the contemporary present. Memory is an active and dynamic process: performative, adaptive, imaginative; it functions as a primary *mechanism*, whereby we make the past present. Nostalgia locates, amplifies, and intensifies memory; a longing for the past in the present, nostalgia is a powerful *force* that can drive the dynamic process of medievalism with its need for presencing the past. Memory takes material form in heritage, where we witness the *performance* of the past in the present; therefore we also see how the present makes a product (or products) of the past.

In their displays of medieval narratives, the museums in Worms (The Nibelung Museum) and Wolframs-Eschenbach (Museum Wolfram von Eschenbach) also demonstrate the practice of memory through the process of adaptation. Like the literature they put on display, the museums open up a discursive space that facilitates the work of memory and adaptation by making the past present. Further, the museums exploit the dynamic process of memory and narrative that underlies medieval romance. As medieval texts are interpreted and adapted by various audiences over time, local communities engage in the practice of medievalism as a way to situate themselves in a given place at a given time through an understanding of what is "medieval." Local communities, like Worms or Wolframs-Eschenbach, thus select and interpret the past for audiences of the present (for local residents, for tourists). In doing so, through these museums, the communities seek to establish their medieval heritage anew by putting literature on display. Finally, this chapter will also situate the museums in Worms and in Wolframs-Eschenbach in the context of other museums that have exhibits of literature (such as the *Literaturmuseum der Moderne in Marbach* or the Austrian *Literaturmuseum der österreichischen Nationalbibliothek*) or exhibits of literary topics (such as the Grimmwelt museum in Kassel or the Siegfried Museum in Xanten).

The museums in this study share an interactive and multimedial intertextuality with the medieval narratives they display. Chapter 2 ("Adapting Medieval Narratives") will provide a thorough introduction to the German medieval texts and adaptations that shape the medievalism each museum enacts in its display. The medieval source texts reveal themselves as inherently adaptive and intertextual, in part because of their origins in oral tradition but also in part due to generic characteristics. Adaptation and medieval literature, particularly romance, go hand in hand. The genre of Arthurian romance has demonstrated its intertextual malleability since Geoffrey of Monmouth. The chapter will trace the development of the textual material from origins to the high-medieval texts to which the museums respond as well as the key reappropriations since the medieval period—particularly in the nineteenth and twentieth centuries. Since our primary case studies involve museal display of literature, we will also look at visual adaptations of the medieval source material. In this context, for example, we can consider the early-thirteenth-century murals of Hartmann von Aue's *Iwein* at Rodenegg (South Tyrol) and Schmalkalden (central Germany), for instance, as the beginning of a visualizing trajectory that leads to the modern museums in Worms and Wolframs-Eschenbach. The chapter will begin with a brief examination of the medieval literary sources: the Middle High German

Nibelungenlied as well as the works of Wolfram von Eschenbach from *Parzival* and *Willehalm* to *Titurel*. After introducing the literary sources, the chapter traces the broad outlines of reception history that adapted the source material in text (medieval continuations), in image (visualizations in murals or tapestries), in music (the operas of Richard Wagner), and eventually also in film (Fritz Lang). These are the adaptations that each museum creatively and critically engages.

The overview of sources and adaptations in Chapter 2 provides necessary background for a detailed analysis of the museums in Chapters 3 and 4. In Chapter 3 ("A Knight at the Museum: Medieval Literature and/as Local Heritage at the Museum Wolfram von Eschenbach"), we take up the first case study: the Museum Wolfram von Eschenbach from 1995. The chapter introduction will recall statue of Wolfram von Eschenbach from the book's introduction. Like the museum, the statue beckons to passersby with an invitation to dialogue. The statue leads to the question the museum asks and answers in greater detail: "Can literature be displayed?" In the museum, the poet Wolfram and his texts become the intertextual vehicles of the medievalism that engages the visitor. The chapter will explore the museum's depiction and interpretation of Wolfram's texts, primarily *Parzival, Titurel*, and *Willehalm*. The museum's displays offer interpretations of the literature that show a very distinctive process of adaptation and past presencing at work, reflective of the cultural landscape in the mid-1990s when the museum opened. As with the town's name change in 1917, the exhibits show a town constructing its modern, and now postmodern, public identity around the medieval poet of *Parzival* and his texts. In this process, the museum uses Wolfram von Eschenbach and his texts as devices to open and guide the dialogue that can shape this communal sense of self.

Chapter 4 ("The Machinery of Myth: The Nibelung Museum and the Interrogation of Cultural Memory") turns to the more recent Nibelung Museum. Opening in 2001, the Nibelung Museum focuses primarily on the modern history of the *Nibelungenlied* text and the material of the Nibelung legend in the last 200 years. In its signature display, the Nibelung Museum highlights the proliferation of visual intertexts that have emerged from the story. By enumerating the images, the museum dismantles the story that has become inextricably intertwined with modern German history and attempts to recontextualize it as a story within a more appropriate history, like the literary history of the *Nibelungenlied*. Throughout, the museum insists that the audience participate in a larger conversation about the machinery of myth (what the museum calls the "Mythenmaschine"), about its creative power, and about the audience's responsibility to deal knowledgeably with the stories it generates. Hutcheon's concept of "palimpsestic intertextuality" accommodates the museum's complex depictions of nineteenth- and twentieth-century cultural history that situate and shape modern understandings of the older text. The displays in the Nibelung Museum offer interpretation of the literature that show an equally distinctive but different process of adaptation and past presencing than that in Wolframs-Eschenbach.

Chapters 3 and 4 demonstrate how the museums, in the absence of historical or archaeological artifacts, uniquely visualize and interpret literature in exhibits that emerge from a complicated nexus of accumulated intertexts. Chapter 5 ("Presencing the Narrative Past: Old Structures, New Stories?") takes the next step to offer a comparative analysis of both museums: their interpretations of medieval narratives and subsequent afterlives, their roles in the community as repositories of local history, their function as monuments and heritage. The chapter will also situate the museums in their respective geographic and cultural landscapes. Both museums, for example, have been built into the existing historical cityscapes of their respective towns. The Museum Wolfram von Eschenbach replaced the former local museum ("Heimatmuseum") in the old city hall ("Altes Rathaus") of Wolframs-Eschenbach; the Nibelung Museum was built into the medieval city wall of Worms. The latter is now a modern structure literally ensconced in the older medieval wall. Physically located both in the past and in the present, each museum seems to pull an immaterial story back into a material and three-dimensional space. In their practice of medievalism, through the display of their respective texts, the museums transform the older structures of each town into new narratives for modern communities.

To conclude the study, Chapter 6 ("The Future of the Past") addresses once again the book's subject of medieval literature on display in the context of medievalism. This chapter begins by integrating literature, medievalism, and memory through reference to the active medievalizing processes revealed through the museum case studies discussed in Chapters 3, 4, and 5. The case studies reveal how memory, through the lens of the Middle Ages, creatively shapes modern cultural identity and heritage. In this way, medievalism becomes the medium by which the communities of Worms and Wolframs-Eschenbach exploit place and space in their museums to make the past present: the literary past, the remembered past, the conflict-ridden and difficult past. Chapter 6 will conclude by placing the Nibelung Museum in Worms and the Museum Wolfram von Eschenbach in the ongoing process of creating heritage.

Medieval cultures were memorial cultures; memory, expressed through literary narratives, becomes part of real lived experience: collective, interpersonal, interactive. As Macdonald and others have shown, modern European culture continues to deal with memory in unique ways, especially since the end of the twentieth century. Such discussions grow out of the European, and German, preoccupation with memory following the Second World War. In literary, cultural, and historical studies since the mid-twentieth century, the term *Erinnerungskultur* recognizes the importance of memory in creating a "culture of remembrance" that became particularly important after the Holocaust. Over time, the term has also come to refer not only to remembering the Holocaust— and this across Europe—but to remembering various other traumas of the German experience in the twentieth century. Memories do not exist as closed systems, says Assmann; in any given social reality, memories intersect, they touch, they strengthen, they modify, and they become polarized in connection with other processes of remembering and forgetting.[35] A dynamic dialogue between individual and collective memory takes place in the long shadow (as Assmann describes it) of a traumatic past.

The events of 1989 propelled memory work in new directions. Assmann asserts that the dissolution of the bipolar political structure of Europe after the events of 1989 that led "zu einer eruptiven Wiederkehr von Erinnerungen und einem 'Wiedererwachen von Geschichte.'"[36] Older national myths and conventional (previously accepted) versions of history came into question. In this environment, as we might expect, the physical landscape and the objects of memory continue to play a significant role. Macdonald's work shows this not only in the context of Europe (*Memorylands*) but also in Germany (*Difficult Heritage*), as does Neil MacGregor (*Germany: Memories of a Nation*). As the political landscape has continued to change since 1989, inhabiting a physical landscape still indelibly marked by two world wars and forty years of division, we see how memorials change and are changed by those in power to shape public memory. For historian Rudy Koshar, this fluidity of memory and physical manifestation characterizes the *Erinnerungslandschaft* or memory landscape of Germany. Koshar coined the term "emergent evolution" to describe how the modes of representation contribute over time to a constantly replicable process that, for him, creates "the history of German memory." Over time, it "becomes an innovative recombination of previously existing elements rather than an unambiguous departure from the past."[37] Both museums of *Medieval Literature on Display* testify to the durability and continuity of images, not just from the *Nibelungenlied* or *Parzival* offering creative examples of how such previously existing elements and ideas can recombine to frame new memories and to create new institutions. The museums in Wolframs-Eschenbach and in Worms show, in other words, how memory becomes also institutionalized as part of the process of musealization.

Museums cultivate a desire for preservation, a need to go back to the past, as it were, and to surround oneself with remnants or souvenirs of the past. Heritage is the tangible or intangible product of presencing the past, as memory (perhaps driven by nostalgia) becomes concrete or real. Heritage is where memory becomes a looking back and a longing for the past (nostalgia) that desires to re-create an authentic past experience in the present to be remembered into the future as constitutive of identity. In this context, the museums from 1995 and 2001 reside securely in what Macdonald calls the European memorylands. They offer examples of memory culture—heritage, monuments, collections, shared experience—living with the ideas of the past and finding a way to create artifacts to put them on display, presencing the past in a very unique way. They offer an unusual example of displays of heritage at/as sites of literary, cultural, and historical memory.

And all of the above come into play as part of the medievalism of these museums. The remembered past is longed for and becomes present in a shared experience that is emplaced into the city's history as story occupies material space in the old Rathaus of Wolframs-Eschenbach or the medieval city wall of Worms. Both museums exemplify the concept of display as an interface that can transform what is shown into heritage.[38] Medievalism becomes the medium by which the communities of Worms and Wolframs-Eschenbach negotiate difficult heritage to become part of the new and developing memorylands of a global Germany and a global Europe.[39] The medievalism of the museums therefore provides a model for how other communities might participate in the European memory complex into the future.

1

Medievalism and Memory

What is now plain and clear is that neither future nor past things are in existence, and that it is not correct to say there are three periods of time: past, present and future. Perhaps it would be proper to say there are three periods of time: the present of things past, the present of things present, the present of things future.[1]

(Augustine, Confessions)

Indeed, it seems that people like the Middle Ages.[2]

(Umberto Eco, Travels in Hyperreality)

In book XI of his *Confessions,* Augustine muses on the insistent present-ness of time. We tend to speak of the past and the present and the future as though they exist; yet, they actually do not. Like Augustine, we can never locate them precisely, though we might wish to do so. Augustine reflects:

> If future and past things exist, I would like to know where they are. And, if that is impossible for me, at least I do know that, wherever they are, they are not there as future or past things, but as present. For, if they are there also as future things, they are not yet there; and, if they are there as past things, they are already not there. So, wherever they are, whatever they are, they do not exist unless as present things.[3]

Things of the past or things of the future can only be apprehended as part of the present; as Augustine says later in this section, we grasp the future in the present as expectation and we recall the past into the present as memory. But the things themselves are either already gone (past) or not yet there (future). Only the present exists for us at any given moment, and this present must encompass any past and any future because they only exist "as present things" regardless of where or what they may be. Augustine concludes that the categories of past, present, and future are insufficient:

What is now plain and clear is that neither future nor past things are in existence, and that it is not correct to say there are three periods of time: past, present and future. Perhaps it would be proper to say there are three periods of time: the present of things past, the present of things present, the present of things future.[4]

Instead of familiar generic categories (past, present, future), we have rather "the present of things past, the present of things present, the present of things future." These terms reflect how the various periods are actually experienced—we sense as discrete the past of things that were and the future of things yet to be. But both tomorrow and yesterday are mediated by the present of today. Augustine's fourth-century ruminations might seem to have little connection to our case studies of modern German museums. Augustine, however, gives voice here to ideas about time and memory that remained influential throughout the medieval period.[5] Furthermore, the presence of the past is our main concern as is the process by which the past becomes present. In the following, I will argue that medieval literature translates Augustine's present of things past into process, thence into practice, and ultimately into collective memory. If the presencing of things past is also the modern process of memory that drives medievalism, then *Medieval Literature on Display* understands medievalism as the process of presencing the medieval past. Communities look backward to look forward, to understand the present as they do so. In this chapter, we want to examine memory and medievalism as they intersect in the museums and in the literature on display. Looking back and presencing things past, to paraphrase Augustine, is the work of memory. For *Medieval Literature on Display*, the process of presencing the medieval past illuminates the choices communities make when they do that work: how and why and when do they choose to look back the way they do—and whose middle ages do they choose to (re)present or perform.

Introduction: The presence of the past

The first words of the *Nibelungenlied* insist on the shared experience of the story:

> Uns ist in alten mæren wunders vil geseit
> von helden lobebæren, von grôzer arebeit,
> von fröuden, hôchgezîten, von weinen und von klagen,
> von küener recken strîten muget ir nu wunder hœren sagen.

> In ancient tales many marvels are told us of renowned heroes, of great hardship, of joys, festivities, of weeping and lamenting, of bold warriors' battles—now *you* may hear such marvels told.[6] (emphasis mine)

This is the first stanza of the C version of the *Nibelungenlied*. General consensus is that this was added later and that the older versions of the *Nibelungenlied* began with the second stanza of C and the focus on Kriemhild growing up in the land of the Burgundians. I want to highlight here how the added strophe programmatically establishes a balance between presence (we/us) and distance (older tales), as we might expect from a poem that comes from oral sources but was clearly composed in writing. Unlike other heroic Germanic epics, the narrator does not speak overtly (no "I" as in the *Hildebrandslied*, for example).[7] Yet, the first word ("uns") draws us in. Before we go any further, we have to acknowledge that this perhaps most famous opening stanza of the epic is generally believed to have been added later; there are A and B versions that do not have it, beginning instead with the description of the beautiful maiden Kriemhild.

Nevertheless, for our purposes here, this is one now familiar invitation to which we as audience respond. The narrator exhorts us to recall familiar stories of heroes and their toil, of celebrations and sorrow, of great deeds; we should prepare to hear more of those wonder-filled tales ("muget ir nu wunder hoeren sagen"). The poet draws us immediately into the circle of the narrative's audience as we find ourselves included in that initial first-person plural pronoun. We are both included yet excluded or set apart. While the poet does bring his audience into his narrative, he also emphasizes the distance between the audience ("uns") and the *alte maeren*, of which he will sing; the narrative offers us a distinct then opposed to a very clear now ("muget ir nu wunder hoeren sagen"). And who are we? On the one hand, the pronoun "uns" constructs a "we"/us (just like the pronoun "ir" constructs a "you") who must be historically and culturally defined by the thirteenth-century Middle High German courtly text produced in the area around Passau. On the other hand, the first-person plural "us" can also include the speaker and audience over time; successive iterations of "we" must inevitably expand any narrow historical and cultural definitions tied to the origins of the text. We are the enthusiastic nineteenth-century readers, like Jacob Grimm and Friedrich von der Hagen, who celebrated the *Nibelungenlied* as the German *Iliad*.[8] We are perhaps the Austrian soldiers exhorted by Emperor Franz Joseph in 1914, on the eve of what would become the First World War, to demonstrate that same deep unwavering loyalty toward comrades and country (*Nibelungentreue*) shown by the Burgundians (the Nibelungs) to their king in the face of certain defeat at their last battle. We are perhaps the audience of Michael Verhoeven's 1987 *Das schreckliche Mädchen*, a film about uncovering the suppressed history of a fictitious but all-too-realistic southern German town during the Nazi period. As the film opens, we see these first lines of the *Nibelungenlied* on the screen; the dissonance is jarring between the medieval

German verse and the pub scene that follows showing the youth who later threaten the main character as she tries to uncover the truth about a history many would prefer to forget.[9] We are perhaps in the audience at a church near the campus of the University of Wisconsin Madison in the late 1980s, listening to a performance of the *Nibelungenlied* in Middle High German by Austrian musician Eberhard Kummer, the sound of his voice and his harp contrasting oddly with the flicker of passing headlights on the fairly busy street outside.[10]

We may also be tourists in the city of Worms, standing on one of the several landings in the second tower of the Nibelung museum in Worms. On this landing of the Nibelung Museum, on the right in the photo, we have several high-backed rather uncomfortable looking seats (**Figure 4**). They might be taken for thrones; after all, we are here to learn about a tale of kings. Visitors are invited to take a seat, to tarry, and to hear excerpts of that tale. These thrones are placed at various stations where visitors to the Nibelung museum are invited to sit and listen to some of the verses of the *Nibelungenlied*, read both in Middle High German and in modern German translation. As we take a seat on one of these throne-like chairs, and we will return to this idea later in Chapter 4 with a more detailed analysis of the museum, the museum literally wants to place us within the story. Names of the main characters are etched into the transparent sides of the chairs, as visitors are asked to consider themselves perhaps part of the medieval story—or at least a member of its larger audience over time. A nearby window throws the process of medievalism into even greater relief. Through the opening in the medieval tower, we look out at the variegated facets of the contemporary landscape represented in the neighborhood below, part of the more encompassing memory landscape of Worms today. We see apartment buildings that recall the architecture of the 1950s along the street that leads to the majestic Romanesque cathedral from the twelfth century. Our view is partially obstructed, however, by the names on the window. Forming another multilayered palimpsest of their own, the names appear in a kind of word cloud. We must read them backward, from right to left, but we can make them out at least partially or entirely: Siegfried, Gunther, Brünhild, Etzel, Kriemhild, Giselher, Hildebrand, Hagen von Tronje, Dietrich von Bern. If we look closely, we glimpse the logo of the Nibelung museum as well. Whimsical and yet thought-provoking in its design, the window invites visitors to linger and to take a look—and then to look maybe even a second or third time. This reflective playfulness reflects the museum itself, as well as the museum's critical attitude toward the narrative it tries to display. In this way, the window compels museum visitors to view the city of 2019 around, because of, and despite, the letters that

Figure 4 Nibelung Museum window in the *Hörturm*, author's own.

form the names that create the story (one of many "alte maeren") which has brought us ("uns") to that very spot in the tower in Worms to begin with.

The poet of the *Nibelungenlied* could not possibly have imagined these audiences, along with the myriad others between the thirteenth and the twentieth centuries. In this first strophe of the C version, however, the poet arguably does make room for all later listeners and readers encompassed by that plural inclusive "us." In the reception history of the *Nibelungenlied*, we witness a process of entanglement that ranges over centuries and takes myriad forms. But it brings us to the point where we look, as through the window I described above, through the text at the city of the present day. We look through the names in a word cloud designed in 2001, signifiers of a medieval epic poem that has literally been constructed into a museum. We look through those names at a city whose history stretches back across a millennium; the layers of the palimpsest thickly crowd our view. The past and the present seem to converge and diverge simultaneously. When we read the *Nibelungenlied* now, when we hear the poem performed in an authentic setting, when we observe the window in the Nibelung Museum, we enable the medieval text and its story to become (our) contemporary lived experience.

In the remainder of this chapter, I would like to place the museums and their work in the context of current research on medievalism and memory. There are several interlocking concepts that we need to identify, clarify, and briefly define in the context of this project. First, we will return in more detail to the concept of **past presencing** in order to frame more broadly the other key terms that constitute the theoretical framework of *Medieval Literature on Display*. First, we will address **memory** as the primary *mechanism*, whereby we make the past present. The work of memory is deeply embedded in the medieval literature the museums put on display; it also prompted the modern need to design the museum. **Medievalism** is the *process* of presencing the medieval past in the contemporary present. **Nostalgia** plays a significant role in the process of medievalism; described most simply as a longing for the past in the present, we might see it as a powerful *force* that often drives the dynamic process of medievalism with its need for presencing the past. Nostalgia locates, amplifies, and intensifies memory. Memory takes material form in **heritage.** The concept of heritage straddles the immaterial and the material, the intangible and the tangible, the abstract and the concrete. Each of these concepts (memory, medievalism, nostalgia, heritage) has been researched extensively; I cannot do justice to it all here, except to acknowledge my own debt to that scholarship in my focus on the museums at the heart of *Medieval Literature on Display*. The museums touch facets of each concept as they reconfigure their respective medieval texts for the present, giving them material form. In the Museum Wolfram von Eschenbach and in the Nibelung Museum, medievalism drives memory in the creation of new heritage through a unique and an intentional emplacement of the medieval literary past in the landscape and architecture of the present.

Memory: Presencing things past

The subjects of memory, remembrance, and commemoration have filled volumes of research by sociologists, psychologists, historians, and literary scholars since the end of the Second World War. Maurice Halbwachs opened the door by describing how social experience structures individual memory. Jan Assmann shifted focus from the individual to the collective, articulating critique of Halbwachs' theory, which essentially locates memory in the individual, even though the individual is embedded in a social context. Whenever people join together in larger groups, they generate a connective semantics, thereby producing forms of memory that are designed to stabilize a common identity and a point of view that span several generations.[11] Memory is not only social, for individuals and communities; memory is also communicative and connective, says Astrid Erll, in a thorough overview of the development of memory studies in the twentieth century.[12] As mentioned earlier in the introduction, historian Rudy Koshar draws on these aspects of memory research to examine the memory landscape (*Erinnerungslandschaft*) of Germany between 1870 and 1990, describing the way in which Germans have processed their history since the nineteenth century through their monuments; the memory landscape is "a topography steeped in memories and images" that resonate both in personal and public spheres particularly due to "the collective meaning of certain buildings or spaces."[13] He reiterates that memory work is reconstructive, ritualistic, performative; it reveals stratified layers that have collected palimpsest-like over time, in what Koshar calls a "triadic relationship between humans, landmarks, and cultural meanings."[14] Koshar's study examines the role of monuments in this relationship, as they resonate with ideas and metaphors, containing and perpetuating collective memory over time for the communities in which they are located. People imbue them with meaning, meaning that can be shaped and adapted over time as memory becomes part of real lived experience.

The desire to share and to preserve lived experience brings us back to the general project of museums; as suggested earlier, musealization is one way in which modern European culture is dealing with memory now, especially since the end of the twentieth century. In *Memorylands*, Macdonald describes the wide-ranging responses to the identity issues that have emerged since the fall of the Berlin Wall in 1989—these responses are presented in various kinds of museal display. As Macdonald uses the term, a "memoryland" may refer to a particular geographic location. The term may include physical monuments or it may describe a more abstract landscape, a set of objects or even behaviors that reflect a personal or collective approach to, or experience of, the past. Aesthetic or imaginative reactions to past time also shape these memorylands, emerging through the process of past presencing. Memorylands shape the contours of our relationships to past, present, and future not just as individuals but also as communities. They form what Macdonald calls the European memory complex; this describes the wide spectrum of ways in which that memory complex manifests itself in the contemporary cultural landscape: seeing, telling, feeling, showing the past. This is the ongoing process of past presencing that encompasses the many ways in which the past is continually reconfigured in a changing present. The term "is intended to draw attention to the multiple ways in which the past may be (and be made to be) present—as well as represented— whether articulated verbally or experienced and performed in other ways."[15] As we see the past in architecture, tell the past in story, feel the past in an old coat, and show the past in a museum, we incorporate the past into our present.

From our vantage point in the present, we now look back at the Middle Ages; however, we know our medieval counterparts looked back as well. Medieval texts form the deep center of this book. Medieval cultures were unquestionably memorial cultures, and thus memory significantly shaped the literature our museums put on display; this has been firmly established by the work of a number of scholars since 1990, most notably Mary Carruthers in her groundbreaking study *The Book of Memory*. Memory is a dynamic, interactive, and performative process. In the words of Bruce Holsinger, it "necessarily involves the ongoing re-performance of individual and communal pasts,"[16] which is where memory and literature intersect in the semiliterate, visually saturated, multisensory environment of medieval culture. Memory is also "imaginative," to borrow a term from historian Amy Remensnyder. In her book *Remembering Kings Past. Monastic Foundation Legends in Medieval Southern France*, Remensnyder uses the term "imaginative" memory to describe what is usually called "social" or "collective" memory "in order to evoke the creative flair" of monastic foundation legends and their "often fantastic transformations of reality."[17] In her discussion of these legends, the term "imaginative" allows her to emphasize the fact that the stories she deals with are not just fantasy or fantastic; there were elements of those stories that their monastic audiences did believe to be true and that compelled them to celebrate rituals that honored those stories in the present, linking the present to the past the stories represented (or literally re-presented). The concept of imaginative memory is relevant not only because it accommodates the persistent kernel of truth in otherwise fantastical (Arthurian) tales. Imaginative memory, for Remensnyder, is also dialogic and dialectic; it implies "a dialogue between then and now, a dialective relationship of continuity between the two temporal spaces." In this way, imaginative memory has power and authority to create identity and meaning because a group, or an institution or an individual, that shares an imagined past can "establish and reaffirm the cohesion of a group" in the present. The past can be evoked to respond to social needs of the present group, particularly when it is a matter of the community's independence that might be threatened. One may also look to the past when one feels alienated from the present, perhaps "a present characterized by rapid social change" or a present that feels estranged from a too-distant past.[18] Indeed, this is also how Linda Hutcheon describes adaptation, relying on an oscillation between past and present.[19] Such oscillation, whatever generates it, leads to a dynamic narrative environment like the one we experience in the Wolfram monument in Wolframs-Eschenbach. We encounter a similarly dynamic narrative environment at Rodenegg (before 1230) or Schmalkalden (ca. 1250–1275), where we find the earliest Arthurian murals depicting material from the early-thirteenth-century romance *Iwein* by Hartmann von Aue. We will look at the murals in a bit more detail in Chapter 2 when we discuss medieval adaptations. The point here is that seemingly fantastical stories become invested with history, as narratives (fictional or otherwise) become invested with lived experience. These aspects of memory (the social, the collective, the dialogic, the imaginative) connect us to our medieval forebears. Medieval memory and modern memory find their way to one another conceptually in the medievalism of these museums that put the narratives and their afterlives on display.

With the first strophe of the *Nibelungenlied*, the poet similarly establishes a connection to bridge past and present; the story of "things past" enters into and becomes part of the audience's present. Since the focus of *Medieval Literature on Display* is literature, I think it appropriate to supplement the above brief overview of medieval memory with one further example of how medieval literature itself presences the past, this time the Arthurian past. With the first lines of his *Iwein*, Hartmann von Aue does the same; he brings his audience into the space of memory, into the remembered (albeit fictional) past of the Arthurian court; the prologue is worth quoting in its entirety here:

> Swer an rehte güete
> wendet sîn gemüete,
> dem volget sælde und êre.
> des gît gewisse lêre
> künec Artûs der guote,
> der mit rîters muote,
> nâch lobe kunde strîten.

er hât bî sînen zîten
gelebet alsô schône
daz er der êren krône
dô truoc und noch sîn name treit.
des haben die wârheit
sîne lantliute:
sî jehent, er lebe noch hiute:
er hât der lop erworben,
ist im der lîp erstorben,
sô lebet doch iemer sîn name.
er ist lasterlîcher schame
iemer vil gar erwert,
der noch nâch sînem site vert. (Hartmann von Aue, *Iwein* 1–20)

He who turns his mind to true goodness will be attended by happiness and honor. Good King Arthur, who knew how to fight laudably and chivalrously, gives clear proof of this. He lived in such a beautiful way that he wore the crown of honor in his time, and his name does so still. That is why his countrymen are right when they say that he still lives today. He has attained such fame that even though he has died, his name will live forever. Even now, whoever acts as Arthur did is completely protected from shame and dishonor.[20]

The prologue to *Iwein* extols the virtues of King Arthur, praising his deeds and prowess for the audience who ought to follow his example if they seek the true goodness ("rehte güete") that will lead to happiness and honor ("sælde und êre"). Arthur's good name still carries his reputation and his praise into the present ("sô lebet doch iemer sîn name"), although Arthur himself has died ("ist im der lîp erstorben"). Ultimately, as they participate in the continued afterlife of Arthur's name, the text's audience become his countrymen ("lantliute") as well. The current audience may not share ties of blood or nationality with the legendary king; nevertheless, by hearing the story, they have joined those faithful followers who practice the values of chivalry and honor embodied in Arthur and his knights of the Round Table. As King Arthur's name lives on in the hearing of any new company, he will serve as a model for others to emulate ("nâch sînem site") now and in the future; those members will share in Arthur's exemplary reputation ("completely protected from shame and dishonor"), joining the ranks of others who have preceded them, thus ensuring the continued life not only of Arthur's name but also of his values and his story in perpetuity. The deeds of Arthur belong to a past that becomes present for the audience.

Hartmann's prologue describes the process of memory; this present "even now" ("doch iemer") invites the audience (the listeners, the readers: us) to share the experience of the story. The poet invokes a remembered and distant, we might even say fictionalized, past and brings it into a tangible present; his words seem designed to inspire a solidarity of feeling, of aspiration, of imagined shared memory among the listeners. Further, it is the tales themselves that will continue to make the past present, in the now of each respective audience, even as the current audience must live their own lives. The past becomes present, even if hypothetically, as people say Arthur may live still. The grammatical conditional ("er lebe noch hiute") expresses the promise of the past in the present, which becomes the indicative of "now" when we consider obeying the injunction to live according to this example: "sî jehent" (they say) and that person will be completely protected from shame and dishonor "der noch nâch sînem site vert" (whoever acts as Arthur did). Thus, Hartmann encourages his audience (us) to bring the Arthurian past into our present; they say he still lives today; we should act as he did.

Hartmann von Aue was a contemporary of both Wolfram von Eschenbach and the anonymous poet of the *Nibelungenlied*. In the next chapter, we will have occasion to explore further details about this vibrant intertextual literary environment around 1200 in Germany. Here, however, I believe that Hartmann's clear expression of the relationship of then and now—the present-ness of deeds from the Arthurian past—recalls Macdonald's concept of presencing the past. Admittedly, the term "past presencing" applies best to the twentieth-century context from which Macdonald derives it. The concept also seems fairly "presentist" in focus as it is concerned with the mobilization of the past at particular moments. However, in her definition, Macdonald emphasizes that any particular points at which we choose to mobilize the past "may themselves be moments in the past and, indeed, any recorded moment is already past." The present can be set at any point in time where there is a clear sense of a time before a time that is experienced as now.[21] I suggest that, in his prologue to *Iwein*, Hartmann situates us intentionally in the ongoing process of past presencing as the Arthurian "then" converges with the audience's "now." In this effort to keep Arthurian time ever-present at court, despite a sense of time passing or having passed, there is a sense of the simultaneity of experience and perhaps also time in that the narrative becomes part of the audience's present. And it will hopefully become part of its future.

Thus, Hartmann encourages his audience (us) to bring the Arthurian past into our present; they say he still lives today, and we should act as he did. Things past thus provide an anchor for the present of narratives like *Iwein* or the *Nibelungenlied* for their medieval audiences. Certainly, I do not intend to draw a direct line from Augustine to the Nibelung Museum in Worms; any line would be tenuous at best. As I said above, however, I do wish to follow a long arc of influence and reception. For Augustine, the task of presencing the past was the work of memory; indeed, it still is. For its own audiences, if we take Hartmann at his word, *Iwein* offered a kind of mechanism for presencing the past. Though the *Nibelungenlied* ultimately has a much different message than courtly romances contemporary with it, its poet also situates us in that ongoing process in the first strophe from the C version. Successive iterations of "we" over time expand any narrow historical and cultural definitions tied to the origins of the text.

Medievalism: Presencing the medieval past

In Eberhard Kummer's performance of the *Nibelungenlied* described above or in our contemplation of the window in the Nibelung Museum, we witness the reception and translation of text and narrative into contemporary lived experience. Reception brings us to medievalism as a process for how we look back now. We can see that the idea of the present in the past inheres as deeply in medieval literature as it does in the contemporary museum displays we will discuss in Chapters 3 and 4. The medieval literature on display is displayed precisely because it participates in the memorial characteristics of medieval culture. The process of past presencing is a process that employs memory both to enact and perform various pasts, notably as part of the preservation and display of heritage in the museums of today. And the medieval past is one that continues to "enthrall" us, to fascinate us; as Pugh and Weisl put it, the Middle Ages is simply "magic."[22] We do not simply "like" the Middle Ages, as Umberto Eco said over three decades ago; we are completely smitten, infatuated by the medieval and the Middle Ages. As a plethora of medieval festivals and reenactments, films, theme parks, museums, and fantasy novels emphatically attest, the Middle Ages "is continually reborn in new stories, new media, new histories,"[23] as a result of our unflagging enthusiasm—and this book itself obviously contributes to the ever-growing list.

This perpetual cycle of regeneration is medievalism at work; "the continuing process of creating the Middle Ages,"[24] as the discipline's founder Leslie Workman put it, is alive and well. In the following section, I want to look briefly at current research on medievalism. Given the sheer volume of work done in the last decade alone, this overview will necessarily be selective; more comprehensive treatment on the discipline itself can be found in publications such as David Matthews' thorough study *Medievalism: A Critical History*, the slim yet provocative volume *Medievalism: A Manifesto* by Richard Utz, or the recent *Cambridge Companion to Medievalism* edited by Louise D'Arcens.[25] For purposes of the museum case studies in *Medieval Literature on Display*, I want to emphasize an understanding of medievalism as both product and process. The museums are not only examples of medievalism. They also enact the process of medievalism for their visitors on a daily basis, and they show us medievalism as adaptation; indeed, Hutcheon identifies three aspects of adaptation as both product and process. An adaptation is first a formal entity ("an acknowledged transposition of a recognizable other work or works"). It is also a process of (re)creation or (re)interpretation ("a creative *and* interpretive act of appropriation/salvaging"). Finally, adaptation is also a process of reception marked by intertextuality ("an extended intertextual engagement with the adapted work").[26] Ultimately, I also seek to align medievalism as adaptation (product and process) with Macdonald's concept of past presencing: medievalism is the process of presencing the medieval past. The museums in Worms and in Wolframs-Eschenbach will show us a medievalism that is both product and process, where the Middle Ages is also reborn at intersections not only of (hi)stories and media but also of heritage and memory.

Medievalisms

Medievalism as product describes the creation, the interpretation, the study of different versions of the Middle Ages. This was part of Leslie Workman's original definition in the late 1970s, when he began the journal *Studies in Medievalism*. The current edition of the *Oxford English Dictionary* reinforces this very basic definition of medievalism with a focus on product: "beliefs and practices (regarded as) characteristic of the Middle Ages" as well as "medieval thought." The definition hints at the process with "the adoption of, adherence to, or interest in medieval ideals, styles, or usages" and occasionally "an instance of this."[27] The term first appeared in English in the nineteenth century[28] and was first used to describe an "engagement" with the period known historically as the Middle Ages or with what was believed to belong to that period.[29] Dialogue has always been central to medievalism in the recognition of the Middle Ages as a lens to interpret one's own contemporary milieu—whether this involved amateurs exploring the medieval, as Dinshaw traces the increasingly blurry lines of disciplinary definition in *How Soon Is Now?*, or whether medievalism became a vehicle to criticize the academy as the seat of mainstream medieval studies in the twentieth century. There, as Utz reminds us, the debate between professionalism and amateurism (still) continues to complicate progress.[30] Shippey makes this clear as he moves in the direction of process as amends the OED entry to include "any post-medieval attempt to re-imagine the Middle Ages, or some aspect of the Middle Ages, for the modern world, in any of many different media."[31] Pugh and Weisl refer to "the art, literature, scholarship, avocational past-times, and sundry forms of entertainment and culture that turn to the Middle Ages for their subject matter or inspiration," but the process lies in reaction to or engagement with the contemporary environment of the artist "explicitly or implicitly, by comparison or contrast."[32] For Matthews, medievalism involves cultural production that has two manifestations: the first is "based largely on medieval elements incorporates modern references or motifs," whereas the second is a product "essentially of its own time" that looks back to the Middle Ages "with greater or lesser explicitness." Overall, Matthews proposes a working model for medievalism as a discourse that employs three modes on a spectrum from portrayal of the Middle Ages "as it was" or "as it might have been" or "as it never was."[33] Multiple discourses facilitate modern reimaginings of the Middle Ages, demonstrating the deep cultural resonance of medieval images and narratives ("memory matter") and revealing medievalism to be a powerful vehicle for what Astrid Erll calls remediation across a wide spectrum of media.[34]

In fact, we refer increasingly now to medievalisms in the plural; for Pugh and Weisl, the singular is no longer possible. Categories vary. Emery suggests three: creative medievalism for cultural productions, spectacular medievalism for entertainment, and living medievalism for experiential activities (e.g., reenactments).[35] Shippey develops a more extensive list that would include more specific categories like philological medievalism (Grimm), musical medievalism, and touristic medievalism.[36] Pugh and Weisl also include the creative (here as music and the visual arts) as well as the experiential and they add a section on political medievalisms. The latter has only attracted more interest in the time since *Medievalisms* was published in 2013, as recent publications by Andrew Elliott (*Medievalism, Politics, and Mass Media: Appropriating the Middle Ages in the Twenty-First Century* in 2017) and Daniel Wollenberg (*Medieval Imagery in Today's Politics* in 2018) attest. We can see in these pluralities, reflected in the continually developing and expanding categories, not only the proliferation of products but the developing dialogue with and about process. For Emery, the advantage of Workman's definitions is his characterization of medievalism as method, which leads her to characterize the method further as "an active process of engagement with things medieval."[37] Thus she favors a definition that emphasizes evolution and process; medievalism is "a constantly evolving and self-referential process of defining an always fictional Middle Ages."[38] And it is this process-oriented definition that applies best to the argument in *Medieval Literature on Display*, though the museums are also certainly products of that process. The focus on process connects the museums with memory and the act of remembering as well as the act of presencing the past in the physical embodiment of the medieval past in museal display.

Medievalisms and *Mittelalterrezeption*

Because *Medieval Literature on Display* is attempting to navigate medievalism through the Anglo-American and the German contexts, I would like to take just a moment to address both scholarly traditions.[39] If we consider "the reception, interpretation or recreation of the European Middle Ages in post-medieval cultures,"[40] as the 2016 *Cambridge Companion to Medievalism* defines medievalism, Anglo-American and German studies have until recently tended to follow somewhat comparable but seldom intersecting paths, divided by language as well as academic focus. The German tradition of medievalism as the reception of the Middle Ages is the overarching focus of German *Mittelalterrezeption*, following the long arc of reception as a process over time in the context of reception history (*Rezeptionsgeschichte*) as articulated in the 1960s by Hans-Robert Jauss. Early research on *Rezeptionsgeschichte* tended to focus very specifically on intertextuality and reception in the Middle Ages or on the incorporation or adaptation of medieval German materials into literature of later periods (from the early modern era through the nineteenth century). Scholars in Germany also tended to pursue research projects on local history or on documents found in local archives. In addition, scholars of German medieval literature preferred text-based, close readings of literary texts in their research much longer before embracing the broader culturally based questions that have tended to characterize North American scholarship. This again may be in part the result of how German scholars reacted to the Second World War. In the years immediately following the war, they retreated into text-based criticism; medievalists in particular tried to distance themselves from the Nazi misappropriation of German medieval literature found in much of the propaganda of the 1930s. Not sharing this history, North American medievalists in German more quickly embraced broader thematic and cultural questions, applying cross-disciplinary perspectives to a range of medieval genres. On the other hand, while German scholarship hesitated to apply new approaches to medieval studies, it laid a firm methodological and historical foundation, both philologically and disciplinarily sound, for later research to incorporate more contemporary theoretical perspectives. Finally, much of German medievalism has also concerned itself with the long shadow cast by nineteenth-century composer Richard Wagner; many scholars have written eloquently in attempts to rescue German medieval literature from the wide-reaching political, ideological, cultural effects of Wagner's visions and re-visions of the German Middle Ages.[41]

Change has been slow but steady.[42] The language barrier has long persisted, for example. Until the 1990s, much German medieval scholarship was published in German; the Germans tended to write their scholarship in German, the Anglo-Americans tended to write their scholarship in English, though a number of scholars did cross the linguistic boundaries. Scholars are now publishing and working in both languages much more frequently. In addition, German scholarship now more frequently addresses the medievalisms described earlier, as the recognition grows of the Middle Ages as an almost infinitely adaptable site of memory ("Erinnerungsort") for postmodern culture.[43] There is a slowly developing acceptance of popular culture as part of the medieval memoryscape ("Erinnerungslandschaft") in contemporary culture. In the introduction to their volume of conference proceedings from several conferences on *Mittelalterrezeption* in Germany from 2008 to 2010 in Berlin and Freiburg, Herweg and Keppler-Tasaki broadly assess the current critical landscape from a European perspective but also with an eye toward Anglophone scholarship. Future inquiry should pursue new modes of understanding, including on aspects of intermediality that can better capture dialogic relationships among texts. Focused primarily but not exclusively in German-speaking areas, they suggest that the past changes from present to present, changing for us and with us.[44] These sentiments echo those of the Swiss historian Valentin Groebner, whose 2006 volume says it all in the title *Das Mittelalter hört nicht auf*: the Middle Ages will not cease. We find our Middle Ages in the texts we interpret as these texts reflect our own interests and needs; the past changes, Groebner says.[45] If the past can change, present scholarship can do so as well.

Medievalisms offer, for Pugh and Weisl, "various modes of meaning" that enable us to commence "building our very selves," to work "through a relationship with history" that is both the past as it was (however that may be determined) and "the magical past that we wish it might have been." Furthermore, as we imagine and make the past, we also make our present, "and thus remake the meanings of both."[46] Certainly, medievalism involves making the past present. Generally, each definition of medievalism says this more or less explicitly, often choosing these exact words. I want to complicate this a bit with Macdonald's idea of "presencing the past" because its cross-disciplinary elasticity applies to the key subjects of *Medieval Literature on Display*. Both the term and the grammatical form are intentional. At its most basic, of course, the term "past presencing" is a synonym for making the past present. However, the use of the word "presence" as a verb allows greater potential in its application, as does its use in the present progressive tense to connote activity in continual process, grammatically and thematically. It is not finite; it is not closed—and it remains progressive in any tense (past, present, future) or mood (indicative or subjunctive) we choose. Presencing the past, says Macdonald, also implies less intentional construction and less defined purpose than the phrase "making the past present." When we talk about making something, we imply that a product will result from our activity. The term "presencing" is more creatively indefinite. The term "past presencing" can also subtly encompass both conscious and unconscious actions that bring any given past into any given present. Hartmann's *Iwein*, for example, engages in the process of presencing the past to its audience with respect to an Arthurian past that can only be imagined. The large arc of my argument in this book is that the process of presencing the medieval past has been going on since the Middle Ages. The museums do this now, particularly with respect to the literature that is put on display in our case studies, for example, the museums in Worms and in Wolframs-Eschenbach. And past presencing is integral to framing this dialogue and to continuing it as it accommodates, creates, and supports cultural memory.

Nostalgia: Longing for the medieval past

Medievalism seems aptly described as an active and dynamic process like that of memory: performative, adaptive, imaginative. The museums of *Medieval Literature on Display* participate in the work of medievalism, which also engages with the project of living with the past and "using" the past to make sense of and interpret the present. This is the process of past presencing at work. In a place like Wolframs-Eschenbach, for example, which wants very much to remain significant to its surrounding communities (Franconia, Bavaria, Germany), the process of presencing the past is the process of making heritage. Designing its museum, using physical elements of the town's history like the previously existing building of the old city hall and its proximity to the monument to create the town's newest attraction, Wolframs-Eschenbach also capitalized on its capacity to tap into the "affective resonance of history presented as heritage"[47] for present and future visitors. This affective resonance brings us briefly to the second term that bears on this study: nostalgia.

Nostalgia expresses a peculiar kind of memory: the longing or desire for the past in the present as for a home that no longer exists or for a different time altogether. This sometimes physical and often deeply emotional "ache of temporal distance and displacement,"[48] as Svetlana Boym describes it, is a powerful driver of memories that then mold the shape of past experience into the present. In the *Future of Nostalgia*, Boym explores two primary categories of nostalgia: restorative nostalgia, delimited often by national sentiment, more constrained in terms of future vision; and reflective nostalgia, channeled through individual and cultural memory, less burdened, more generative. Boym eventually joins these two categories to form another: creative nostalgia, which "reveals the fantasies of the age" in which "the future is born."[49] In this case, the object of our longing is not the past the way it was but rather the past the way it could have been. This last is a key factor that motivates a turn toward the medieval, the desire to use the medieval as a way of understanding the present, the desire to interpret that distant past now as we imagine it could have been in our need to juxtapose what we want to be "old" with how we see the "new." The work of Boym and others on nostalgia has had a significant impact on scholarship in medievalism. D'Arcens talks about the way in which the medieval past "becomes a nostalgic corrective to modernity."[50] Weisl suggests that medievalist performance, as it "embodies both past and the present simultaneously" and as it "looks directly into the present by setting the contemporary world up against the past," demonstrates a tension between "nostalgic yearning and presentism": the past can be longed for or it can be incorporated into the present moment in a way that does not privilege what was over what can be.[51] This tension leads, I think, to what Dinshaw calls a temporal complexity within nostalgia; it is not linear, just moving from past to present or the reverse. Rather, in a formulation that we might more commonly apply to popular fantasy fiction, Dinshaw comments, "the present is ineluctably linked to other times, people, situations, worlds."[52] This temporal complexity attracts and fascinates and inspires. It is what has inspired fantasy just as it has inspired the many amateur scholars of the nineteenth century to follow their passion for antiquarian literature and ancient languages; the fact that we carry the medieval past so constantly and asynchronously with us is the reason why the issue of temporality figures prominently in current studies of medievalism.[53] To examine these complex relationships in the passionate affair that we have with the past, Dinshaw advocates for a critical nostalgia, a kind of third category that could be added to the two put forward by Boym (reflective and restorative). The reflective dimensions of nostalgia can ultimately lead to a "broader understanding of the shared, collective possibilities of life now."[54] In short, nostalgia has the capacity to create community in the memory we create of a past we long to share. This capacity to inspire and create memory leads us to narrative. Nostalgia has been seen as kitsch or sentimentality, and it can be that, but it is also more: "memory inflected by desire."[55] And it is always a paradox, it is unstable; it may be a fantasy, but it is one that is "constantly shown up as inadequate, constantly in need of improvement, constantly jettisoned, constantly retrieved and renovated."[56] This is also where memory comes into play, adjusting, adapting, recombining, and recollecting experiences, those that are real or those that are made real through their narratives.

And this brings us back to the idea of presencing the past, connected with the modern anxiety caused by the rapid and seemingly inexorable spread of globalization in the twentieth century. In their essay "Before the trains of thought have been laid down so firmly: The premodern post/human," the introduction to the first volume of the journal *Postmedieval*, editors Eileen Joy and Craig Dionne address the effect of globalization on our conceptions of our present. In an era of "hyper-globalization" that seems simultaneously "saturated with and drained of" historical memory, we should take a moment to "consider the complex web of relations that inhere between the Now(s) and Then(s), the Here(s) and There(s)" that make up the time we find ourselves in.[57] The longing of nostalgia to presence the past (an always-already lost time) enables a creative environment in which there are "many different Nows existing alongside each other."[58] We continually create a Middle Ages that we cannot ever retrieve or fully know but which remains more than a mere palimpsest in the present. Furthermore, we have our "own nostalgias, fantasies, identities" even as we build upon the Middle Ages created by our predecessors.[59] The question is what to do with the desire to, or the need to, remember. The desire to reclaim former glory, or the desire to be "put on the map" again—the desire to reconnect with medieval roots—such desires arguably fuel nostalgic feelings and inspire the work of memory. For our purposes, this work takes shape in the medieval literature on display and in the museums designed to display it.

Heritage and museums: Performing the present past

The museums lead us to the final key word, namely "heritage." Heritage emerges through place as the past is made present, where the emphasis is not only on the relationship between a Now and a Then but also on a very tangible Here. Macdonald stresses the role of place in nostalgia:

As a prime mode through which the past can be experienced as a powerful physical presence, "place" is variously "made up" not only in rooted locations but also through memory and imagination and the various media that enable them. That the term *nostalgia* might be interpreted as longing for, and yearning to return to, either the past or home is, perhaps, a significant elision, for it is the past as potentially suitable "home" that nostalgia summons up; and it thus also makes sense that forms of nostalgia emerge and proliferate at times when people are challenged by displacements of various sorts.[60]

Place and heritage play a role in the desire for home, the need for security, the search for rooted-ness. Heritage is indeed the performance of, and the emplacement of, the past in the present. It is, for Macdonald, a "noisy form of memory materialization,"[61] where the past emerges through place and "its specific physical elements, such as buildings or natural features."[62] Place, that is, physical location, is very significant for the museums in Wolframs-Eschenbach and in Worms, in the communities that built them and that continue to support and promote them. The museums would not have come about without the firm anchor in place: in the buildings they inhabit, in the towns that they are part of.[63] They also have a very firm anchor in a particular historical period (the Middle Ages) that each community wants to celebrate as its past: not just any past but the medieval past. And not just any medieval past but the past inscribed in the literature of the early thirteenth century. The communities, particularly Worms, seem to want to go back to the literary and historical roots of their medieval narratives, which resonated so wildly and destructively in the last 200 years. The medieval past and the literary past are "pasts" and "memories" that can be claimed by all because the real medieval heritage is not as controversial as the themes that were promoted by nineteenth- and twentieth-century nationalists, as well as National Socialists. In this, the museums exemplify the process of medievalism in the service of imagining community as medieval literature becomes a vehicle for presencing the past and for shaping a future. The cities seem to express a hope that the texts, their themes, and their history become more visible and more firmly established as part of the respective community's heritage.

In general, the museums we will discuss in Chapters 3 and 4 can be seen as part of the museum boom of the late twentieth century. The trend toward musealization reveals an underlying cultural need for "temporal anchoring in the face of loss of tradition and unsettlement" brought about by the increasing speed "of technological and related change."[64] Macdonald describes heritage as "sticky." Like glue, heritage connects and binds the members of a community together. As it also clings and constrains, heritage can also be difficult, which is how she characterizes the relationship of the city of Nuremberg to its history, particularly with the still-existing grounds of the 1934 Nazi party rally. Certainly, we could characterize German history generally, after the Second World War and after 1989, as difficult—perhaps even doubly so, amplified by the different experiences of the two Germanys before and after reunification. Indeed, one still makes reference to the old states ("die alten Bundesländer") and the new states ("die neuen Bundesländer") in talking about the West and the East almost thirty years later. The term "Ostalgie"—a play on the word east (Ost) and the German cognate for nostalgia ("Nostalgie")—describes a kind of nostalgia for East Germany (i.e., life in the former East Germany) that has developed particularly in the late 1990s and early 2000s. As Macdonald suggests, drawing on the work of Daphne Berdahl, the phenomenon expresses a longing not necessarily for the return of the past but more for the sense of community that people perceive to have existed then. "Ostalgie" began as a characteristically German phenomenon that resonated powerfully with other nostalgias, emerging and colliding as the two former Germanys worked to unite. German collective memory had been contained and perpetuated over time, says Koshar, by monuments and images carefully cultivated in the German memoryscape.[65] These images and monuments transcended Cold War divisions; the Wartburg castle would be an example of the powerful continuity of metaphor in German collective consciousness. In the late 1980s and early 1990s, I want to suggest, various nostalgic impulses regionally and nationally support a more local longing for the medieval past. The literary past, for Worms or Wolframs-Eschenbach, is not recoverable in any real sense; yet changes in the modern present encourage thoughts of former greatness, or awaken the desire to be "put on the map" again, or inspire the connection with medieval roots—such desires fuel nostalgic feelings and facilitate the work of memory. This work takes shape in museums that choose to put medieval literature on display; this is where memory becomes heritage.

Literary museums

The rather traditional museum landscapes in and around both Worms and Wolframs-Eschenbach make the literary museums stand out. These two museums also stand out in the museum landscape of Germany. For that reason, we will take a moment here to situate the museums in Worms and in Wolframs-Eschenbach in the context of other literary museums in Germany and in the context of museums of medieval culture. For purposes of comparison, I will highlight here several museums with related exhibits and installations; all of the museums share a mission to display literature and/or literary activity. Some of the museums also see themselves as guardians of local or regional culture (Schloß Neuenbürg and the Siegfried Museum in Xanten) as well as proponents of their respective narrative traditions. Other museums have a more traditional focus on literary texts as artifacts or on literary history and literary reception as part of a national/global cultural legacy that also complements the work of associated literary archives (Marbach, Zurich, Vienna). The Grimmwelt museum in Kassel combines all of these areas of emphasis—regional culture, national legacy, literary texts—in its presentation of the life and work of the Grimm brothers. All of these museums seek to engage their audiences in a conversation with literature through creative, unique, often interactive displays.

There are a number of literature museums that we might look to for comparisons and context with respect to the museums at the center of this study. The museums generally fall into two categories: national and regional. Indeed, if one does a brief Google search for "Literaturmuseum," three turn up, one in each major German-speaking country. The oldest and most well known is the *Literaturmuseum der Moderne* in the German town of Marbach. This is the premier literary museum in Germany, built alongside the German literary archives that were established in Marbach, the home of Friedrich Schiller. The *Literaturmuseum der Moderne* is part of a complex that houses the German literature archives (*Deutsches Literaturarchiv*) as well as the national Schiller museum (Schiller National-Museum). Literature is its focus. As its information says about its permanent exhibition "Die Seele" ("The Soul"), writing is at the center of this exhibit's focus ("Im Mittelpunkt der Dauerausstellung steht das Schreiben").[66] And literature, the written word, is very much at the center of the museum's mission. There are also newer museums of literature in Vienna (opened in 2015)[67] and Zurich—the latter was just approved for funding in 2017 to expand the Museum Strauhof into a more comprehensive museum with literature as its primary focus.

The museum of Austrian literature, the *Literaturmuseum der österreichischen Nationalbibliothek*, opened in 2015 to glowing reviews. Under the auspices of the Austrian national library, the museum came about in a happy coincidence of events: in 2006 the old imperial archives consolidated their files and the old Grillparzer house in central Vienna became available. Franz Grillparzer (1791–1872), one of the leading authors and dramatists in mid-nineteenth-century Austria, had also served as the court archivist from 1832 to 1856; the museum's second floor offers a look into his study. The museum incorporates the history of the building as archive, displaying documents (such as letters and manuscripts) as well as objects (such as uniforms or travel suitcases), with the story of Austrian literature from the late eighteenth century through the present day. One can see Peter Handke's hiking boots or a director's chair in which Ernst Jandl sat. One can view plenty of objects from the personal and professional lives of Austrian authors from the nineteenth century to the present. One reviewer remarks on the museum's humorous undertone, offsetting the enormous amount of material that the museum has to display; the concept favors a jaunty stroll rather than a reverent pilgrimage.[68] In addition, as the museum strives to be not just a new archive but also a space for the present day ("Gegenwarts-Ort") the written and the spoken word feature prominently as exhibits show readings of various works, whether by actors or by contemporary authors reading from their own material. And the museum eschews a chronological display, offering instead a more thematic view of Austrian literature situated firmly a larger European context. The museum aims to cultivate the love of literature, leading visitors from what they see and what they hear to the written word and back again.[69]

At this writing, plans are also underway to create a museum of Swiss literature, incorporating the current Literaturmuseum Strauhof into the more comprehensive project.[70] A pilot project, the museum has recently received approval (and funding) to go ahead into the next phase that should lead to a more permanent exhibition. The location had sponsored a number of literature exhibits since 1989. The city had plans to close the Strauhof in 2013; a jury was commissioned to find new sponsors by the end of the 2014 year.[71] Planning for two development phases (2013–2015 and 2015–2018), the museum has remained open since 2015 in the old city center of Zurich. Currently, it is gearing up for the 200th anniversary of Swiss author Gottfried Keller (1819–1890), a major proponent of nineteenth-century realism. The museum's motto seems to reflect current trends in literary display: it is a place for the reality of literature. A space for imagination. Going beyond languages and borders. ("Ein Ort für die Wirklichkeit der Literatur. Ein Raum der Imagination. Über Sprachen und Grenzen hinweg.") Like other contemporaries, this museum proclaims its intention to be more than just a museum ("im engeren Sinn kein Museum"), as it inhabits the intersection of literature and its staging in three-dimensional space. In this museum, like its Austrian counterpart, we can clearly see the desire to celebrate a distinct national literature. All literature written in German, the Swiss and the Austrians insist, is not the exclusive purview of Germany.

The other category of museums that centers on literature includes museums that are actually most relevant for this study. Rather than focusing on national literatures, they turn their focus instead toward literary interpretations as regional or local history. In this context, I would like to mention three museums in particular, all built since the year 2000. The oldest of these is a museum located in the small town of Neuenbürg nestled among the hills of the northern Black Forest region. Utilizing several rooms of the castle (Schloss Neuenbürg) that overlooks the town, the museum focuses specifically on a three-dimensional display and narration of *Das kalte Herz* (*The Cold Heart*), a well-known literary fairy tale by the regional author Wilhelm Hauff (1802–1827). Opened in 2001, coincidentally the same year as the Nibelung Museum, the museum in Schloss Neuenbürg is a branch of the Badisches Landesmuseum (the state museum of Baden), whose main museum is in the city of Karlsruhe, a bit further to the south on the Rhine River. The castle was looking for new opportunities, and the state museum had been involved in a project to reinvigorate regional museums, some of which were in new buildings and some of which were in areas that needed renovation. Indeed, while Neuenbürg is a picturesque town in the middle of a beautiful landscape, it is most easily accessible by car and is not necessarily a frequented stop on the main tourist routes. Similar to both the museum in Wolframs-Eschenbach and the Nibelung Museum, the museum in Neuenbürg has also been described as a "begehbares Hörbuch," an audiobook that one can walk through; the museum's website calls it a walkable mise en scene.[72] Closely following Hauff's tale, the display tells the story of a poor woodcutter in the Black Forest, Peter Munk, born lucky on a Sunday ("Sonntagskind"), who has three wishes granted to him by the good forest spirit (the "Glasmännlein"). The young man squanders his good fortune, goes into debt, makes a deal with an evil forest spirit (the "Holländer-Michel")—he gives up his living heart for one of stone—earns his fortune, and destroys his loved ones in the process until he learns his lesson, repents, gets his heart back. The rooms of the museum tell the story with beautiful dioramas, colorful lighting, rich soundscapes. The creativity of the storytelling is counterbalanced by a more traditional interactive display about the Black Forest region and the culture of the region in the nineteenth century (forestry, etc.) when Hauff wrote his story. The purpose is to make the history of the castle, the city, and the region of the northern Black Forest tangible—so visitors can experience it in the moment. According to the most recent museum information, the museum has had more than 200,000 visitors since 2001 (that is an average of 12,500 a year). Here again is the need to design a concept that is new and exciting and able to establish a museum that does not have any basis on a long-standing collection.

The result is an "animierte, multimediale Präsentation" that combines film, silhouette/cut-outs, music, narration, creative lighting.[73]

The Grimmwelt museum is perhaps the most recent addition to the landscape of German literature museums.[74] The new museum took shape over the course of several years, beginning around 2012, when the city of Kassel determined that it was time to upgrade the previously existing museum for the Grimm brothers, who had made their home in Kassel from 1798 to 1848. Additional incentive came from the 2005 decision to make the primary work of the Grimm brothers, the *Kinder- und Hausmärchen* (*Children's and Household Tales*), part of the UNESCO's Memory of the World. A referendum passed to approve the museum's location in 2012, the original museum closed its doors for the first time in its fifty-five years. Whereas the first museum had emphasized language and literature, and was not exactly designed for children, the new design would strive to make the museum a place that visitors could experience, a place that brought the Grimms to life, where exhibits would actually allow the visitors and the artifacts to change roles.[75] The museum, with a price tag of at least 20 million Euros, would fit into an existing museum landscape in the region that includes thirty-four museums and galleries.

Built on the Weinberg on the city's edge, the museum opened to rave reviews in September 2015 and it has remained popular since, wildly exceeding expectations in attendance. The museum has three main sections. The first highlights the work of Jacob and Wilhelm Grimm as philologists, lexicographers, and scholars participating in the nineteenth-century intellectual landscape of Europe, literally shaping the language of the German nation with the massive undertaking that becomes the *Deutsches Wörterbuch*. The museum's second section focuses on the Grimms' best-known legacy, offering interactive displays of fairy tales where one can enter the cottage of Red Riding Hood's grandmother to confront the wolf or where one can take a turn gazing into the mirror of Snow White's evil stepmother. A fascinating exhibit on Rumpelstiltzchen allows the visitor to hear the story told in numerous world languages, as well as several German dialects; as the story proceeds from one teller to another, from one language to another, the narrative flows seamlessly. The words may change, the gestures of the storyteller may change, but the familiar narrative continues from beginning to end without interruption, and the visitor realizes that the tale remains constant as the telling varies in a most effective display of the story's reach across languages and cultures. Finally, the third section of the museum places the Grimm brothers and their family in the context of nineteenth-century German culture and society.

For the reviewer of the *Frankfurter Allgemeine Zeitung* (11.09.2015), it is the combination of whimsical play ("Spiel") and content ("Gehalt") that makes the museum so successful. *Die Zeit* (10.09.2015) calls the museum both a temple of language ("Sprachtempel") and a fairytale forest ("Märchenwald"). Interviewed by the *Freie Presse* (17.09.2015), in the week of the museum's opening, museum director Susanne Völker insists that the Grimmwelt is no house of poets ("Dichterhaus"), no literature archive ("Literaturarchiv"), and no ordinary run-of-the-mill museum. Rather it is a place where the wider public can feel welcome and included in a space oriented toward the experiences and the active engagement of a wide audience: "ein Ort der erlebnisorientierten, aktiven Einbeziehung des breiten Publikums." The museum seems to thrive on its combination of interactive and traditional displays: the Grimms were linguists, after all, and knew that language was a living thing. The museum therefore keeps the living transmission of language and literature at its center, and it does not overemphasize historical content. After all, the goal is not to overwhelm the public with information; rather, the museum aims to engage visitors actively to in a positive learning experience.

Since its opening in 2015, the Grimmwelt museum has seen well over 100,000 visitors on average per year—in fact, in its first year it saw close to 160,000. The 200,000th visitor crossed the threshold in March 2017. This shows an unqualified success. It is an audience magnet ("Publikumsmagnet")[76] that blends into the park landscape at its location, offering a walkable sculpture dedicated to language and literature. The museum is part of the current economic and cultural upswing for Kassel, as the *Süddeutsche Zeitung* describes it; more than 75 percent destroyed in 1943 and close to the border with East Germany after 1949, the city remained culturally, economically, and geographically on the periphery of the German Federal Republic until 1989. The new Grimmwelt museum has received numerous awards for, among other achievements, its architectural and conceptual rejection of any connection to Disney. In December 2015, the *Guardian* named the Grimmwelt museum one of the ten best new museums in the world.[77]

Finally, we come to newest museum that related most closely to the medieval literature on display in Wolframs-Eschenbach and Worms: the Siegfried Museum in Xanten is newer.[78] In 2010, the museum opened under the name of the "Literaturmuseum Nibelungen(h)ort" (Das Museum Nibelungen(h)ort Xanten). This original name contains a smart play on words that reveals much about how the museum sees itself and its purpose, designed as a literary museum with a dual focus: first, on the treasure hoard ("Hort") of the Nibelungs and, second, on the city of Xanten as a significant place ("Ort") for those same Nibelungs. Xanten is, after all, the alleged home of Siegfried according to the *Nibelungenlied*. In 2013, the museum changed its name to the more generic tourist-friendly Siegfried-Museum; though a Germanist like myself enjoys the clever double entendre, the word play of the original seems to have been a bit clumsy as a marketing tool. The name may have changed, but the museum from its opening had offered a creative mix of exhibits that display artifacts of medieval culture, whether originals or replicas. It also tells the story of the medieval *Nibelungenlied*, as well as the story of the text´s reception history from the thirteenth century through the twentieth century. The museum display in general is straightforward, chronological, and informative. If one were to ask a visitor what he or she learned, it would be relatively easy to tick off main points—both of the narrative and of its history. We know the main characters of the tale, we can follow their journey through its real geography, we learn not only a brief history of the city of Xanten but also have glimpses into medieval material culture. Finally, the museum offers a detailed chronology of the *Nibelungenlied*'s reception in the nineteenth and twentieth centuries through literature and music and, eventually, film. There are distinct similarities to the Nibelugnenmuseum in Worms. The museum is located in the middle of the downtown (*Altstadt*) in Xanten. In addition, the museum is built into a portion of the old city fortifications, not unlike the museum in Worms. Perhaps most importantly, like the museum in Worms, the museum in Xanten establishes its authenticity by drawing upon the fact that the *Nibelugnenlied* names Xanten as the birthplace and home of Siegfried. The city of Worms serves the same function for the Burgundians and for Kriemhild. Both Xanten and Worms are existing places with documented and identifiable histories since the time of the Romans. They provide not only a geographical anchor for the narratives but also geographical anchors for those interpreters who have come after and who want to place themselves literally/concretely into the narrative.

Not surprisingly, the Siegfried Museum understands itself as a response to and perhaps even a corrective to the Nibelung Museum in Worms. Trost, for example, expresses his gratitude to the museum team from Worms in the acknowledgments to his 2012 museum catalog *Vom Umgang mit Helden*. I find it significant that Trost frames the Nibelung Museum in the context of further Nibelungen reception, along with the Nibelungenfestspiele in Worms—as well as in terms of the importance for tourism and marketing ("Stadtmarketing").[79] The activities of the museum promote the many facets of the narrative's reception history. Several comments seem to echo rather veiled critique of the Nibelung Museum, or perhaps an attempt in Xanten to differentiate the more recent museum from the older one. On the other hand, it does seem quite clear that Xanten is trying (in its exhibits) to respond to the rather over "over-the-top" innovations that have elicited negative comments about Worms. Trost offers a characterization of the Nibelung Museum as an example of how it seems easier for our time to deal with the legend in a more ironic or more unburdened way.[80] In comparison to Worms, which describes itself as a "begehbares Hörbuch" (a walk-able audiobook), the museum in Xanten promotes itself as an opportunity to achieve a goal/task that the other does not: it presents the myth of the Nibelungs historically and in the context of its reception.[81] Indeed, the exhibits are carefully constructed around the reception history of the *Nibelungenlied*; they are creative but fairly traditionally and chronologically organized. Visitors go through the museum literally from the beginnings in the legends that arose from sagas originating around the time of the migrations ("Völkerwanderungen") to the present day (in film, comics, advertising, young adult literature). The task of the Xanten museum is to show this variety in the reception history of the *Nibelungenlied*—allegorically, dramatically, musically, or satirically—implying that the Nibelung Museum in Worms does not display this variety.[82] Or, at least, that Worms does it so differently that Germany needs another museum to serve as a kind of counterbalance, as though a bit more tradition offsets the innovation in Worms.

Conclusion

The process of past presencing is a process that employs memory both to enact and to perform various pasts, notably as part of the preservation and display of heritage in the museums of today. It is also a process that enables a creative convergence of medieval and modern memory in the display of literature in the Nibelung Museum and in the Museum Wolfram von Eschenbach. The Wolfram monument is one example of this convergence, and before we proceed to the next chapter, I would like to offer one more example from the Nibelung Museum in Worms. After moving through the first twelve stations in the *Hörturm*, one arrives at the top floor of the tower, with a beautiful panoramic view of Worms. On the table at the center of the room, we find the replica of a twelfth-century map; as one approaches it, the poet (in the audio guide) invites the visitor into the Nibelung's land, to look at the poet's world from each compass direction. We will talk in more detail about the construction of the exhibit when we discuss the museum in Chapter 4. For our purposes here, I want to use one example as a small teaser to illustrate how place, memory, and narrative come together in a simple but effective display that reveals the palimpsests in which we participate. The view to the east, entitled "Erinnerungen an Attila" ("memories of Attila"), looks toward the land of Attila and the Huns. Attila, or Etzel, figures in the *Nibelungenlied* as the second husband of Kriemhild, first married to the doomed Siegfried. As we stand at the window, our view moves eastward across the Rhine and the Neckar rivers to the Danube. We are prompted to note familiar landmarks along the way: the countries of Austria and Hungary; the cities of Regensburg, Passau, and Budapest. Our gaze only extends actually perhaps to the Rhein. But the act of looking, with the map as a visual aid, overlays the museum's medieval tale onto modern Europe's familiar geography, as our knowledge of that geography simultaneously maps back onto the story. We feel ourselves at the intersection of the present and the past, similar to the feeling we have when we stand at the window and look through the names of the characters about whom we have heard so much. The layers of the palimpsest materialize before us, enfolding us and hinting perhaps at layers yet to be discovered. We find ourselves in a dynamic creative space, on multiple thresholds: between the medieval and the modern, between the tangible and the intangible, between old(er) and new(er) histories, between then and now.

This kind of creative space demands considerable effort of visitors to find their place in it, piecing together remnants of histories and narratives to do so. The work asked of visitors resonates, I suggest, with Bhabha's concept of "the join," inasmuch as this idea relates to the role of literature in exploring a modern condition fragmented by deep traumas. In the introduction to *Location of Culture*, Bhabha addresses the need for group "cohesion" as the task of artistic endeavor in a time of change and perhaps uncertainty:

> When historical visibility has faded, when the present tense of testimony loses its power to arrest, then the displacements of memory and the indirections of art offer us the image of our psychic survival. To live in the unhomely world, to find its ambivalencies and ambiguities enacted in the house of fiction, or its sundering and splitting performed in the work of art, is also to affirm a profound desire for social solidarity.[83]

Perhaps connections to actual historical events seem unsettlingly tenuous ("historical visibility has faded") in a world that often feels uncomfortable and even alienating, full of "ambivalencies and ambiguities." Bhabha uses the word "unhomely" to translate *unheimlich*, a world that may feel unsettling, alienating. The "indirections of art" embrace and challenge those ambiguities, giving them shape and expression, offering readers or viewers (or listeners) an anchor for "psychic survival" in an environment marked by anxiety, discomfort, discontinuity. When the house of fiction provides a stage on which the ambiguities may be enacted or performed, says Bhabha, literature and art evoke "a profound desire" for solidarity, for belonging, for community. Audiences affirm this desire, he suggests, by responding, "I am looking for the join ... I want to join ... I want to join."[84] Memory (an earlier version of the essay uses the term "distortions of memory"[85]) would seem to offer a mechanism to enable this join, a potential to fulfill the desire for solidarity affirmed so powerfully by literary or visual arts. As memory displaces, it also re-places, re-assembles, re-members; the join emerges in this creative (also imaginative) space.

Bhabha draws his image of the join from the poignant scenes in Toni Morrison's *Beloved* where the voice of the eponymous figure speaks of "looking for the join," of seeking a place to be alone no longer and to touch another, to become whole and reunite fragments of body and identity, of mother and child, of history and home, of death and life. Though I admit I take perhaps a sizable cultural and historical leap here, I do want to suggest an associative resonance in the way the museums invite visitors to anticipate a kind of "join" that will reassemble previously scattered fragments.[86] To be sure, these fragments are not the remnants of an identity brutally shattered by a racially oppressive past, as Bhabha reads Morrison's portrayal of the African American experience of slavery and its aftermath. However, I suggest that the museums present an identity perceived to be similarly fractured by its own disquieting history: the German identity of the late twentieth century, imagined anew in the communities of Wolframs-Eschenbach and Worms through their museal adaptations of medieval German literature. The museums invite visitors to see, to imagine, to participate in, or to experience for ourselves the wondrous things we have heard ("muget ir nu wunder hœren sagen") in those old tales ("in alten mæren") that now take shape before us. This anticipated encounter is also the work of imaginative memory in creating new meaning from inherited story. As these modern German museums display the medieval past and thereby interrogate the twentieth-century past, they ask visitors to consider a kind of "join," to pull fragments of a traumatic past into a present narrative. Whether real or hyperreal, whether found or made, whether authentic or fake, the Middle Ages is "presenced" as the literary cultural past in the Nibelung Museum and in the Museum Wolfram von Eschenbach through the medieval literature on display. The ability to accommodate multiple perspectives, multiple temporalities, and myriad intertexts is what the museums pull from the literature they display—even as they make the display of literature into the museum objects and artifacts that they lack. Janus-like, the museums draw on this history and their medieval texts as they simultaneously try to look backward in order to look forward. The museums also seek to capitalize on the ubiquity of the Middle Ages in popular culture, where it builds fantasies across genres and media and frames a variety of narratives. By taking up and engaging the question of whether it is possible to exhibit not just any literature but medieval literature, they place themselves squarely between alterity and modernity.

2

Adapting Medieval Narratives

My lord Hartmann von Aue, a guest of mine is coming to Lady Guinevere, your mistress, and to your lord, King Arthur, to their castle.[1]
(Wolfram von Eschenbach, *Parzival*)

Part of this ongoing dialogue with the past, for that is what adaptation means for audiences, creates the doubled pleasure of the palimpsest.[2]
(Linda Hutcheon, *Theory of Adaptation*)

Wolfram von Eschenbach pays homage to Hartmann von Aue in book III of *Parzival* just before the eponymous hero comes to King Arthur's court. It is morning as young Parzival eagerly hurries toward King Arthur, who is holding court in the city of Nantes. Parzival is dressed in the fool's garb (sackcloth shirt and breeches) his mother made for him; he rides a nag, and he carries his javelin with him. His cousin Sigune, whom he has just met, has given him (and us) his name; he has also just left the lady Jeschute, whom he assaulted in order to take her ring and brooch. His behavior and his appearance seem most unbecoming for an aspiring knight: impulsive, crude, unconsidered. Wolfram knows this and breaks into his own narrative to address Hartmann von Aue, the poet of *Erec*, which heralded the debut of Arthurian romance in the German vernacular around 1185. Wolfram asks that his newcomer Parzival be treated well:

> My lord Hartmann von Aue, a guest of mine is coming to Lady Guinevere your mistress and to your lord, King Arthur, to their castle. Pray protect him from scorn. He's neither fiddle nor rote—let them take another plaything! Let them, out of courtesy, rest content with that. Otherwise your lady Enite and her mother Karsnafite, will be dragged through the mill and their reputation crushed. If I am to wear out my mouth with mockery, I will defend my friend.
> (*Parzival*,143,21–144,4; Edwards, p. 61)

Wolfram appeals to Hartmann to be kind to Parzival, whose rough appearance and uncouth behavior may be deceiving. He is asking his fellow poets, their shared audiences, to look kindly and generously on this newcomer to King Arthur's court. Otherwise, he threatens to disparage Hartmann's own works in the person of Erec's queen Enite.

Wolfram's appellation to Hartmann is the perfect way to start the chapter on literature and adaptations. With this intertextual flourish, Wolfram declares not only Parzival's but his own arrival on the Arthurian scene. He sets himself up as Hartmann's contemporary; he indicates that he knows Hartmann's work and is doing something completely different with his naive hero that is slowly wise (*Parzival* 4, 18) and does not appear to be the kind of hero that would appear at first like Erec. In the passages immediately preceding and following, Wolfram also skillfully appropriates Hartmann's narrative for his own purpose. Parzival, the clumsy and inexperienced youth, has just left Jeschute (Erec's sister) and Sigune (his cousin), both of whom are connected to other stories both earlier (this would be Jeschute with respect to Erec) and later (this would be Sigune with respect to Titurel). This is one of many intertextual connections that we find in Wolfram, not only to Hartmann—but it is significant that Hartmann features so prominently in the intertexts in this particular book. After Parzival leaves Jeschute and continues on his way to King Arthur's court, the narrator addresses Hartmann to ask that Parzival receive a decent/appropriate reception by Arthur and Guinevere, as befits a young man with such promise. We know, however, that Jeschute is being punished for that encounter with Parzival, forced to ride in rags as her husband seeks to restore his honor. He integrates Erec's story into Parzival's by making Jeschute Erec's sister. Her situation recalls that of Enite, as her husband takes her off into the woods, making her wear rags, punishing her for an indiscretion that was not her fault but that has shamed him. This is essentially what Erec does.

As narrator and poet, Wolfram demonstrates not only his own knowledge and artistry here; he shows us the elasticity of the romance genre. Romance is playful, says Wolfram here—it is adaptive, allusive, and intertextual. Wolfram here appropriates Hartmann's narrative for his own purposes, in addition to demonstrating how well he understands the tradition in which he participates; he knows it well enough to play with it. Intertextuality is a defining feature of Arthurian romance. Poets like Hartmann and Wolfram worked in an interconnected literary environment; they implicitly or explicitly borrowed from one another, adapting one another's works and often molding them into new creations. They borrowed themes (the quest, courtly love), characters (Arthur, Guinevere, Gawain, Lancelot, the swan knight Lohengrin), images (a bleeding lance, a knight with a lion companion, the loathly lady). The inherent intertextuality of Arthurian romance leads to the palimpsests and adaptations we find accumulating over time between the thirteenth century and the present. The *Nibelungenlied* is itself a sophisticated adaptation of a variety of older sources texts; *Parzival* is a translation, a continuation, and an adaptation of the earlier *Perceval* by French poet Chretien de Troyes.[3]

Adaptation and allusive intertextuality were practiced enthusiastically in the thirteenth century, and these processes shape the creative layers of palimpsests over time. The museums in this study share an interactive and multimedial intertextuality with the medieval narratives they display. The Nibelung Museum integrates critical and humorous reflections on this intertextuality not only into its display but also explicitly into the narrative of the museum guide, as we will see in chapter 4. A brief teaser will serve to illustrate: the guide, narrated by the fictional (and still anonymous) poet of the *Nibelungenlied*, mentions Wolfram's allusion to Rumolt as a poor joke by adaptor C (the author who added the first strophe to the *Nibelungenlied* that we discussed at length in Chapter 1) that Wolfram then quoted word for word. The poet-narrator of the museum guide feels quite insulted by this, saying this kind of behavior and misquoting were characteristic of Wolfram, who was "always fond of saying stupid things."[4] Cowritten by German medievalist Joachim Heinzle and architect Oscar Auer, one of the museum designers, the text for the poet-narrator encapsulates the most pointed critique of Wolfram's contemporaries Gottfried, who likens Wolfram's style to that of a hare jumping willy-nilly over a "word-heath."

Adaptation and medieval literature go hand in hand. The remainder of this chapter will introduce the German medieval texts and adaptations that shape the medievalism enacted through the displays in the Nibelung Museum and the Museum Wolfram von Eschenbach. The chapter will trace the development of the textual material from origins to the high-medieval texts to which the museums respond as well as the key reappropriations since the medieval period—particularly in the nineteenth and twentieth centuries. In this context, for example, we can consider the early-thirteenth-century murals of Hartmann von Aue's *Iwein* at Rodenegg (South Tyrol) and Schmalkalden (central Germany), for instance, as the beginning of a visualizing trajectory that leads to the modern museums in Worms and Wolframs-Eschenbach. Hartmann's *Iwein*, as the first literary work put on display, visually translated from text to image and transformed into the first secular murals found north of the Alps in the thirteenth century.

A brief examination of the medieval literary sources will provide a basis for the adaptations to follow: the Middle High German *Nibelungenlied* as well as the works of Wolfram von Eschenbach from *Parzival* and *Willehalm* to *Titurel*. After introducing the literary sources, the chapter traces the broad outlines of reception history that adapted the source material in text (medieval continuations), in image (visualizations in murals or tapestries), in music (the operas of Richard Wagner), and eventually also in film (Fritz Lang). These are the adaptations that each museum creatively and critically engages. Narrative tropes and deictic strategies reveal that the task of making the imaginative past present was a familiar one for medieval literature in a highly memorial culture. The interactive and yet also memorial aspects of medieval literature make it a suitable mechanism over time for adaptation through intertexts and other narrative entanglements. Finally, the museums exploit these interpretively pliant aspects of medieval literature to express community history and identity by making the past present through depiction of the Middle High German narratives most important to them. Thus, the idea of the "medieval" enables each community to engage further in presencing the past.

Wolfram, Hartmann, literature, and memory

With the first lines of his *Iwein*, Hartmann brings his audience into the space of memory, into the remembered (albeit fictional) past of the Arthurian court. As I suggested in the earlier discussion of the prologue, the "even now" of this present invites the audience, medieval listeners, or twenty-first-century readers, to come together in the group; it inspires a connection, a solidarity of feeling. The *Nibelungenlied* similarly seeks to evoke this connection in the first strophe we discussed in Chapter 1. Medieval literature was a communal endeavor in a hybrid semiliterate environment where most audiences heard their texts or saw them performed. Evelyn Vitz describes the audience of medieval romance as a community involved in "an intense, interpersonal, heavily-mediated, and strongly interactive situation."[5] The collective and interactive nature of interpretation, inviting the participation of text and performer, establishes what Vitz terms "an interpretive community," whose members must have "valued the experience of group reception: the sense of a truly shared culture."[6] This sense of shared culture, of collective identity, facilitates the cultivation of memory and the presencing of the past. It is this sense of imagined shared memory among the audience that Hartmann addresses in his prologue to *Iwein*. A wealth of surviving evidence demonstrates that medieval patrons liked to surround themselves with this past and its deeds, particularly with the story of Iwein (the knight with the lion); we will get to this visual evidence in more detail later in a moment.[7] A timeless present, then, potentially gives shape and place to an imagined past.

The remembered past of the Arthurian court, which the first lines of *Iwein* invite us to share, seeks our engagement by making the past present. The past becomes present, even if hypothetically, as they say he may live still; furthermore, the grammatical conditional becomes the indicative of "now" when we consider obeying the injunction to live according to this example. In effect, Hartmann's prologue describes the dynamic and dialogic process of memory; as he encourages his thirteenth-century audience to bring the Arthurian past into their present, seeking a connection with the noble and illustrious king Arthur of legend, he also engages the modern reader of literature, who makes new associations with familiar stories or older texts. Memory is the process woven into the fabric of medieval romance, the process also exploited by the museums at the center of this study. Hartmann expresses this most eloquently in his prologue to *Iwein*, which is why I have devoted so much attention to it here, though this focus on Hartmann appears perhaps tangential to our central texts. The *Nibelungenlied* poet and Wolfram von Eschenbach are later contemporaries of Hartmann; the museum case studies in Chapters 3 and 4 showcase their works. Hartmann, however, establishes a precedent, both in text and in image; *Iwein* inspired spectacular contemporary visual adaptations in the murals at Rodenegg (South Tyrol) and Schmalkalden (Thuringia), which date from around or very close to the time of Hartmann's text around 1200. Generally considered to be the first examples of secular wall painting in northern Europe, the Rodenegg murals in particular offer a unique precursor to our museum case studies as a medieval example of adaptation.

Detour: Visualizing *Iwein*

General consensus is that the Rodenegg murals were painted first and that both sets are from at the first third or the first half of the thirteenth century. Taken together, of course, they offer stunning visual testimony to the popularity of the text from which they are literally drawn. I want to take a moment here to describe the murals very briefly.

The Rodenegg *Iwein* tells its story in a compact but open space, the powerful and large figures moving the plot forward in scenes with bold gestures, intense action, and vibrant color. At Rodenegg, the story is clearly Ywain; the figures are labelled with names (Ywain, Aschelon, Laudina, Luneta) that make a very explicit connection to the story if not to the actual text of Hartmann von Aue—the figures are clearly identified, and the intertext is unmistakable.[8] As one enters the space, one also enters the story told "around the room" from the right-hand side of the door. A knight (Ywain) encounters a fearsome-looking herdsman as the knight is on his way to a garden or forest clearing where he pours water (liquid) on a stone. A red knight (Aschelon) appears to challenge and fight Ywain, who deals him a mortal wound (**Figure 5**). As Aschelon is mourned by his lady and his retainers, Ywain watches from a tower window, having been safely hidden from view by Luneta, who has spirited him away using a ring that renders the wearer invisible. The courtiers search in vain for their lord's assailant and the mystery remains until Luneta brings Ywain before Laudine, where he kneels and reveals himself to her. The Rodenegg narrative that we have ends here; there is space on the wall for one more scene, in addition to the wall that has the door. The story would suggest, as Rushing and other scholars speculate, that there may have been a wedding scene.[9]

The murals were initially interpreted as an incomplete version of Hartmann's epic. General consensus now holds that the images tell their own story; the

Figure 5 Images of Ywain at Rodenegg, South Tyrol, *Wikicommons*.

murals are not an incomplete understanding of a literary source; rather, they are rather complete narratives sufficient unto themselves. What story does the Rodenegg *Iwein* tell? This tale seems to focus on knightly exploits, the dangers of *aventiure*, the establishment of order (if not authority). There is the challenge, the duel, the pursuit, the search for Iwein, the revelation to Laudine. These are scenes of actions and their consequences; they feel immediate and urgent and dramatic. They also feel somewhat unfinished or open. The last scene that has been preserved is one in which Iwein kneels before Laudine. In Hartmann's text, she has vowed to marry the man who could defend her land, and this man turns out to be Iwein. The images do not offer this background. The figure of Laudine evokes authority; whether she exercises judgment, condemnation, or mercy is unclear, though Hartmann's narrative unequivocally emphasizes the love between Laudine and Iwein as well as her political expediency in choosing a knight who can defend her land. Schmalkalden's *Iwein* uses the same narrative to tell a different story. The space is close, the ceiling low, the images somewhat unclear (as at Rodenegg), but the colors definitely muted. Instead of extending around the walls of the space, the story is told in multiple registers, read both horizontally and vertically across a vaulted ceiling. The pace of this *Iwein* seems to have slowed, perhaps because the figures are smaller and there is a greater number of scenes that have been drawn in the multiple registers. The largest image is that of the wedding feast, a scene of celebration and of rejoicing—whereas the larger scenes (that remain in tact) at Rodenegg are of the duel and of Laudine mourning. The physical layout of the murals requires more effort and attention on the part of the audience, as one must look around and above to participate in the story.[10] Schmalkalden's story emphasizes courtliness, highlighted (as James Rushing notes) by the preponderance of scenes depicting conversation rather than knightly combat or endeavor.

The murals at Schmalkalden and at Rodenegg demonstrate, in Hutcheon's words, a mode of adaptation that does not merely show or tell—it enacts. It is story that becomes experience in an act of self-conscious self-representation: the process of telling story and narrating history falls along the spectrum of orality and literacy, offering a new kind of cultural autonomy, according to Curschmann, a new dimension of active participation in the poetic process.[11] We witness this active participation in the ways the visual story deviates from the literary source, which the artist must have known in some form. The murals suggest that the interest in the literature must have been considerable for people to want to "live" with the stories like this, to inhabit the same space as these narratives and the figures in them. They demonstrate the mode of adaptation that Haiko Wandhoff suggests that medieval spaces like these, particularly the "Gesamtkunstwerk" of the medieval church, closely resemble what we now call "virtual realities."[12] Audiences (albeit certain select audiences) have their chance to step into a kind of virtual reality, as they look for the "join." Both examples of Rodenegg and Schmalkalden show the reuse of figures in a context intentionally designed to evoke a sense of community and encourage solidarity for an audience that liked to imagine and represent itself—remembering itself into fictions of its own design.

Thirteenth-century poets like Wolfram von Eschenbach and the poet of the *Nibelungenlied*, along with Hartmann von Aue, directed their literature toward discerning audiences who should appreciate the truth value of what they hear or see or read. The courtly audience was a participatory audience, encouraged to perform the text before their collective mind's eye, to become part of the narrative.[13] In the context of *Medieval Literature on Display*, which examines the practice of imaginative memory through the adaptation and reception of medieval German literature over time, the murals at Rodenegg and Schmalkalden show us a beginning. I suggest further that the museums in Worms (the Nibelung Museum) and Wolframs-Eschenbach (Museum Wolfram von Eschenbach) offer a modern variation of these visualizations. In their displays, the museums make use of intertexts that have accumulated over time to form what Hutcheon terms a palimpsest, as she describes the process of adaptation in *A Theory of Adaptation*. Before we continue, it will be useful to look at Hutcheon's analysis in more detail.

Palimpsests

Familiar in medieval studies as a manuscript in which later writing has been superimposed on earlier effaced writing, the term has also come to refer more broadly to anything similar to such a writing surface especially when it has been reused or altered while retaining traces of its earlier forms. Generally, then, a palimpsest describes a multilayered record. In a provocative yet fitting pun, Hutcheon describes adaptations as inherently "palimpsestuous" works, emphasizing the relatedness of the layers that form any palimpsest over time. Based on prior texts, often demonstrating an "overt relationship to another work or works," adaptations are "haunted at all times by their adapted texts," says Hutcheon. We inevitably feel the presence of the prior text "shadowing the one we are experiencing directly," at least if we know those prior texts. The palimpsest offers a way to address ongoing debates about the derivative or the creative nature of adaptations in this context. Hutcheon insists that adaptations are "autonomous" as "aesthetic objects" in their own right, even as they remain "inherently doubled or multilaminated" works as well.[14]

The framework of the palimpsest neatly accommodates Hutcheon's three-part definition of adaptations. First, adaptations transpose prior works. They also creatively interpret prior works to produce new ones. Finally, adaptations engage in an intertextual dialogue with prior works.[15] The prior works accumulate as palimpsest. It is this extended engagement of adaptations with other recognizable works that leads Hutcheon to her term "palimpsestuous intertextuality."[16] This describes a relationship among texts and intertexts, where layers accrue and entwine in successive iterations to form palimpsests that in turn seem to become deeply, almost inextricably linked. This is the process of adaptation over time. As a creative and interpretive transposition of a recognizable other work or works, adaptation is not only a kind of extended palimpsest; it can also involve very often a kind of transcoding into a different set of conventions altogether.[17] Palimpsests support an "ongoing dialogue with the past" that also generates what Hutcheon describes as the "doubled pleasure" of the palimpsest. When we experience a palimpsest, we derive pleasure from "knowingly" experiencing more than one text.[18] Over time, as these palimpsests accrue, they can develop complex narrative interrelationships; entanglements occur that may crucially shape not only discourse but memory, leaving what Bakhtin would call a trace in narrative layers or complicating and enhancing its expression. While Bakhtin is talking primarily about textual narratives (e.g., the novel), the advantage of the term "palimpsest" is it can apply in transtextual and transmedial contexts, as our earlier discussion of the Wolfram monument in the introduction demonstrated. Bakhtin's traces are what allow the palimpsests to resonate in memory, enabling us to recognize the works that form the multiple layers that our adaptations incorporate and that we enjoy as we experience them. Hutcheon characterizes this experience in part as a kind of the interpretive doubling or "conceptual flipping back and forth between the work we know and the work we are experiencing."[19] I would like to connect entangled narratives, palimpsests, experience, and media by further connecting adaptation to memory. As product and as process, adaptation exploits a familiarity we acquire through repetition and memory, a familiarity that ultimately enhances "both memory and change, persistence and variation."[20]

It is here that I would like to situate the museums in Wolframs-Eschenbach and Worms as well as their medievalism, where we can see adaptation as a form of intertextuality in the process of reception. Like Bhabha, whom I have referenced earlier, Hutcheon is not talking about premodern texts or the premodern experience. Both, however, speak to the modern experiences from which the museums emerge, born of the need in their respective communities to enact the medieval literary past in the present. We can see the layers of the palimpsest in the statue of Wolfram von Eschenbach as well as in the window I described above at the Nibelung Museum. The statue represents a historical figure, the poet Wolfram of *Parzival* and the town's famous son, in the form of a literary figure, the minstrel Wolfram of the fictitious song contest. The statue blurs the boundaries between history and fiction, between literature and reality, inviting passersby to engage in a dialogic encounter between the past and the present by tapping into the kind of imaginative memory we find addressed in Hartmann's prologue.[21] In other words, the process of adaptation is the practice of memory. As we will continue to see, it is also the process and practice of medievalism. But because their subject is literature, the museums also take part in a process of literary reception and adaptation. The literary sources of the museums are first and foremost medieval German texts that originate around the beginning of the thirteenth century. It is time to explore how this process works with a look at both the medieval source material and major works that have adapted the medieval sources in the modern era. These various products, as adaptations, become part of the medievalisms over time, which contribute to presencing the medieval past in Worms and in Wolframs-Eschenbach.

Medieval literature I: Source material and themes

Each of the individual texts on display is a topic of study in its own right. In the Museum Wolfram von Eschenbach, these include: the Grail romance *Parzival* and its "prequel" *Titurel*, the Crusader epic *Willehalm*, and various *Minnelieder* (love poems). In the Nibelung Museum, these works include: the *Nibelungenlied* and several of its source texts, such as the *Prose Edda*, medieval German continuations, such as the *Klage* (*Lament*) or the later *Rosengarten* (Rose Garden), the nineteenth-century opera cycle *Der Ring des Nibelungen* of German composer Richard Wagner, and the 1924 films *Siegfried* and *Kriemhild's Revenge* by Fritz Lang in 1924. In the following, I want to give a very brief overview of these works, their content, and their major themes. Given the volume of both primary and secondary material, this overview by no means aims to be comprehensive. Rather, for readers unfamiliar with the primary texts, this overview will hopefully provide background for the literature and the texts on display in the museums. Furthermore, we will also begin to get a sense of how the modern adaptations have taken shape through a process of reception already ongoing since the medieval period.

The Nibelungenlied

The Nibelung Museum in Worms has one primary medieval German source text, namely the *Nibelungenlied* (*Lay of the Nibelungs*), which is generally accepted to have been written around 1200. The *Nibelungenlied* was also probably written before *Parzival*, since Wolfram makes reference in book VIII to the Burgundian cook Rumold, alluding to the fact that the cook does not want to accompany the Burgundians on their ill-fated journey to the land of the Huns.[22] The *Nibelungenlied* itself is an adaptation and a compilation of a number of older narratives, particularly in the Germanic tradition. These source narratives are summarized below; two particularly good resources for further background in English would be *The Nibelungen Tradition: An Encyclopedia* (2002) and *A Companion to the Nibelungenlied* (1998).[23] Certain core elements of the story remain constant in the retellings, while others vary, depending upon time period or cultural contexts. The museum window has given us the names of the main actors in the narrative: Kriemhild, Siegfried, Gunther, Hagen, Etzel, Dietrich. A brief plot summary of the *Niblungenlied* will place them in the context of that version of the story. This will also provide a basis against which to compare the older and later versions of the story that also feature prominently in the museum displays.

> The Burgundians rule on the Rhine in Worms. There are 3 kings: Gunther, Gernot and Giselher. They have a beautiful sister, Kriemhild, who is wooed by Siegfried of Xanten. After serving Gunther, and helping Gunther win Brunhild for his queen, Siegfried marries Kriemhild. Years pass; however, Brunhild has always been troubled that Siegfried does not behave appropriately as a vassal should. She and Gunther invite Siegfried and Kriemhild to Worms. The question of Siegfried's status leads the queens to have a very public argument on the steps of the cathedral about who should enter first. Kriemhild insists that she is married to the stronger man, the one who subdued Brunhild on her wedding night, and she then reveals that she is wearing the girdle Siegfried took from Brunhild at that time. Publicly humiliated, Brunhild demands retribution, which Hagen delivers by killing Siegfried on a hunt organized by Gunther. The second part of the *Nibelungenlied* follows Kriemhild after Siegfried's death. Most significantly, she commands that Siegfried's treasure (the Nibelung hoard) be brought to Worms; this is the treasure that Hagen tosses into the Rhine to prevent Kriemhild

from distributing the wealth and gaining support. Word of the beautiful widow reaches Etzel in Hungary, also recently widowed. Etzel seeks and eventually wins Kriemhild's hand and she joins him in Hungary. Kriemhild continues to harbor a deep desire to avenge Siegfried's death and to regain her dowry from Hagen. After a decade passes, she convinces Etzel to invite her brothers to visit them in the east. The Burgundians, now called the Nibelungs, make the journey to Hungary despite ill omens and predictions that they will not return. Etzel receives them warmly and courteously, but the situation/visit/mood deteriorates to the pointwhere Kriemhild has the Huns set the guests' hall on fire while they are locked within. Kriemhild's final demand for the treasure meets with Hagen's defiant refusal, even after she shows him Gunther's head. Kriemhild beheads Hagen finally with Siegfried's sword and she is in turn ignominiously hewn to pieces.

The *Nibelugnenlied* has fascinated and puzzled scholars for the last 200 years. Surveys of medieval German literature in the twentieth century generally considered the *Nibelungenlied* to be the most significant example of the high medieval courtly epic, defining the genre.[24] Heusler, one of the early critics who attempted a complete study of the poem, praised it as the zenith of courtly poetry in Germany; he placed the poem among the well-known epics (Homer, Beowulf, Roland).[25] Critics now generally agree that the *Nibelungenlied* shows characteristics of both epic and courtly traditions, in creative and sometimes uneasy tension.[26] Themes include courtly love, loyalty and betrayal, honor and decorum as well as family, guardianship and kinship, and revenge.[27] Later versions highlight the tension evident in the *Nibelungenlied* between the courtly ethos/code and the heroic Germanic ethos at the core of the source materials. This tension can be seen in the conflict between friendship and loyalty that emerges in the relationship between Hagen and Etzel's liegeman Rüdiger at the court of the Huns.[28] Haymes sees the *Nibelungenlied* as "a very political poem" and "almost certainly composed at a very political court."[29] The text also seems to have been popular, as forty surviving manuscripts and fragments attest.[30] Of the main manuscripts (A, B, C), only C has the first strophe I quoted earlier.[31] The latest one is in the Ambraser Heldenbuch that was compiled between 1504 and 1516, according to translator Cyril Edwards, and then the text disappeared for about 200 years to be discovered again in 1755. The St. Gall codex, which contains the version of the *Nibelungenlied* generally accepted as manuscript B, also contains a manuscript of *Parzival* and of *Willehalm*.[32] This indicates that the texts on display in these museums were among the most popular of the medieval period in German-speaking areas.

The medieval German *Nibelungenlied*, however, also has a number of source texts; the Nibelung museum highlights three main sources. One of these is the

Prose Edda of Snorri Sturlusson, a kind of handbook for young poets. Believed to have been written in the early thirteenth century, the *Prose Edda* is one of the most complete narratives of Norse mythology. There is also the poetic Edda (or the elder Edda), a collection of anonymous lays that fall generally into two groups: mythological lays and heroic lays. Most of the heroic lays deal in some way with the story of Sigurd. One narrative strand deals with the story of Sigurd and Brynhild (the *Lay of Sigurd*), while the *Lay of Fafnir* and the *Lay of Regin* relate the tales of the young Sigurd. The *Lay of Attila* (or Atli) tells of the defeat of Burgundian king Gunnar by the armies of the Huns led by Attila. This lay is also clearly an older version of the Nibelung legend because Gudrun fights at the side of her brothers and kin to defend against the enemies; here, she remains true to her kin; she does not forsake them for her husband, which is what she does in the medieval German *Nibelungenlied*.

The *Saga of the Volsungs* has a particularly clear relationship to the *Nibelungenlied* since both works connect the legends of Sigurd/Siegfried to the downfall of the Burgundians, although the Norse version "reflects the undoubtedly older version of the Burgundians' destruction by the Huns."[33] The saga tells the story of the children of Volsung. Sigmund, whose backstory includes the relationship with his sister Signy, has a son, Sigurd; the saga tells of Sigurd's birth, his childhood in the forest after the death of his mother, his killing of Fafnir the dragon and his invincibility, his acquisition of Fafnir's treasure, and finally Sigurd's pledge to marry Brynhild after he finds her tied to a slab of stone encircled by fire. The next part tells the story of what relates to the second part of the *Nibelungenlied*, where King Gjuki and his wife Grimhild have four children: sons Gunnar, Hogni, and Guttorm; and a daughter, Gudrun. Gudrun ends up marrying Sigurd, who has forgotten his promise to Brynhild because of a drink that causes amnesia. Sigurd swears brotherhood to Gunnar, urges him to marry Brynhild, and helps him win her; eventually, Gudrun and Brynhild quarrel, Guttorm kills Sigurd, Brynhild takes her own life on his pyre, and Gudrun goes on to marry Atli. Atli desires the treasure that Gudrun's family possesses and tries to take it, but Gudrun fights with her brothers against Atli. To avenge the death of her brothers at Atli's hand, she kills Atli's sons and feeds Atli their hearts, as she does in the Lay of Atli. Eventually, Gudrun kills Atli with the sword of her brothers.[34] In the *Saga of the Volsungs* we can see elements that later appear in Wagner's synthesis of the Nibelung conflation: the hero's youth in the forest, the incest between brother and sister, the broken pledge/forgotten promise to Brunhild, among others.

Finally, we have the saga of Dietrich of Bern (the Old Norse *Thidrekssaga*). The saga of Dietrich of Verona tells the story of Thidrek, a legendary figure based on the historical king Theoderic the Great of the Ostrogoths, who reigned in the late fifth century in Italy. A large portion of this saga treats the material of the Nibelung legend that the *Nibelungenlied* leaves out. We hear the story of young Sigurd found, and later adopted, by the smith Mimir, who has a brother (Regin) in the form of a dragon. Mimir punishes Sigurd by sending him into the forest, hoping Regin will dispatch him. Sigurd battles Regin, kills him, bathes in the dragon's blood, and is then able to understand the birds around him. They tell him that Mimir is plotting against him; Sigurd dispatches Mimir, leaves the forest, and meets Brynhild. The second part of the story involves the Niflungs (Gunnar, Gernoz, Gislher, Grimhild, and their half-brother Hogni) in the now-familiar plot that closely resembles the *Nibelungenlied*: Gunnar's pursuit of Brynhild, Brynhild's anger at Siegfried's betrayal, the bridal night where Sigurd must help Gunnar tame his new wife, the fight between Brynhild and Grimhild over seating rights in the hall, Hogni's killing of Sigurd at Brynhild's request (after she has appealed to Gunnar), Grimhild's subsequent marriage to Atli, and the destruction of the Niflungs.[35]

These brief sketches of selected source material illustrate the broad outlines of how the poet of the *Nibelungenlied* took the old epic out of its original mythology and created a new narrative for a different historical and cultural context. The figure of Attila consistently appears as the queen's second husband, for example. The figure of Dietrich comes from another narrative altogether, yet the poet inserts strands of Dietrich's story into the *Nibelungenlied* to make Dietrich the staunch liegeman of Etzel in his story—the liegeman whose retainer, Hildebrand, delivers the final swordstroke to end Kriemhild's life. The narratives differ on the question of the queen's allegiance. In the older Norse versions, the queen maintains her loyalty to her family and her clan, taking revenge on Attila for his treatment of her brothers (older Norse versions). In the *Nibelungenlied*, Kriemhild avenges Siegfried by killing her brothers and all of their retainers. Nevertheless, the motif of the Burgundians' fall and the vengeance of Siegfried's widow remains constant—whether it is Gudrun or Grimhild or Kriemhild who takes it, whether she avenges her own kin or her dead husband.

Wolfram von Eschenbach

For the museum in Wolframs-Eschenbach, the source texts are basically the complete works (as far as we know them) of the medieval poet Wolfram von Eschenbach. We do not need here to take up the question of his biography;

we will return to it in the next chapter when we visit the museum. Wolfram does name himself in his works several times, and there seems to be broadly established consensus about Wolfram's authorship. Wolfram's actual identity, or whether he was indeed a real person, is another question altogether.

Wolfram composed three major works that belong to the category of courtly epic; in approximate chronological order of composition they are: *Parzival* (around 1205, before 1210), *Titurel* (a continuation of *Parzival*; time of composition remains unclear), and *Willehalm* (composed between 1210 and 1220). *Titurel* consists of two fragments of 131 verses and 39 verses, respectively. In the chronology of Wolfram's works, the only thing that seems certain is that they were composed after *Parzival*. One cannot determine whether they were composed before *Willehalm* or if they were Wolfram's last works. *Parzival* can be found in over eighty manuscripts (generally sixteen complete manuscripts and over sixty fragments);[36] *Titurel* is only complete in one manuscript (Munich G); *Willehalm* can be found in more than manuscripts, twelve complete versions and approximately fifty-eight fragments. In addition, there are approximately nine lyrics attributed to Wolfram as well, and most of these belong to the genre of the dawn-song (*Tagelied*). Given the number of manuscripts and manuscript fragments, Wolfram's works seem to have enjoyed considerable popularity in the Middle Ages. Furthermore, just as he indicates in his appellation to Hartmann von Aue in *Parzival*, Wolfram himself receives mention from his contemporaries, notably Gottfried von Strassburg in his *Tristan*. Wolfram's characters or Wolfram himself also receive mention by other poets or in other works; the story of the swan knight Lohengrin, one of Parzival's sons, and the tale of the song contest at the Wartburg castle (*Sängerkrieg* or *Wartburgkrieg*) represent two of the most widely circulated. For a much more comprehensive overview of Wolfram's works, I would refer the reader to a very thorough summary by Bernd Schirok at the beginning of the first volume of the two-volume *Wolfram von Eschenbach. Ein Handbuch* published in 2011.[37]

Wolfram's creative period is generally assumed to be from approximately 1205 to 1220. *Willehalm* is often dated between 1210 and 1220; this dating is more by inference than any other verifiable source. The prologue to *Willehalm* mentions the reception of *Parzival* by a contemporary audience (*Willehalm* 4, 19–22). This, as well as other references, strongly indicates that *Parzival* was probably written before *Willehalm*. There are two accepted fixed moments ("Fixpunkte"), as Schirok terms them.[38] In book VII of *Parzival*, the narrator mentions the vineyards near Erfurt that still show evidence of having been trampled. This passage refers to a documented conflict in 1203 between Philip of Swabia and Hermann of Thuringia, during which Philip besieged Hermann around Erfurt. Scholars have suggested that visible evidence of the siege would still be detected perhaps as late as the end of 1204 or the beginning of 1205. This is the time generally set for the composition of *Parzival*. *Willehalm* contains a reference to the coronation of Otto IV in 1209, such that *Willehalm* was likely composed after that. In book VIII of *Willehalm* as well as in *Titurel*, according to Heinzle, the narrator makes mention of Hermann of Thuringia in terms that seem to indicate one is speaking about Hermann after his death in 1217. After 1220, there are no references to Wolfram, so that is assumed to be a logical date of death. Wolfram's works themselves have French source texts that the museum does take up in the guide's explanatory material; however, in contrast to the Nibelung Museum, the Museum Wolfram von Eschenbach does not place particular emphasis on the sources—nor do they figure overly prominently in the museum's design or interpretation of Wolfram's texts. The museum guide provides a synopsis equivalent to the information that we might find in a literary history or reference book.

Parzival

Parzival is the story of the Grail knight. The main source for Wolfram's text is the French *Perceval* by Chretien de Troyes, written sometime before 1190. Wolfram added considerably to the next, notably the narrative strand concerning Gahmuret as well as the detailed story that follows Gawain on his own for seven books out of the total sixteen. Prominent themes in Wolfram's text include community, family, the Arthurian court juxtaposed with possible alternatives, the nature of knighthood, and the chivalric code. Will Hasty's edited volume *A Companion to Parzival* provides a good introduction to themes that remain relevant in current scholarship.[39]

The tale begins before Parzival's birth with the story of his parents. His father, Gahmuret, is a second son of the house of Anjou, who seeks knightly fame in the east. He has a child with the Moorish princess Belacane before he returns to France and marries Herzeloyde. Adventure lures him back into the field, and soon after Herzeloyde gives birth to their son Parzival, she receives word of Gahmuret's death in combat. Although she determines to raise her son far from the temptations and dangers of knightly pursuits, Parzival ends up leaving her to seek King Arthur's court. He makes a name for himself among the knights of the Round Table, marries the princess Condwiramurs, gains great renown—only to be humiliated in front of the entire court when the Grail messenger Cundrie berates him for having failed a test at the Grail castle. Parzival leaves the court in shame to spend almost five years searching for the Grail. While he is engaged in that task, the focus of the narrative actually turns to Gawan, who experiences a series of parallel adventures until he comes face-to-face with Parzival in a duel once more before Arthur's knights. Parzival gets another chance to ask the question that eluded him during his first visit to Munsalvaesche, after he faces his fiercest opponent—who turns out to be his half-brother, the speckled child (both white and black) of Gahmuret and Belacane. Parzival succeeds his uncle Anfortas as the Grail king. The text ends telling us that the son of Feirefiz (Parzival's brother) and the Grail queen Repanse is Prester John. One of Parzival's sons is the knight Loherangrin, who becomes known as the swan knight when he saves the duchess of Brabant.

Titurel

Titurel picks up on of the narrative strands in *Parzival* and literally writes a backstory for the figure of Sigune. From *Parzival*, we know that Sigune is the cousin of Parzival on his mother's side; in other words, she shares in the Grail lineage. There are five children in the family of the Grail royalty: two sons (the ailing Grail king Anfortas and the hermit Trevrizent) and three daughters (the Grail keeper Repanse de Schoye, Parzival's mother Herzeloyde, and Sigune's mother Schoysiane). We see Sigune three times in *Parzival*, as her path seems to run parallel to his on his search for the Grail; indeed, she seems to lead Parzival to the Grail: first, she is mourning in book III by a rock's edge with the body of Schionatulander in her lap; in book V, she is in the linden tree, cradling her lover's lifeless body; next, at the beginning of book IX, before he meets Trevrizent in the forest, Parzival encounters her in a hermit's cell, praying over Schionatulander's coffin; finally, on his way to the Grail castle in book VI, Parzival finds her dead beside that same coffin, and he buries the two of them together.

In *Titurel*, we see how the relationship develops between Sigune and Schionatulander and we also see how he meets the untimely end that Sigune mourns in *Parzival*. Young Sigune seeks an opportunity to be the object of a knight's love service, and Schionatulander steps up; he is actually the squire of Parzival's father, Gahmuret, before Gahmuret's death and Parzival's birth. His love-service for Sigune has to do with a unique dog leash that has a story Sigune wants to read—she sends Schionatulander after the dog when it runs away still wearing the leash around its neck. Schionatulander ends up in a duel that costs him his life. The devastated Sigune remains with him and we follow the end of her story in *Parzival*.[40] *Titurel* has been interpreted as anti-Arthurian, critical of the courtly ethos, intentionally open-ended, and enigmatic—or an unfinished but beautiful story of young love. Besides the expected themes of courtly love and the ideals of love service in the context of the Grail family relationships, *Titurel* also concerns itself with text, as the depiction of Sigune illustrates an emphasis on the act of (and the effects of) reading.[41]

Willehalm

In *Willehalm*, Wolfram departs from the courtly romance, drawing on the traditions of crusading epic and *chanson de geste*. *Willehalm* derives from the narrative of William of Orange, which emerges out of the legends of Charlemagne in the French tradition in the twelfth and thirteenth centuries. Wolfram's narrative has a structure very much like Parzival, in rhymed couplets each arranged in thirty-verse units. Some scholars believe that *Willehalm* is a fragment, because some of the narrative strands remain incomplete and open. In addition, the last verses of the epic do not necessarily seem conclusive. On the other hand, other scholars (particularly recently) seem to think that the work is complete as we have it.[42]

Willehalm is the story of two major battles, the first of which is won by the Saracens and the second in which the Christians are victorious. Simply stated, it is a story of war and the devastation it causes; it is also the story of a crusading conflict that is far from simply a clash between the Christians and the Saracens. Willehalm, the oldest son of the count of Narbon, has established himself as the ruler of Orange. Taken prisoner in an earlier battle against the Saracens, Willehalm had escaped with the help of his adversary's wife Arabel, with whom he has fallen in love. Arabel has since been baptized, and she takes the name Gyburg. The action of the narrative begins on the eve of a battle between the Christians and the Saracens, after Tybalt has returned to take back his wife. The armies meet one another on the battlefield at Alischanz. The Christian army is eventually overpowered in this conflict. Willehalm eventually retreats to his castle at Orange with the few men he has left. Willehalm then goes to seek assistance from the French king, leaving Gyburg in charge of the defenses. While waiting for the reinforcements to assemble in Orleans, Willehalm makes the acquaintance of Rennewart, a kitchen boy of unusual size and extraordinary strength. Though Willehalm would like to train him as a knight, Rennewart prefers his great staff. As the French army approaches Orange, they can see the flames of the burning city. Gyburg rejoices to see Willehalm, and there is a banquet for all of the guests. Unfortunately, the banquet ends in a brawl after Rennewart drinks too much and loses his temper when the squires lay their hands on his staff. Later, he ends up killing the cook, who accidentally singes his beard while he is asleep in the kitchen. Willehalm vouches for Rennewart and gives him into the care of Gyburg—who suspects that Rennewart is actually her brother, though Rennewart will reveal no information about his family. At a council meeting, the French princes (though initially reluctant) take the cross and vow to continue the campaign. Gyburg makes an impassioned plea to spare the Saracens because they are God's creatures also.

The armies set out for Alischanz, where they meet the superior Saracen forces. Wolfram departs from epic tradition here and describes strategy, planning, and tactics rather than just the heroic deeds of knights in battle. The tide changes in favor of the French, however, when Rennewart follows one of the Saracen kings back to his ship (off the coast of Provence, which is where the battlefield is). Rennewart takes the ship, vanquishes the crew, and frees the Christian prisoners. Later, Rennewart's great staff splits in the middle of a duel with the Saracen king Purrel. The battle turns after Rennewart, having continued to fight with his bare hands, takes up a sword and kills numerous opponents. Ultimately, the victory is a costly one; after the French search for friends and relatives, and after they plunder the battlefield, the dead are collected, mourned, buried. Willehalm also allows one of the surviving Saracen kings to gather the other Saracen kings who had fallen. The narrative ends with this king's departure.

Prominent themes include the conflict between Christian and Saracen; the values of knighthood, kinship, and honor; and the clash of cultures. Many interpreters have seen in the narrative a courtly humanizing of the heathen.[43] Wolfram goes beyond the superficial treatment of Feirefiz in *Parzival* for de Boor, who sees *Willehalm* as a mature work that is actually aesthetically and intellectually superior to *Parzival*.[44] For Bertau, the combination of courtly form and historical content allows the fatality of the chivalric code to unfold in an epic manner.[45] In her 2012 study *Reading the Medieval Book*, Starkey offers a detailed reading of the epic, with particular attention to issues of language and communication in text as well as image.[46] As the guide to the Museum in Wolframs-Eschenbach comments, all attempts to justify war (as defense of Christendom, as defense of the empire, or as defense of love and marriage) are contradicted by the end result: to be a knight means to be a murderer.[47]

Medieval literature II: Selected medieval adaptations until around 1600

The Nibelungenlied

The Nibelung Museum takes up three major adaptations or continuations of the *Nibelungenlied* and its source material that appeared in the Middle Ages. As with the *Nibelungenlied* and its sources, I want to give a brief overview of this reception with equally brief summaries of the adaptations.

The *Klage*, or the *Lament*, is the earliest evidence of the immediate reception of the *Nibelungenlied*, since both texts often appear in manuscripts together. This seems to be a continuation of the tale of the *Nibelungenlied* but is also "a commentary and interpretation" of its precursor, which places the *Nibelungenlied* in a Christian framework of good versus evil.[48] This text summarizes the events of the second part of the Nibelungenlied and also continues to follow Kriemhild through her grief at the downfall of her family while also praising her for her loyalty to her first husband. Indeed, Kriemhild should be seen as free from all guilt and blame for her loyalty to Siegfried, appearing "as the loyal wife who behaves according to Christian principles and whose place in heaven is assured."[49] Heinzle calls the *Klage* a "Glücksfall" (stroke of luck) for the reception of the *Nibelungenlied* because we have evidence of an almost immediate reaction to the work in the *Klage* and in the C version of the poem, a reaction that involves a "consistent and linear unburdening of the character of Kriemhild."[50]

There are two other adaptations of the *Nibelungenlied* that the Nibelung Museum takes up. The *Rose Garden* (*Rosengarten*) is a text that dates from the middle of the thirteenth century; at its center we find Kriemhild. In Worms she has a splendid rose garden, where twelve heroes stand watch. She wants to see her betrothed Siegfried fight Dietrich and so she lets Dietrich be challenged. She provokes Dietrich to challenge her warriors, saying that she will award the winner with a garland and a kiss. Each of Dietrich's warriors challenges one of the guardians of the rose garden. There are twelve duels and each time Dietrich is victorious. The climactic confrontation occurs between Dietrich and Siegfried, and it is eventually decided by Dietrich's ability to blow fire.[51] The fire melts Siegfried's horned skin. Haymes sees the Dietrich of the *Rosengarten* as a parody of the Dietrich in the *Nibelungenlied*, who functions ultimately as a peace-maker. Print versions of the second adaptation, the *Tale of Siegfried and the Skin of Horn* (*Der Hürnen Seyfrit*), circulated widely in the sixteenth century. Here, the hero Seyfrid must rescue Krimhilt from the dragon who has abducted her, returning with her to Worms, after he has tossed the treasure he won from the dwarves into the Rhine, so as not to arouse envy. This does not sit well with Krimhilt's brothers (Günther, Gyrnot, and Hagen) and they murder him in a manner roughly corresponding to the events of the *Nibelungenlied*. This text is significant for the material it includes— Scandinavian sources that are otherwise not so explicitly evident in Germany. This tale also seems to represent the convergence of popular traditions of the Siegfried legend with the older narrative material of the *Nibelungenlied*. In twenty-first-century Worms, the Nibelung Museum treats this bewildering array of medieval adaptations with humor. The poet-narrator of the Nibelung Museum's *Book of the Anonymous Poet* playfully comments on the fact that the *Rose Garden* features the episode with the dragon that he had omitted from the *Nibelungenlied*: he had not wanted to propagate lies. He acknowledges less courtly, folk traditions here and takes offense. The poet expresses that he is greatly offended at the seeming popularization and bastardization of his work in this particular adaptation.

Wolfram von Eschenbach

Wolfram was well known in the medieval period, and there is a fairly well-established reception history. His characters seem to have captivated listeners and readers well into the modern era. Figures from Wolfram's works found their way into the visual arts, as the fourteenth-century murals at the Haus zur Kunkel in Konstanz attest. And certainly, the number of surviving manuscripts of his works—particularly *Parzival* and *Willehalm*—also indicates Wolfram's popularity in the Middle Ages. As we have already seen in earlier examples, such as Wolfram's appeal to Hartmann von Aue on behalf of young Parzival or Gottfried's critique of Wolfram's poetic style (or lack thereof), Wolfram was himself intensely aware of his contemporaries and he actively and openly engaged with their work through his own. Throughout the Middle Ages, we also find many examples of texts that continue, complete, expand, or change Wolfram's works, as in Albrecht's *Jüngerer Titurel* from around 1271–1280.[52] The *Jüngerer Titurel* and *Lohengrin* are based on *Parzival* and *Titurel*, respectively. The *Jüngerer Titurel* was a continuation of *Titurel* completed around 1270–1275 and became quite popular, especially after a print version was done in 1477. Composed by a poet assuming the guise of Wolfram, later revealing his name as Albrecht, the work was popular in the medieval period as evidence by eleven extant manuscripts and forty-five fragments. Its popularity was acclaimed in 1462 by Jakob Püterich von Reichertshausen, who is celebrated in the Museum Wolfram von Eschenbach. For Gibbs, Albrecht's work is not a "failed Arthurian romance" nor a "clumsy and ill-conceived attempt to outdo Wolfram"[53]—rather an achievement in its own right.[54]

Later writers seem to have ascribed works to Wolfram fairly often that he did not actually write; again, Albrecht's *Jüngerer Titurel* is an example. Finally, new narrative strands emerge around Wolfram, like the Wartburg song contest (ca. 1221–1230), that eventually take on a life of their own. The story of the swan knight *Lohengrin* represents a case in which the Wartburg narrative combines elements from Wolfram's *Parzival* (Lohengrin is his son) into a work eventually that examines the nature of fiction and the relationship of literature and history. Wolfram's integration into the narrative of the *Wartburgkrieg* also reflects the intertextuality that is a characteristic of later thirteenth-century Arthurian romance in German. While most of these romances have been interpreted as local narratives having only local importance, they are being reexamined now in current scholarship.[55] And we see a variation of the local emphasis manifested in the Wolfram monument of 1861. Mertens comments that, in contrast to other medieval poets, Wolfram was never completely forgotten.[56] This has not only to do with Wolfram's role in the tale of the Wartburg song contest—this also had to do with the story of St. Elisabeth of Hungary. Elisabeth's story had its own hagiographical and historiographical tradition that connected the *Wartburgkrieg* poems to the regional interests of the Thuringian court.[57] The song-contest narrative only solidified Wolfram's reputation as the lay poet who succeeds in defeating the necromancer Klingsor. The confrontation of the two poets seems to have contributed to the popularity of the story.

While the thirteenth and fourteenth centuries saw numerous continuations of Chretien's *Perceval*, the German version did not seem to inspire similar artistic response, though the tale of Parzival continued to circulate as evidenced by the fact that both *Parzival* and the *Jüngerer Titurel* appeared in print in Strassburg around 1477. Furthermore, also in the late fifteenth century, Ulrich Füetrer's *Buch der Abenteuer* (*Book of Adventures*) testifies to a continuity in German Arthurian literature. With the *Buch der Abenteuer*, however, new adaptations of the courtly romances practically ceased. The last great compilation was the Ambraser Heldenbuch in the early sixteenth century, which contains manuscripts of the *Nibelungenlied* and *Titurel*, among others.[58]

Adaptations after 1750 in text and image

After gathering dust for about 200 years, our texts fairly burst back on the literary scene in the mid-eighteenth century, and texts are translated and edited at a rapid pace. We can orient ourselves by means of the Wolfram monument of the introduction: the verses inscribed on the pedestal from 1861 in Wolframs-Eschenbach come from Simrock's translation of *Parzival* in 1842 based on Lachmann's edition from 1833, after *Parzival* had been (re)discovered by Bodmer in 1753. The *Nibelungenlied*, whose first edition appeared in 1782, had been found at the Swiss castle of Hohenems by Austrian physician Jacob Herrmann Oberreit in 1755; Oberreit gave the manuscript to Johann Jacob Bodmer, who then published it under his name. As a result, Bodmer's name was long the one primarily associated with bringing the *Nibelungenlied* back into German literary consciousness. A version of *Willehalm* was first printed in 1784. In general, however, Wolfram's works gained popularity more slowly than the *Nibelungenlied* as the latter was translated into modern German and published quickly. Bodmer worked hard to publicize the new discovery and to make it suitable as national literature, attempting to place it in the context of the new patriotism that had grown as a result of the Seven Years War (1756–1763).[59] The *Nibelungenlied* also found its way rapidly into the visual arts through the work of Johann Füssli, an English artist of Swiss heritage who produced the first illustrations of the narrative.[60]

We see here the beginning of the process by which the *Nibelungenlied* arguably became, at least for Ulrich Müller and Francis Gentry, the most influential and important medieval work in the popular and scholarly reception of the German Middle Ages.[61] In the late eighteenth and early nineteenth centuries, new interest in the Middle Ages inspired by a reaction against the Enlightenment associated with the French helped to fuel growing patriotic feeling around the idea of Germany as a culture nation ("Kulturnation")—and this feeling was buoyed by the enthusiastic endorsement of the *Nibelungenlied* as the German *Iliad*.[62] German intellectuals around 1800 repeatedly expressed enthusiasm for the texts that they hoped would lead them to a sense of nationhood and common culture growing out of a shared and illustrious past after the French occupation.[63] Herder and his contemporaries had seen the need for a well-ordered past to serve as the foundation for a stable future; they thus began a process, which continued well into the next century, of constructing a homogenous Middle Ages. Groebner describes this reconstituted Middle Ages a kind of glue ("Klebstoff") to bind emerging national sentiment to the people who were supposed to feel it.[64] Jacob and Wilhelm Grimm, as authors and editors of numerous German linguistic, cultural, and literary texts, exemplify what Groebner calls a desire for roots,[65] as they set about imagining Germany in the first half of the nineteenth century. In this desire for cultural and intellectual "rootedness," lacking a positive "foundational myth," the Germans sought one in the early nineteenth century.[66] Enthusiasm for the Nibelung saga, and a desire to appropriate literature for history, was evident at the court of Frederick William IV, who commissioned eighteen Nibelung frescoes for the royal residence in Potsdam.[67]

From the early 1800's, reception of the Middle Ages in Germany had a more ideological slant than in other areas of Europe, reflecting the complexity of the relationship between medievalism and nationalism in Germany in the nineteenth century. In general, before and after 1815, the Middle Ages "could act both as a reminder and as an admonition for patriots who yearned for the unification of their nation."[68] In other words, the newly revived interest in, and engagement with, the medieval past provided a vehicle for imagining a "German" community. History, "especially the glorious time of the Hohenstaufen dynasty," provided the means "to legitimate longings for national unity and national power which obviously could not be realized in the present."[69] Furthermore, at least the academic interest in the past, the research on "common German(ic) cultural and linguistic roots," was for German scholars such as Jacob Grimm "a conscious act of civil disobedience" in German-speaking areas against autocratic rulers, who "staunchly opposed" any unification after the Congress of Vienna.[70] Of course, and this is a current subject of much discussion in medievalism studies, the Grimms and their contemporaries were also participating in another endeavor in their pursuit of German(ic) stories for Germany. As Helen Young puts it, "European ethnic nationalist identities have, since the late eighteenth century, been widely constructed as having their roots in the Middle Ages." This gives rise to a kind of nostalgic medievalism that, for Young, functions as a "whitewash" to perpetuate an ideal Middle Ages that served colonial and imperial ideals.[71] This idea of the Middle Ages remains problematic; focused on literature and textual narrative, we will see that the museums prefer to avoid directly addressing the relationship of modern identity to the homogeneity of this constructed past and its history.

Richard Wagner

The large arc of the *Nibelungenlied*'s reception history in the nineteenth century, the rediscovery of the text along with the narrative's reappropriation by Romanticism and national sentiment, features prominently in the displays of the

Nibelung Museum. The museum also highlights three particularly significant aspects of the narrative's reception history from the nineteenth through the twentieth centuries: the operas of Richard Wagner (1813–1883), the films of Fritz Lang (1890–1976), and the nationalist propaganda of the nationalists (including the National Socialists. Any discussion of German medievalism in the nineteenth-century must deal with the long shadow cast by Wagner's work and legacy. Many scholars have written eloquently in attempts to rescue German medieval literature from the wide-reaching political, ideological, cultural effects of Wagner's visions and re-visions of the German Middle Ages. Wagner's influence can scarcely be overestimated. He interpreted anew many of the works that we have already encountered in this review of literary reception, both in music and in text, resulting in works that have become staples of the operatic repertoire. We have already mentioned Wagner's version of the Wartburg song contest in *Tannhäuser* (1845, Dresden; 1861, Paris). Wolfram von Eschenbach appears here as Tannhäuser´s counterpart in the opera, the faithful and devoted friend who sings of courtly love and worships the same Elisabeth, who in turn favors the tortured Tannhäuser. Wagner also continued working on his version of the Nibelung story throughout much of his life, based more on Nordic myth and legends than on the *Nibelungenlied*. He had begun much of this work on the *Ring* in the late 1840s, notably after the revolutions of 1848: "one of the most ambitious works of art ever conceived."[72] In this, Wagner continued in the vein of his contemporaries in the early 1800s, who saw the Middle Ages as a way to escape form the "sordid reactionary present" to a "past in which Germany had once been united and strong."[73] Wagner and others creatively express an intense nostalgia, a longing for the past, though Wagner happened to go back "further in time than his Romantic predecessors." Thus "by tapping into the *völkisch* thinking of his day," Wagner early laid the foundation of his works, "in which the palimpsest of Romanticism is overwritten by mythicized history and secularized myth."[74] The four operas of the Ring were finished by 1876. Wagner's last work was his reworking of the Grail story, which becomes a story of temptation and redemption in a world that is much less expansive and inclusive than that of Wolfram's *Parzival* world and with a story that very much reflects Wagner's values of abstinence, repentance, asceticism. Wagner and Wagnerism dominate the twentieth-century reception of *Parzival* and the Grail in German-speaking countries. Parzival is seen by some as a brother of Faust, the prototypical seeker on a quest for knowledge and for salvation.[75] Indeed, as with all of his works based on medieval literature, Wagner claimed to have communicated the essence of each of these tales; they offered ideas and inspiration for his own artistic purposes.

Medievalists have spent much time wrestling with Wagner's medievalism and have reluctantly come to accept that Wagner had little interest in the Middle Ages, or medieval literature, for their own sakes. It was the Icelandic sources of the Nibelung legend that captivated Wagner, ensnared his imagination, and renewed his enthusiasm for the subject of the *Nibelungenlied*, which he found too medieval. Wagner also ignored Arthur and the Round Table altogether, focusing his operas only on individual figures, such as Parsifal or Tristan, and their stories as he chose to interpret them.[76] No longer was Siegfried the knightly warrior of the medieval courtly epic, though the educated middle class (*Bildungsbürgertum*) energetically invested Siegfried with what they considered Germanic values: courage in battle, honor, loyalty. One can see Hagen and Siegfried vying for the status of hero: Siegfried dies because of his youthful rashness and exuberance; Hagen is the coolly calculating statesman. This essentially mirrors the two halves of the narrative of the *Nibelungenlied*. Von See describes Siegfried as a rather odd choice for a national hero, but in the end, the figure is characterized by a certain polyvalence (rather like Wilhelm Tell) that could be applied almost as needed in a variety of political contexts over time. Each phase of his life as a legendary hero could lend itself differently to ideological manipulation: Siegfried as a young innocent and impressionable hero (young Germany in the nineteenth century, also as the young/new empire), as the maker of his own sword (Bismarck), as the dragon-slayer, as the victim of deceit and betrayal (stabbed-in-the-back legend).[77] The *Nibelungenlied* becomes a source of patriotic fervor that should inspire the nation's youth in a way that would have puzzled medieval readers or listeners.[78]

Fritz Lang

Wagner's enormous influence cast a long shadow that shrouded the reception and impact of the *Nibelungenlied*.[79] Indeed, seen by some as a "prototypically modernist work,"[80] Wagner's cycle *Der Ring des Nibelungen* finds expression in the new medium of cinema. Bettina Bildhauer places Lang's films in a trajectory, with Wagner and Hebbel "turning the medieval poem into an expression of German nationalist identity."[81] Heinzle calls the films the most fascinating new adaptations since Wagner.[82] Lang's two-film series *Die Nibelungen* is an UFA double feature shot in 1923–1924; the films, *Siegfried* and *Kriemhild's Revenge*, generally follow a narrative arc that conflates the mythological world created by Wagner's *Ring* with aspects of the *Nibelungenlied*.

The script was written by Lang's wife Thea von Harbou, who freely took liberties to make her own story, deconstructing the literary material/Nibelung myth for purposes of creating her own program.⁸³ Lang said repeatedly in interviews that he had turned to *Die Nibelungen* after coming to a conscious decision to make a film to give Germany a lift after years of economic and political turmoil.⁸⁴ Lang wanted to create a film about the "epic legend" of Siegfried to counteract the "pessimistic spirit"—he wanted to deal with "Germany's legendary heritage" as Germany was searching for an ideal past "even during the horrible time after World War I." Staunchly refuting Kracauer's claim that the films were a precursor to Hitler,⁸⁵ Lang insisted he wanted to bring a film to people that would belong to them and not be something for the privileged and cultured few (unlike the Edda or the Middle High German *Nibelungenlied*).⁸⁶ And the gesture needed to be a grand one with figures placed on a pedestal larger than life because one does not place monuments on flat pavement.⁸⁷

Regardless of Lang's insistence to the contrary, *Siegfried* shows its debt to National Socialist aesthetic and ideology in the presentation of the Nibelung legend. Lang and Harbou exploit the very first mass medium in what Heller calls a flight forward ("Flucht nach vorn").⁸⁸ They make visual what the poem can only express in words; there is, after all, only one illustrated manuscript of the *Nibelungenlied* (the fourteenth-century Hundeshagen Codex). The gestures, costume, décor in the films become ornamentalized in static frames that then fix the eclectic motives and fragments of the Nibelung story in the specific ideological horizon of the 1920s with mythological and Christian overtones.⁸⁹ For Lembke, the film shows the danger of a destructive fascination with heroism that looks backward and has therefore no future for those who refuse to look forward.⁹⁰ *Siegfried* was re-released by the Nazis in 1932 with a Wagnerian soundtrack, while *Kriemhild's Revenge* was left in the vault. The revenge plot was apparently too discomfiting. In sum, in his films *Siegfrieds Tod* and *Kriemhilds Rache*, Lang "transferred part of a national heritage into permanent visual form"⁹¹ that strengthened the appeal and influence of the Nibelung narrative through the 1920s, both for political manipulation well as for commemoration.

The *Nibelungenlied* and national sentiment had gone hand in hand through the nineteenth century, and the nationalism read into the story had permeated a spectrum of cultural expression from music and the visual arts to politics and literature. I referenced earlier the fact that Emperor Franz Joseph in 1914, on the eve of what would become the First World War, encouraged Austrian soldiers to demonstrate the same deep unwavering loyalty toward comrades and country (*Nibelungentreue*) shown by the Burgundians (the Nibelungs) to their king in the face of certain defeat at their last battle. A propaganda postcard from 1915 recalls the young Siegfried in its depiction of Hindenburg as a smith—with the figure of

Germania standing behind him. During the Second World War, a field edition of the *Nibelungenlied* allowed soldiers to read it on the battlefields, thus using the *Nibelungenlied* as part of Nazi propaganda to persuade soldiers to sacrifice everything and fight like the Germanic warriors of old rather than lose one's own honor or that of the fatherland. Another striking example of the medievalism of the Nazis can also been seen in the painting *Der Bannerträger* ("The Flagbearer"), which portrays Hitler himself as a knight against the backdrop of the Nazi flag. Nazi ideology advanced through the idealization of such images, many of which were drawn from medieval sources, both chivalric and heroic. Laurie A. Finke and Martin B. Shichtman devote a chapter to the Nazi fascination with medieval knighthood in *King Arthur and the Myth of History*.[92] In their work, Finke and Shichtman focus primarily on chivalric narratives that have been easily appropriated by twentieth-century fascism. Finke and Shichtman address this not only in their book *King Arthur and the Myth of History* (Chapter 7 is devoted to "Paranoid History") but also in their more recent work, where they talk not just about the exploitation of Arthurian narratives by fascists but specifically about the appropriation of the Round Table.

As described by Finke and Shichtman, the Nazi appropriation of older narratives has two aspects that each of the museums (particularly the Nibelung Museum) later address explicitly or implicitly. First, the Nazis used older narratives similarly to medieval aristocrats who used (as Finke and Shichtman show in *King Arthur and the Myth of History*) "the genealogies provided by historical narratives of King Arthur to justify and promote their own, often oppressive, exercise of power."[93] Arthur becomes the representative of order and religion—the utilization of the Arthurian world enables the displacement of violence and persecution into a realm of fantasy. This is how the chivalric narrative serves to justify the violence of those who claim that narrative as their values and ideology. The second aspect of Nazi medievalism involved the appropriation of older literature and its metaphors to capitalize on a potent nostalgia in Germany, where "the recollection of an idealized past brought comfort to those for whom the past held dangers and insecurities" as it also "held out the prospect of mobilizing fascist desire."[94] One of the things we can also say is that Arthurian narratives (like the *Bannerträger* or the well-documented search of the Nazis for the Grail—not just a fiction for Indiana Jones—or the new "Round Table" that Heinrich Himmler sought to create for the SS at the Wewelsburg castle) also support the vision of a new utopia and the building of a new world. The Nazis not only used chivalric but also heroic narratives in the establishment and support of ideology. As Finke and Shichtman put it, "Nazi medievalism was not the fantasy of a single individual, but part of an ideology that pervaded German life."[95] This might be kind of "framing strategy," to hearken back to Koshar's term, as a way to co-opt these cultural memories for ideological and propaganda purposes. As we know, the Nazis were nothing if not opportunistic in their cultural appropriations, liberally and indiscriminately mining older literature for their purposes. As Heinzle points out, in the declaration of the Nibelung loyalty (*Nibelungentreue*), it was Hagen who represented Germany—defiant and loyal to the death despite grim odds— and, in the story of the betrayed victim stabbed in the back, it was Siegfried. Heinzle comments further on this convenient inconsistency that came from discrepancies inherent in the medieval text itself: "the Nibelungenlied was used as the quarry from which one extracted whatever one needed at any given time." ("Das *Nibelugenlied* wird als Steinbruch benutzt, aus dem man herausbricht, was man gerade gebrauchen kann.")[96] In a way, in their embrace of Wagner, the Nazis could elide the chivalric and heroic traditions into a medievalism that suited their needs through a "hypermasculinity mobilized in the service of a persecuting society intent upon domination."[97] Both Siegfried and Parsifal could become narratives for the new man or the new world. Wagner's Siegfried represented a man buffeted by forces beyond his control, succumbing to them even as they destroy the world so it can be reborn. The Grail fantasy—similarly loosed by Wagner from its narrative moorings—could be reinterpreted as a story of racial purity that functioned "as a corrective to Nazi anxieties" of contamination.[98]

It therefore comes as no surprise that, after 1945, the *Nibelungenlied* and other medieval literature landed in a kind of ahistorical bubble; scholars and writers focused on close reading of texts, for example, on philological analysis, or on narratives in medieval context. They could thereby avoid overt connections to politics or media or other areas that had so contaminated beloved medieval texts in the hands of the Nazis. Popular culture, however, never lost interest completely in the older stories. The story of the Nibelungs continued in the 1950s and 1960s, but the adaptations were retellings of the story in abridged form. While the idea of the German national epic has lost its effect and usefulness, perhaps fortunately, the story certainly has enjoyed continued popularity. The publication of at least two new novels in 1986—Wolfgang Hohlbein's *Hagen von Tronje* and Jürgen Lodemann's *Siegfried*- demonstrated for Bernhard Martin the pull of a myth that had life in it yet.[99]

Arthurian tales, on the other hand, never reached the same level of popularity in the German-speaking areas as in England or America. Müller and Wunderlich suggest three reasons for this in their essay on the modern reception of the Arthurian legend. These reasons include the challenge of exporting the figure of Arthur as a national figure (since Arthur embodied for most the quintessence of Britain), the German fixation on other legends and myths like the *Nibelungenlied*, and the overwhelming influence of Richard Wagner. Müller and Wunderlich also suggest that the only medieval literature that Germans paid any attention to for a while dealt with the texts that Wagner set to music, aside from the *Nibelungenlied*, of course, but that narrative was being pulled into history as a national epic of Homeric proportions in a way that the Arthurian story was not.[100]

In contrast to the reception of the Nibelung sagas, the German reception of the Arthurian legend does not often draw parallels between Arthur´s world and German history and German political ideology. Stories of the Round Table and the Grail Quest occur in the German-speaking countries more as "rich" metaphors for the "failure of utopianism," for the inability of history to "reach a state of peace, freedom, and progress" and as persistent patterns "for the demonic power of love and sexuality."[101] Old myths become a space to illuminate contemporary concerns; Wunderlich explains the comeback of Arthurian literature in the 1980s in Germany this way:

> Distrust of the effects of nuclear power, concern about the deterioration of the environment, natural catastrophes such as famines, fear of war itself: all of these influenced personal and public beliefs so that, on the one hand, we find nightmarish visions of a tormented future and, on the other, a deep-rooted desire for a solution in which hope, peace, idyllic nature and brotherhood are united.[102]

In 1989, Parzival comes to the theatrical stage in Christoph Hein's *Ritter der Tafelrunde*, and interest has continued in Wolfram and the Grail with works by authors such as Peter Handke, Tankred Dorst, Adolf Muschg. The reception in popular culture in German-speaking regions has been steady and reflects sustained interest, even if, as Müller and Wunderlich observe, the reception is not as vigorous or as commercial as the reception of the Grail romances/Arthurian romance in the French and English traditions, with the latter reverberating exponentially on both sides of the Atlantic in a steady stream of new works of fiction and fantasy in multiple media. The postmedieval modern reception of, and increasing interest in, the Arthurian legend in translations of fantasy works have an "unbroken record of success." Furthermore, the reception trajectories in German-speaking and in Anglophone regions have been steadily growing closer under the broader umbrella of postmodernism in contemporary European and American culture, where both resonate with "the often fragmented interactions of past and present, myth and history, fiction and reality which characterize recent reinterpretations of Arthurian material."[103] The turn of the twenty-first century saw Anglo-American medievalisms continued to proliferate through electronic media, Hollywood films, and myriad variations thereof. Looking toward a new millennium, a once more united Germany was again confronting insistent questions of past and present, of myth and history.

And these are questions that both museums address with smart, creative, and thought-provoking displays, seeking local answers not drawn from the fantasies of elsewhere. In a sense, whether focused on the works of Wolfram von Eschenbach or on the *Nibelungenlied*, both museums grow out of the legacy left by treatment of the Nibelung material in the nineteenth and twentieth centuries in art and politics. The Nibelung legend became one of the great paradigms for the power of nationalist symbols, where the symbols and the narrative tapped into the deep emotional yearning for the nation, giving rise to a perilous nostalgia for a constructed medieval imaginary. At the same time, treatment of the Nibelung ideology in Germany in the post–Second World War era has become a paradigm for how to deal with the traumas connected to the nationalist traditions in Germany.[104] The ways in which *Nibelungenlied* has been interpreted over time reflect various understandings of German history; we cannot hold the myth responsible for its misuse.[105] Furthermore, we need the myth to hold ourselves accountable for the future. We need both an understanding of the myth freed from the constraints of the mis-use that history has occasioned as well as a critical awareness of these same misapplications and misappropriations. We do not need to shut our eyes to them; rather the best defense against them and against their ideological oversimplifications is awareness.[106] We engage the palimpsests of older narratives in an artistic and aesthetic dialogue but they also urge us, at least in the Nibelung Museum and the Museum Wolfram von Eschenbach, to contemplation and perhaps eventually to action.

Thus, we come back to the visualizations and display of medieval literature. Indeed, as the museums create an environment that actually capitalizes on the simultaneity and heterogeneity inherent in the medieval literature they exhibit, they facilitate the dialogue for their visitor. They want us to echo Hartmann's suggestion about Arthur ("sî jehent, er lebe noch hiute"); this echo does not necessarily reverberate in new Arthurian exempla, or in a wistful nostalgia for the Middle Ages, or in the utopic fantasy that a dream frame could invent. The echo surrounds visitors with an insistent connection to today but in terms of the past that has changed and adapted for the present that contemporary audiences now inhabit. As entangled as they are in numerous intertexts of their own, the medieval narratives become part of yet one more intertext, yet another adaptation that entices contemporary audiences to imagine as integral and relevant not just to their immediate surroundings but also to the global community.

In short, tales persist now as then. The dynamism, permutation, and adaptation of popular narratives, the accumulation of afterlives, are well known to the Middle Ages. *Iwein* first took impressive shape in the thirteenth-century murals at Rodenegg and at Schmalkalden, demonstrating the responsive, malleable nature of Hartmann's narrative for medieval audiences captivated by it. The relatively rapid adaptation from text to mural suggests that people wanted to "live" with the story, inhabit the same space as the narrative, bring the fictional/imagined past into a real present. The visualizations reinforce a sense of community, as the visual connections to a narrative past seem to "concentrate the constitute power of imaginative memory."[107] In their multidimensionality, allowing audiences to invest variously in (re)claiming an older story, *Iwein*'s early adaptations reveal creative medieval responses to the need for bridging the divide between a then and a now.

Max Siller suggests that the world of King Arthur has consistently offered its audiences welcome and open opportunity for self-identification.[108] The allusive interplay of narratives and images realizes this potential, reinforces the creative process of past presencing that resonates through Hartmann's prologue to *Iwein*. Hartmann has situated us intentionally in a persistent process that, as we know, certainly does not apply only to *Iwein*. The process continues through the literature's own appeal to become part of the continued lived experience and imagined memory of its audience. Visual reminders of Hartmann's *Iwein* as at Rodenegg suggest that patrons wanted to continue making that Arthurian past present however they could—giving their admired narratives tangible shape, physical location, and material substance. In this, the museums exemplify the process of medievalism in the service of imagining community, as medieval literature becomes a vehicle for presencing the past and for shaping a future. Audiences have the chance to step into a kind of virtual reality, as we seek to participate actively and energetically in the remembering and recollecting, in the reassembling and reinterpretation of the older narratives we encounter.

We should enjoy this engagement; however, we should also learn from it. It has a serious purpose. The Rodenegg *Iwein* offers a powerfully compelling re-presentation of Hartmann's story as a critique of knightly frivolity and as a subsequent reestablishment of manorial authority. The museums likewise have a serious mission, which aligns with literature's role in uncertain times. I want to revisit here briefly Homi Bhabha's idea of the join: the yearning to reconnect emerges from an abject brokenness—the broken past, strewn with broken bodies and relationships and promises, seeking to join again or anew by bringing the fragments together. Bhabha takes this idea from Morrison's *Beloved* and in turn from the unique history of slavery in America. This history appears to have nothing whatsoever to do with Germany or with the Middle Ages or with medieval literature. And yet I believe that there are two kinds of useful connections to be made for the mission that prompts the museums in Worms and Wolframs-Eschenbach to put medieval literature on display. First, we see the role of literature to provide a beyond, a space to encounter the unhomely, a space to navigate borders between a here and an elsewhere (or a past and a present)—whether those borders are between modern present and medieval past, for example, or between modern city and medieval literature. Second, the application of the join from Morrison via Bhabha is all the meaningful, I wish to argue, because words—literature and of art—have restorative power; they can re-assemble memory (collective or individual) that has become fragmented and dislocated over time. These museums open a space where history, literature, and memory meet.

I would like to take the liberty of paraphrasing Bhabha then for a moment. When the medieval is overtaken by the modern (when historical visibility has faded), when the historical past continues to recede from view or when the generations who fought in the Second World War begin to pass away (when the present tense of testimony loses its power to arrest), then the museums offer a way to pull the memory of literature and of the medieval past into the present— in a dynamic and creative environment where the lives and voices of older texts show us how to seek in "the indirections of art" the answers to questions that we ask in the modern world. As we will see in the next chapters, both the Museum Wolfram von Eschenbach and the Nibelung Museum insist that literature can not only be displayed but also that we engage with that display actively. We must navigate the installations through medieval texts that feel familiarly unfamiliar as their imprint is still deep in the modern landscape we inhabit. In this way, the older narratives should inspire new dialogues.

3

A Knight at the Museum: Medieval Literature and/as Local Heritage at the Museum Wolfram von Eschenbach

WÄLDER ZU LANZEN!¹

(*Museum Wolfram von Eschenbach*)

dîz vliegende bîspel
ist tumben liuten gar ze snel,
sine mugens niht erdenken:
wand ez kan vor in wenken
rehte alsam ein schellec hase.²

(Wolfram von Eschenbach, *Parzival*, 1,15–19)

In this chapter, we take up the first case study: the Museum Wolfram von Eschenbach from 1995. Recall the statue of Wolfram von Eschenbach from the introduction: the figure of Wolfram gazes resolutely toward the church tower, in front of and below which we also see the old Rathaus, which now houses the Museum Wolfram von Eschenbach, the town's museum (**Figure 6**). With its accumulation of entangled narratives from Wolfram's *Parzival* and the Wartburg song contest to the renaming of the town in 1917, the statue beckons to passersby with an invitation to dialogue. The statue looks toward the museum, guiding us literally to the question the museum asks and answers in greater detail: "Can literature be displayed?" The Museum Wolfram von Eschenbach offers a creative, discursive space devoted to the literature, the figures, and the ideas of that same laurel-crowned Wolfram von Eschenbach.

Figure 6 Museum Wolfram von Eschenbach exterior-entrance, *author's own.*

Introduction: Entering the museum

As we enter the museum's main space on the second floor of the old city hall, the wooden floor boards creak, our eyes adjust to the contrast between the natural light outside and that within, and the display in the corner gradually takes shape. Constructed as a room within a room, the entrance space offers a transition from the world of the present into the world of the Middle Ages, a transition from the world of the original old Rathaus and from the world of the town Wolframs-Eschenbach into the world of the poet Wolfram von Eschenbach, a transition from the world of the everyday into the world of literature.[3] The room's inner structure adapts the half-timbered style of the supporting outer walls into a grid, or perhaps an oversized chessboard pattern; the grid has a simple form: a wooden frame outlines bright cassette squares that effectively lighten the room (recall Figure 1). The simple design allows the visitor to focus first perhaps not on the frame but on the more conspicuous bulletin board set out from the left-hand wall, offering information about the Middle Ages in the form of notes, questions, and answers. But the squares of this first room are not all white or blank. Text catches the eye: some of the squares show cobalt blue letters on white background, while others have the reverse, with white letters gleaming on a cobalt blue background. Visitors will recognize the color and the text from the museum's logo seen on the design of the sign outside the museum as well as on the tickets: the figure of a wolf standing on the one square slightly askew.

The text reveals itself on each square as a variation on the museum's central question: "Kann man Literatur ausstellen?" ("Can literature be displayed?"). One square may have the single word "Literatur," while others display the sentence and its mirror image, or the question paired with its response, verb and subject reversed to transform the query ("Kann man Literature ausstellen?") into the declarative statement that answers in response: "Man kann Literatur ausstellen." In the left-hand corner, adjacent to the next room, the question is offered very imaginatively as an exhibit itself, as it is playfully displayed in a series of interlocking cubes, whose wooden frames replicate in new form the half-timbers of the building's original architecture. Because the text is printed in block letters, the elements of the question can be rearranged to make the affirmative answer as a declarative statement without needing to follow rules of capitalization or punctuation. The question is assembled, reassembled, taken apart, put back together again. This representation plays with language and plays with the question of putting literature on display. It encapsulates for us the museum's message as well as its process: the whimsical yet thought-provoking variations on the question ("Kann man Literatur ausstellen?"), on the response ("Man kann Literatur ausstellen"), and on the keyword ("Literatur") create a playful display of word art, just as Wolfram von Eschenbach plays with language and with medieval literature in his own works and just as the museum arguably plays with Wolfram's texts and with literature in general. We saw the resonance of several intertextual layers in the monument that watches from the town square: the figure of Wolfram the medieval poet, the figures from Wolfram's works or from the works of others about Wolfram, and finally the figure of Wolfram as the native son, whom the town proudly celebrates. Furthermore, the museum aims not only to offer a comprehensive presentation of Wolfram the poet along with his works in historical and literary context; in its creative and thought-provoking exhibits, the museum also seeks to establish the continuing relevance of Wolfram's ideas for audiences of the twenty-first century.[4]

The need for creativity in designing the museum was apparent from the outset for a very practical reason: How does one design a town museum around a famous son when one has few if any artifacts of that person to put on display in the museum? There is an obvious dearth of traditional "stuff"; on the other hand, one does have text and ideas and 800 years of reception history. Not surprisingly, then, the museum in Wolframs-Eschenbach focuses on those texts and ideas. It engages visitors with at least three related questions: Can one display the literature of Wolfram von Eschenbach? Medieval literature? Literature in general? The museum answers each of these questions with a resounding "yes!" In doing so, juxtaposing the question (Kann man Literatur ausstellen?) with an unambiguously affirmative answer, the museum counters arguments in the late 1980s about the challenges and near-impossibility of putting literature on display.[5]

In its presentation, the museum demands an agile and intelligent audience to follow its quick shifts from topic to topic, much like the famous flying image example of Wolfram's prologue to *Parzival*, which the museum takes as its guiding design principle, translating some of the poem's most famous lines:

> This flying image is far too fleet for fools. They can't think it through, for it knows how to dart from side to side before them, just like a startled hare.[6]

This text is featured prominently on the first page of the museum's guide book as one of the mottos for the Museum Wolfram von Eschenbach. The museum thus sets a humorous tone for itself and its visitors, exploiting here Wolfram's own words as well as the well-known critique of Wolfram offered by his contemporary Gottfried von Strassburg in the famed *Dichterexkurs* of *Tristan*. Wolfram says, in his prologue to *Parzival*, that the flying example ("daz vliegende bîspel") is too quick ("ze snel") for dull-witted folk ("tumben liuten") who cannot follow its darting path ("wand ez kan for in wenken") as it moves like a quick hare ("ein schellec hase"). Gottfried, for his part, scornfully dismisses those who would prefer to be the hare's companion ("des hasen geselle"), hopping around on the fields of poetry ("wortheide"), looking for scraps of artistry among the words strewn about. Wolfram is one of those inventors of strange tales, "vindaere wilder maere, der maere wildenaere,"[7] whose apparent propensity for disorganization and confusion Gottfried does not appreciate. The museum organizers, however, have embraced the flying image ("dîz vliegende bîspel"), and it aptly describes the museum's design concept and its purpose: to give dynamic new shape to older narratives.

In the museum, the poet Wolfram and his texts become (inter)textual vehicles of the medievalism that engages the visitor as both product and process. The museum depicts and interprets Wolfram's texts, primarily *Parzival*, *Titurel*, and *Willehalm*, through a series of "begehbare Lektüren"[8] ("walkable readings") that visitors can walk into, literally as though crossing a threshold into one of those texts. Physically and figuratively translating the medieval texts into three-dimensional exhibits, the displays enact a very distinctive process of literary adaptation. In that process, they also become an example of past presencing at work in the cultural landscape in the mid-1990s that uniquely claims medieval literature as the cornerstone of a modern town's identity. As with the construction of the Wolfram monument and the town's name change in 1917, the exhibits show a community constructing its modern, and now postmodern, public image around the medieval poet of *Parzival* and his texts. The town's marketing campaign for tourists shows that its efforts have succeeded: the city has a solid presence in the region as the city of the *Parzival* poet ("Stadt des Parzivaldichters") and as the home of the poet Wolfram von Eschenbach ("Heimatort des Dichters Wolfram von Eschenbach").[9] In this process, the museum uses Wolfram von Eschenbach and his texts as devices to open and guide the dialogue that shapes this communal sense of self. The local poet lends his prominence to the place that calls itself his home. Perhaps more importantly for the medievalism at work, the poet's works on display serve to anchor visitors in a modern world where medieval narratives continue to resonate with contemporary messages.

The museum: Introduction

The Museum Wolfram von Eschenbach took up residence on the first floor of the old city hall and was opened in 1995, after five years of planning. **Figure 7** shows an outline of the museum's organization. There are ten rooms altogether, organized thematically and for the most part chronologically, given what we know about Wolfram's life and work. The rooms are dedicated to various aspects of Wolfram's life and career, inasmuch as this information can be determined from sources available. Visitors can technically explore in any order, although there is only one entrance to the museum; one must begin at the beginning with the introduction (Einführung) in Room I, with the display of the bulletin board and the museum's central question. From Room I, the visitor can proceed either to Room II (Biographie/Biography) or to Room X (Bibliothek/Library). After Room II, if one goes through the rooms in order, the first exhibits deal with Parzival in Rooms III–V. Next in the sequence, Room VI focuses on Titurel, Room VII illustrates Wolfram's Minnesang in the form of his dawn songs (Tagelieder), Room VIII displays Willehalm, and Room IX concentrates on the reception of Wolfram's works from the thirteenth to the twentieth centuries. The final room, Room X, contains a small library of representative critical works.

Figure 7 Museum Wolfram von Eschenbach diagram of museum interior from museum guide, *Museum Wolfram von Eschenbach*.

In Rooms III–VIII the museum lays out the texts that are the focus of the display (*Parzival, Titurel*, the *Tagelieder*, and *Willehalm*). As indicated above, the displays are creative readings of Wolfram's works; the detailed analyses of each work in each dedicated room have a primary focus on one particular theme that can also encompass other aspects of each respective work; in the case of *Parzival*, given the scope of the work, there are three rooms around three themes: the first room tells the story and offers a brief overview of Arthurian romance, the second room is devoted to not only Parzival's family but also human family relationships, and the third room is dedicated to the Grail (also human compassion). The *Titurel* room highlights the dangers hiding in the game of courtly love, while the room of *Willehalm* illustrates war. Each of these latter rooms distill the main themes from their respective texts into a single, powerful visual image: Sigune in the tree mourning her lover, Willehalm's battlefield suffused in a fiery glow.

The museum offers extremely detailed and dense ("thick") exhibits as sophisticated interpretations of Wolfram's works, where the structure of the display thematically reflects the content or the ideas on display. One example would be the aforementioned lances that seem to form the forest that surrounds Arthur's tent in Room III. The lances evoke knightly pursuits, they hint at the danger lurking behind the façade of chivalry, and they also recall the trees of the forests razed to provide the spears used in tournaments and battle. Together with the quotations visible on the walls, the tree-lances form a thematic thread that connects all three major narrative works (*Parzival, Titurel, Willehalm*) on display in the museum. We move through the rooms roughly in the assumed chronological order of each text's composition. The room that displays the dawn songs (*Tagelieder*) is the place where we approach what we might consider to be more personal experiences and voices from the Middle Ages. This is the room that discusses Middle High German and that offers opportunity to read the poems in the original. The literary rooms are framed (Rooms I and II, Rooms IX and X) by rooms that bring us into the Middle Ages and then back into the present. Rooms I and II offer first an encounter with intangibles: literature and ideas, the past and the Middle Ages. The question is simple: Can literature be displayed? This is the answer, of course, that the museum seeks to answer. Rooms IX and X bring the visitor back through a representation of Wolfram's empty grave, acknowledging the lack of concrete historical information about the poet, and finally a small library of resources that stands for the modern reception of Wolfram's works in many more volumes of editions, translations, adaptations, and scholarly criticism.

In the following, I would like to offer a more detailed description of each room accompanied by analysis of the room's design, highlighting how the details elucidate the room's overarching theme. The museum, in its focus on the literature and on the ideas the literature communicates to its audiences across the centuries, displays the literature along with those ideas as artifacts—made tangible and present and real in the walls of the museum. The themes themselves, as they emerge from Wolfram's works through the museum's displays, appear universal: love, hatred, compassion, family. They are not marked as necessarily modern or European or German. The museum, however, reveals itself as a very local phenomenon; in this sense, the museum follows the example of the monument as a palimpsest with local symbolic significance that potentially resonates with more extensive overtones. The intertextual elements of the palimpsest, the layers of narrative that have accumulated and entangled over time, are perhaps less evident and more understated in the museum, however. After all, the museum's main object on display is, of course, the work of Wolfram von Eschenbach. The textual interpretations in each room are essentially set pieces, and they seem more closed than open; fixed in their displays, they do not seem to change over time. On the other hand, gaps remain and the interpretations that fill them will vary with each observer, as they inevitably do in any thoughtful and thought-provoking encounter with a literature. Wolfram's texts remain the focal point of each display. While the layers of the palimpsest appear subordinate to the textual interpretation, the layers become more visible upon further examination. The displays nudge the visitors toward connections among the exhibited narratives, suggested interpretations of those narratives, the world of Wolfram von Eschenbach, and the world of the present. The insistent references to the lances being made from forests ("Wälder zu Lanzen") resonate with a modern visitor in 2019, for whom climate change and sustainability are perhaps more urgent issues than potential deforestation of the Black Forest caused by the need for knightly weapons. In fact, the visitor here becomes very much a part of the ever-accumulating palimpsest of intertexts surrounding Wolfram von Eschenbach and his works—just as the museum becomes part of the intertextual palimpsest that is the town (itself an example of Wolfram-reception). The visitor's encounter with the texts on display is actually integral to the museum's program and design, because the analysis of and the dialogue with Wolfram's texts is central to the exhibits—the dialogue extends to medieval literature and the Middle Ages and then to literature in general. As it interprets Wolfram's works, as it inspires us to ponder his message and perhaps read more for ourselves, as it forms a bridge between new readers and older narratives, the museum takes its place as a new text, itself a product of (and in) the process of adaptation.[10]

The first room (*Einführung*) is the introduction, which sets the stage, in sound and image and creative display, for the rest of the museum. Three concepts are on display in the entrance hall: literature in general, the Middle Ages in general, and the works of Wolfram von Eschenbach. As I suggested above, the entrance pulls the visitor into another world, visually and intellectually: into the museum, into the Middle Ages, into literature—all of these make up the world of Wolfram von Eschenbach on display. The museum guide underscores the importance of questions as it describes the purpose of the introductory room: "Without questions, there are no answers and no explanations." The guide insists that "the discovery of questions is the beginning of all knowledge" and the museum "will help you discover questions."[11]

Prominently placed near the entrance is a bulletin board that shows us how to begin this journey of discovery; we find notes with questions about Wolfram's Middle Ages and initial answers as an example of the process. The board is a very efficient (and eye-catching) way to disseminate a good deal of information about the twelfth and thirteenth centuries in a relatively small space, conveniently offering visitors background to offer visitors information about Wolfram's world in particular and the world of the Middle Ages in general. Drawn onto the board are "notecards," each with common questions about the Middle Ages, about life in the Middle Ages: "What is a tournament?" or "What is a melee?" ("Was ist ein Turnier? Was ist ein Buhurt?"). Another equally important question, central to the Wolfram's work, is "What is love?" ("Was ist Minne?"). For this question, as for others, there are some answers offered in the form of definitions: courtly love is, for example, the ideal of service to ladies ("Minne ist idealer Frauendienst.") just as a tournament is knightly sport with sharp weapons to which one had to be invited ("Rittersport mit scharfen Waffen, zu dem eingeladen wurde"). There is also a commentary as well; courtly love does not reflect reality ("entspricht nicht der Wirklichkeit").[12] The notes, taken individually and as a whole, direct visitors toward asking central questions that lead further to questions that Wolfram deals with in his texts: tournaments, courtliness, love, service, reality in contrast with chivalric ideals. Finally, after we have oriented ourselves in the Middle Ages with the help of the bulletin board and as we proceed toward the next room, we pause by the provocative word art that displays the overarching question to which the museum offers itself as answer. The interlocking cubes reiterate both the challenge and invitation ("Kann man Literatur ausstellen? Man kann Literatur ausstellen"), a tantalizing sample of the way in which visitors will encounter the process and/as the product as they walk through the museum.

Room II: Biographie

Room II is designed to show Wolfram's world, his biography (such as it is), and his knowledge. The blue color of the introductory display ("Kann man Literatur ausstellen?") becomes the dominant color of Room II, providing a visual connection that accompanies the visitor across the threshold from Room I. In a sense, the color of the word "Literatur" becomes the color of Wolfram's world, aesthetically underscoring the literary nature of Wolfram's world as well as his biography, since most information about his life or his environment is drawn from his own statements about himself; furthermore, the blue color that connects the word "Literatur" with the Wolfram room also underscores the fact that Wolfram's biography is as much literature as "verifiable" history.[13] In the words of the museum guide, "Wolfram looks out at us with many faces from his works: there are only self-portraits, no documents."[14] The transparent outline is an ingenious response to the persistent problem of Wolfram's biography, which characterizes most of his thirteenth-century contemporaries in general: there are no documents, only self-portraits, or portraits (descriptions) from others and what we see or read ourselves. This room also clearly highlights the textual nature of Wolfram's world and his life, dominated by six large transparent panels inscribed with various explanatory texts. Flanked by columns and shaped in the form of what could be a knight's shield, each of the panels offers a different self-portrait of Wolfram, at its center an outline of Wolfram's famous portrait from the Manesse manuscript, created out of lines in white lettering that repeat the statement "ich, Wolfram aus Eschenbach" ("I, Wolfram from Eschenbach"). The museum guide tells us that Wolfram makes this particular statement three times: twice in *Parzival* (185, 7 and 827, 13) and once in *Willehalm* (4, 19).[15]

> The six panels show us self-portraits of Wolfram in six different categories chosen by the museum designers based on Wolfram's own statements about himself and his own life: self-portrait with ladies ("Selbstbildnis mit Damen"), self-portrait in the community ("Selbstbildnis mit Landsleuten"), self-portrait as knight ("Selbstbildnis als Ritter"), self-portrait with family ("Selbstbildnis mit Familie"), self-portrait as illiterate ("Selbstbildnis als Analphabet"), self-portrait as poor man ("Selbstbildnis als armer Mann").

The outline of Wolfram's image is itself "filled in" with the dark cobalt blue of the walls one can see behind the glass; this design cleverly presents the very familiar image in a new context, continuing to emphasize Wolfram's ultimately constructed and fundamentally unknowable biography. The blue color represents the literature that must fill in that biography for us because it is all we have. Quotations from Wolfram's own writings are printed in red on the panels, in modern German translation; his words speak to us about his world and his life as he may have perceived it, at least as he described it, with respect to each of the categories outlined above. As an example, one sees here in red the following quotation from *Parzival*, with a statement by the "I" thought to be Wolfram:

> Every noble woman with understanding and honor—I am certain!—who sees this written will admit: I know how to say more good of ladies than I ever sang cruelly about one once in a song. (337, 1–6).[16]

The text appears in modern German translation with the reference to Wolfram's own texts in parentheses (e.g., *Parzival* or *Willehalm*). The museum designers offer a commentary on each of these major themes printed in yellow on the banner that the figure of Wolfram holds in his hand. They speak to Wolfram's world and about the social relationships that come into play in the aristocratic society of the thirteenth century:

> The well-read Wolfram did not call his own wife a *frouwe*, or a noble lady, rather he uses the term *wîp*, the old word for a dear wife. He says in *Willehalm* that he likes to sleep with her. But he does not want to bring her into this decadent courtly society, on whose applause he depends.[17]

Such explanatory notes seek to bridge the distance between the thirteenth century and the twenty-first century. Wolfram is, in a real sense, the subject of his own work, both inscribed in it and circumscribed by it. The museum guide also emphasizes this very postmodern aspect of Wolfram's work, acknowledging the strong personality of the narrator that consistently asserts himself by stepping out of the narrative's frame to give his own opinion on the current events being related. This is, as the museum guide puts it, Wolfram's Wolfram who can impress and delight as well as shock his audience.[18]

As stated earlier, the designers had to deal with the very real problem of how to display the life of a poet about whom there is very little actual biographical data. One solution is found in this series of six self-portraits. Another solution can be seen in the obvious sense of humor with which they constructed the remainder of the display. The plexiglass panels, for example, are flanked by columns on either side. Each column has a mouse at its base, referring to a famous passage from book IV of *Parzival*. At the beginning of book IV, when Parzival enters the embattled city of Pelrapeire, Wolfram offers a characteristically witty description of the suffering brought about by a long siege. The people have no need for toothpicks as they have no meat or cheese or bread, says Wolfram, and very little fat drips into their coals because they have nothing to cook over them.[19] Tankards and jugs will not spill over with mead, nor will one find a Trühendingen pan with fried cakes.[20] Then Wolfram himself breaks into his narrative:

> If I were to reproach them for this now, that would be very mean-spirited of me, for where I have often dismounted and where they call me master, back home in my own house, a mouse has seldom cause to rejoice, for it would have to steal its food. No one would need to hide food from me—I can't find any lying around in the open. All too often it befalls me, Wolfram von Eschenbach, that I have to put up with such comfort as this. (*Parzival* 185, 1–8; Edwards, p. 79)[21]

Wolfram the narrator describes a physical impoverishment that we also perceive in a historical and biographical sense, presented with the same droll humor in the display.

The humor and the pedagogy continue throughout this room, as they do throughout the museum. In the far left-hand corner, one finds a globe that is cut in half through the middle; it represents Wolfram's world and symbolizes the geographical understanding of the time: the flat portion has been overlaid with a medieval world map and a lance, pointed toward the ceiling, thrusts out of the center. Of course, this is Wolfram's Middle Ages; therefore, the designers took Jerusalem out of the center of the medieval world and replaced it with Wolframs-Eschenbach as Wolfram's alleged home; the poet says: "ich bin Wolfram aus Eschenbach."[22] In fact, the map does illustrate the places that Wolfram mentions in his texts in a geographically and spatially appropriate manner, radiating outward from Wolframs-Eschenbach at the center. Other towns in the region, mentioned by Wolfram in his works, are also on the map, arranged in relative distance from Wolframs-Eschenbach.[23] The lance pointing out of the globe-map reminds us of the story of the Grail king Anfortas and an ill-fated spear. In addition, direction of the lance's tip draws our attention to the stars on the ceiling and to the seven planets that Wolfram mentions in both *Parzival* and *Willehalm*. Depicted with their names in modern German, Middle High German, Arabic (in Roman letters), and Arabic (in Arabic), they demonstrate for us Wolfram's extensive knowledge of the world around him. The number of lights in Room II corresponds exactly to the seven planets Wolfram mentions in *Parzival*. All of the details have been carefully thought through, and there is nothing that has been done without a reason—every detail is intentional.[24] This display, like displays throughout the museum, is extremely dense and multilayered, and all details were carefully considered from the map and the planets to the self-portraits in text and image, with the depiction of the mouse at the base of each column and the calculation of how many calfskins one would need for a manuscript of *Parzival*. The presentations in the museum fairly brim almost to overflowing with details that have to be unpacked and disaggregated so that a new understanding can emerge. When we read Wolfram, the same is true for us as readers and interpreters. In a very real sense, the museum leads us through a process of interpretation similar to that which we use when reading any text, but particularly medieval texts with their modern resonances. The museum reveals various layers of palimpsests and intertexts, suggesting a process of interpretation through its display.

Room III: Parzival I

The next room is the first of three rooms (Rooms III, IV, and V) that focus on Wolfram's *Parzival*. The visitor goes through the rooms in succession, following the key points of the narrative: the Arthurian court (III), Parzival's family (IV), and the Grail castle (V). The museum guide describes Room III as one of the worlds through which Parzival moves in his story:

> Parzival traverses two worlds. The first is the world of knighthood, of worldly fame and renown: of King Arthur and the Round Table. This is also the world of joy and love. It is the world of his father.[25]

Like the youth Parzival on his first visit to Arthur's court, whom we met at the beginning of Chapter 2, the viewer steps into the pastoral space of the court: we enter Room III onto a white floor and into a semicircular tent that covers approximately half of the room. The tent looks onto a meadow painted on the full length of the left-hand wall, and under it, one can see a green semicircle with a white semicircular center. One looks through the poles "out" onto a green meadow of summer dotted with the bright colors of flowers in full bloom. This room brings the visitor into the Arthurian world, in text and image. The text is immediately visible, hanging on sixteen rolls of parchment between the tent poles and offering a brief (but complete) summary of the sixteen books of *Parzival*. The story is read from left to right, and the text for every "chapter" (book) has been printed in a color that denotes the book's topic: blue for the Arthurian books (1 and 2), red for the Parzival-books (3–6, 9, and 15–16), green for the Gawan-books (7 and 8, 10–14)—the red and green colors will figure in the next rooms as well.

With a brief history of Arthurian romance (*Artusroman*) and the synopsis of *Parzival*'s narrative, the museum designers clearly intend the audience to take this information and go along Parzival's journey with him through the next rooms. At the beginning of the text summary, there is also a brief timeline of the Arthurian material from Nennius in the ninth century through Chretien de Troyes and Ulrich von Zatzikhoven in the twelfth and thirteenth centuries to make the point that "the entire world told tales of King Arthur." After the short history of Arthurian chronicle and romance, attention can turn to the scenery that illustrates the joy that "reigns supreme at the Round Table; where Arthur is, there is always beautiful May weather, spring, fertility."[26] On the floor one sees a white circle painted on the green floor, meant to portray a round cloth spread out on the green grass of the meadow in which the tent has been pitched. Around the border of the white circle, there are words of Parzival's question to the first knights he encounters in book III, along with their response: "Tell me, who created knights? King Arthur does that himself!"[27] The circle before us on the ground in this tent represents the Round Table, which is a cloth of silk in book IV, the form it would take when King Arthur was traveling and could not bring the actual table with him (*Parzival*, 309,1–30).

The merry month of May, while full of life and light and sun, does cast its darker shadows. When one turns around, away from the image of the meadow and toward the doorway to the next room, one sees a sign on the wall surrounded by trees (**Figure 8**).

> WÄLDER ZU LANZEN!....
> Der kam mit einem Lanzenwald.
> Stellt Euch vor:
> Im Schwarzwald jeder Baum eine Lanze!

In large print is "Wälder zu Lanzen!" We are supposed to stop at this, to come out of the happy reverie we experienced as we contemplated the idyllic meadow landscape now behind us. We are to wonder what the phrase "forests to lances!" is supposed to mean. The text on the sign seems more complete: He came with a forest of lances. Imagine: Every tree in the Black Forest is a lance! ("Der kam mit einem Lanzenwald. Stellt Euch vor: Im Schwarzwald jeder Baum eine Lanze.") The museum paraphrases here a passage in book VII of *Parzival* as the battle of Bearosch begins:

> What more can I say now? Except that Poydiconjunz was proud. He rode up with such forces that even if the Black Forest's every bush were a shaft, more wood might have been seen there. (*Parzival* 379, 3–8; Edwards, p. 160)[28]

This message in Room III captures the same astonishment one finds in Wolfram's comment about the army of Polydiconjunz having depleted the Black Forest for

Figure 8 Museum Wolfram von Eschenbach Room III: A forest of lances, *author's own*.

its lances. The image of forests being transformed into weapons, destroyed by warrior knights and made into lances, will be taken up and continued in other rooms of the museum, as the museum designers find a common thread in this image that they follow through Wolfram's later works *Titurel* and *Willehalm*.

The museum's message for modern readers is a provocative one: humans destroy our forests in order to kill one another with lances made from good wood that would have perfectly good and peaceful uses. Of course, Wolfram's message is not one of environmental protection; he is criticizing knightly pursuits and the code of chivalry. Nevertheless, says the museum, Wolfram's thirteenth-century critique of forest misuse should resonate with us now, if for different reasons. As if to reinforce the relevance of this question for us as well as for Wolfram, one sees the outer walls of the room lined with trees that seem to have pointed tips: they are transforming into lances before our eyes, the sharp metal heads in stark contrast to the pastoral landscape in soft pastels on the opposite wall. The designers reproduce related verses, similarly paraphrased, in the rooms dedicated to *Parzival* and *Willehalm*, respectively: as a banner on the wall in Room VI next to spear shafts emerging from tree trunks or as the inscription on one of the shields on the battlefield depicted in Room VIII. Wolfram's mention of lances as numerous as the trees of the Black Forests becomes the museum's cry "Wälder zu Lanzen!" ("forests into lances!"); thus the museum modifies and updates Wolfram's verses into a challenge for the twentieth-century visitor that resonates through text and image in each of the displays.[29] In their repetition of the phrase "Wälder zu Lanzen!" throughout the museum, the designers want to echo a frustration that Wolfram himself seems to express with destructive knightly games as forest trees transform into a jumbled mass of lances. Issues with the decimation of the forest to make a vast array of implements for combat hint at the potentially disastrous consequences of knightly pursuits such as tournaments and war and in turn reverberate with overtones of modern-day sentiments toward peace and environmentalism.

And the challenge goes further: when one looks to the right of the tree-lances, one can see the tracks of a small animal, no doubt a hare, leading to a handkerchief that flutters in the wind (supplied by a fan in the corner). On the "snowy" ground, the tracks are also an oblique reference to the three drops of blood from book VI of *Parzival* that mesmerize the hero by reminding him of his absent beloved (282,20–283,19).[30] The fluttering handkerchief should recall the "flying image" from *Parzival*'s prologue; leaving no inference to chance, the designers print the quotation on the cloth. Again, the placement of the quotation and the verses themselves interrogates the visitor and the visitor's modern world: What do we learn from our stories and from our literature? We need not be the dumb folk who are easily confused by the quickly moving hare. The tale may dart back and forth, zig-zag, but if we look closely and if we read carefully, we can still discern the path and we can clearly follow the story—the story that allows the transformation of forests into lances, the one that should give us pause in Parzival's world and in ours.[31]

Room IV: Parzival II

The next room (Room IV) is the "family room" (*Verwandtschaftsraum*), which displays the family relationships among the major figures in *Parzival*. The narrow room looks like it is wallpapered with cards; half of the cards have a design of green falcons on them, while the other half of the cards have a design of red doves. The falcons and the doves symbolize each of Parzival's worlds: the Arthurian world and the Grail world, respectively, the worlds coded green and red from the descriptions in the previous room. The floor is red and white, with a huge card in the middle of the floor, facing the same card painted on the ceiling. Suspended from the ceiling, taking up most of the room, is a huge mobile that depicts Parzival's family tree; the red lines of the Grail family connect to the green lines of the Arthurian family, and among them, one can glimpse the white lines of other characters who are unaffiliated. Wolfram intended to make almost all of the figures in his work related. Considering the importance of family relationships in *Parzival*, the designers chose the mobile as an efficient and effective model for illustrating both those relationships and the interconnectedness of all the characters in the text. They suggest that Parzival's "second world is connected to the first through the family relationships. The mobile illustrates the system of those relationships. All people are hanging together with others. Parzival must learn this."[32] The cards also do not hang freely, as they are all connected together with small rings. This undoubtedly has a very practical reason, namely to hold the cards in the form of the mobile. However, the rings highlight Wolfram's message about the interrelatedness of human beings, since the people represented by the cards are also connected by their family relationships—and almost all of the figures in Wolfram's *Parzival* are related ("Wolfram macht fast alle Personen in seinem Werk verwandt"). The practical consideration enhances the metaphorical level of the representation. Altogether, the large cast of characters in *Parzival* produces a confusing and complex web of relationships, in which Parzival is the only one who connects both the Grail and the Arthurian families.[33]

The pieces of the mobile are cards that look like playing cards; indeed, they are designed to allude to a game: the game of courtly love. Wolfram is the one who often gives us the game metaphor.[34] The characters within this highly effective depiction of Parzival's exceptionally complex family tree are also ingeniously interpreted by the cards chosen to represent them: the museum designers used Tarot cards. The cards represent the game of chance we find in the roll of the dice but they offer an additional dimension, since Tarot is a game of fortune-telling; the courtly game is a game of chance but also a game of fate, in which the participants must also learn to navigate the life into which they are born. On one side of the card, there is an appropriate picture of the figure whom the card is to represent. On the reverse, one finds the color and the symbol of the family to which that figure belongs (dove or falcon, red or green). The audio guide explains the choice of the cards as a result of the episodic nature of the plot, which could resemble a Tarot reading (one learns something new, or Parzival learns something new, every time a new card is turned over), and as a result of the many game metaphors in the text, as we noted above. The designers chose particular cards for particular people (e.g., Parzival, Herzeloyde, Condwiramurs, Gawan, Feirefiz), and then they used more generic cards for those figures in the narrative that have their own names but end up replicating each other's actions in parallel situations. The Eastern queens Belakane and Secundille, for example, play interestingly parallel (though minor) roles in *Parzival*, and for this reason, they are represented by an identical figure (this card also represents Schoysiane and Antikonie); Cardiz, Segramors, and other "miscellaneous" knights (including Vergulaht as well as Isenhart) and others are also each represented by the same image. The mobile asks us to think about the players in this (and, by extension, our) knightly game and the implications if some of them, or perhaps all of them, are interchangeable. How are we to evaluate and assess the game and our own actions (those actions that are determined by our parts in the game)? What is the relationship between the individual (the part) and the whole, between the individual and the family/clan? This interpretation demonstrates how figures play their parts as types and as individuals in the game of courtly love, as they are also all connected and related.

The reverse sides of the cards are also symbolic of the game and its players; there are only two colors: red for the doves that represent the Grail family, and green for the falcons that represent the Arthurian family. The falcon, a bird of the hunt and a symbol of nobility and courtliness, logically represents the world of the Arthurian court. The green color for the falcon picks up on the green of the floor in the previous room, which sought to create the festive atmosphere of a May outing on a sunny spring day. Green emphasizes the motifs associated with Arthur and the Round Table: courtly ritual, life, love, springtime, peace. Red, the color of blood, may seem an unusual choice to symbolize the Grail family in contrast to the court of King Arthur, but the red of the doves resonates with key images from the narrative, including: the blood of the mysterious lance that Parzival sees at the Grail castle; the festering wound of the Grail king (Anfortas) that will not heal until Parzival asks his question; the three drops of blood against the backdrop of pure white snow that remind him of his wife Condwiramurs. The intelligent yet playful representation of Parzival's story in this room is apt and imaginative, reflecting the sense of humor so often expressed by Wolfram the narrator in the text. The didactic element also has a place in this room, as we find on the walls six themes written on white cards, grouped with other images that illustrate the themes and the figures that embody those themes.[35] The combination of the themes/groupings on the wall and the "story" contained in (and depicted by) the mobile tells Parzival's history and the story of Wolfram's *Parzival*—all the while communicating in a creative yet eloquent form one of the basic messages of the text: all human beings are related and we must care about one another.

Room V: Parzival III

The "family" room serves as a transition from the Arthurian world (Room III) to the world of the Grail (Room V). The next room illustrates Parzival's second world, the "zweite Ritterwelt," in which he can realize the "truth" represented by the mobile. The guide describes the room as the "world of the Grail" that is "dark and mysterious" full of pain and guilt and death. This room will tell us the real story of how "Parzival came to his guilt." The walls will show us how he could come to the aid of the Grail world. Also a world of "misfortune in love," it is the world of his mother, for Herzeloyde was a child of the Grail family as we know from the family tree we have just seen.[36]

The subdued, almost candle-like, lighting of the Grail room enhances the feeling of mystery and creates a more somber mood in contrast to the bright colors of the previous "family" room or the pastels of the Arthurian room. Upon entering, the visitor stands opposite a structure that looks very much like a concrete wall with a window-like opening. Stepping closer to look through it, one glimpses the model of a castle and hears a recorded voice. The voice is that of Parzival, as he recalls his first visit to the Grail castle on that day that he remembers as accursed ("an jenem unseligen Tage meiner Erinnerung").[37] In fragmentary utterances, Parzival recounts his memory on that day of an ignorant youth, of an unasked question, and of a lost chance; my translation here of the script in the printed museum guide gives an idea of the conversational, retrospective style (the notes enable a comparison with Wolfram's actual text in book V of *Parzival*)[38]:

> Rode **the entire day**, over fields, through forest, no one around.
> **Dusk**, lying at anchor in a lake, a splendidly attired fisherman, he invited me to his castle, if I could find the path—as if I would ever have been concerned about the path.
> **Friendly reception** at the castle, because of the fisherman's invitation. I don't know any castle of such size… it was odd, though—no traces of combat anywhere.[39]

Since Parzival is telling the story from his own memory of it, he can lament for us his failure at the end of his story:

> **Alas, if I had only** asked then … I departed the castle alone. Suddenly someone pulled the draw bridge up from under me, my horse reacted with lightening speed, and then someone called: If you had only opened your mouth and asked the lord. You are a goose!"[40]
> **The castle gate closed.**

The narration ends and the museum visitor, like the young Parzival at the end of that first encounter, remains in silence, standing, outside that wall and that gate. We are supposed to experience some of his confusion, communicated through the first-person narrative of that visit, and we are to consider that question ourselves. We are also to wonder: what question did he forget to ask?

The window has grown dark by the conclusion of the recorded narrative. On the lower part of the wall, below the now-dark window, we find a hint about that question. Someone who was perhaps there before us, und who finally understood the message, has painted the question in large, colorful eye-catching letters that recall the kind we might expect in a subway station or a city park: "hêrre, wie stêt iwer nôt?" (*Parzival* 484,27). The question seems so innocuous: "Lord, what is the nature of your distress?" Of course, this is the question that Parzival did not ask that evening at the Grail castle. Parzival learns this in book IX of Wolfram's text, when he meets his maternal uncle Trevrizent, who is living as a hermit in the forest. Trevrizent is brother not only to Parzival's mother, Herzeloyde, but also to the long-suffering Grail king Anfortas. As Trevrizent explains to Parzival, there was a knight that came "riding to the Grail. He might as well have left it alone! He of whom I told you before won infamy there, as he saw the true anguish" (*Parzival*, 484,21–25; Edwards, 204) and yet he did not ask his host about how he fared. Parzival must recognize his own culpability here. The depiction of the all-important question as a spray-painted slogan makes it seem even more modern and relevant. We are also called to think about the meaning that the question would have for us in our world. It is not just an empty phrase that young people have sprayed on a concrete wall; even though it is a simple question, it is one that we should all recognize as important. We should know, for instance, to inquire after the well-being of a visibly ill host. Furthermore, we should be able to recognize that, in the final analysis, all human beings are related to one another; we should remember and acknowledge that relationship always. This is the message of the mobile from the previous room; it is the message of the question Parzival ultimately asks the Grail king not only as the gracious host from book V but also, and perhaps even more significantly, as his maternal uncle: "uncle, what ails you?" ("œheim, waz wirret dier?" *Parzival* 795, 29). Addressed to a close relative rather than a lord, to someone familiar rather than a stranger, the second version of question has become more personal, more compassionate, even more meaningful.

On each of the other walls of the room, there hangs a black plaque with the following text: "After four and a half years of restless searching, Parzival learns the mysteries of the Grail on a Good Friday from the hermit Trevrizent."[41] On these other walls, one finds key elements of the Grail mysteries denoted by characteristic symbols and accompanied by sentences that describe what each element means in the context of the Grail: the stone (symbolized by the dove), the Grail/the Grail castle (symbolized by the cross of the Teutonic Order), the king (symbolized by the spear).[42] The writing is constructed to make the viewer look closely: the letters are in white (in other words, they are the same color as the wall), raised from the background so that they are barely visible. In the play of light and shadows created by the dim lighting, one can just make out the words, implying that those who know to look and to read will also understand. Indeed, the most important words are the words of the question, painted in color and set off by their position on the wall. The seemingly haphazard path of the darting hare brings us to the goal we are intended to achieve.

Room VI: Titurel

Opposite the wall of the Grail castle is the doorway into the next room. If the courtly game is part of what leads Parzival astray, clouding his judgment and preventing him from asking the question the first time he has a chance, then the next room takes the visitor to a more jarring encounter with the tragic consequences of that game. This room deals with the two fragments that together form the *Titurel* that tells the story of Parzival's cousin Sigune and her lover Schionatulander. Readers will recall that Sigune appears in *Parzival* only with the corpse of her lover. The *Titurel* fragment, dated after *Parzival*, tells their story in a kind of prequel to the longer *Parzival*. Bathed in a harsh fluorescent light, the room appears constructed of white tile outlined in black. The light, along with the severity of the color contrast, creates an atmosphere of discomfort in a sterile and impersonal space. One enters a room filled with a harsh light, and most noticeable is the stark contrast between the white of the walls and the black of a kind of grid that overlays the floor, walls, and ceiling. One is tempted to ask if this is an inversion of the half-timbers of the entrance or of the older architecture. Perhaps it indicates a cell or a cage. Or perhaps they are visual representations of the fragments that make up the story, fragments that have been pieced together like a puzzle in order to make a story and a room in a museum. The pieces are perhaps too regular for a puzzle, but a huge black gash threatens to rend the floor: a fabric tears; the earth splits; a wound bleeds:

> The world of the Grail and the world of young love are marked by Death. Many of the symbols in *Titurel* illustrate this. Unfulfilled happiness finds expression in this verse-narrative; it consists of fragments.[43]

Other fragments abound. There is a synopsis of the *Titurel* poem in black text on a transparent plastic banner running through the room, and we see a broken lance embedded in the wall. Over the wall that leads to the next room, there is an image from *Parzival* of a mourning Sigune, cradling her dead lover in a tree. The juxtaposition of images in this particular room is thought-provoking. In addition, the room feels like a hospital emergency room. The hospital atmosphere emphasizes the tragedy and finality of the courtly love game when it goes wrong. Sigune challenges her knight to prove his love and pursue a magnificent dog leash that is decorated with a text she has not finished reading. Pursuing for his lady what might appear to be a trivial object, Schionatulander pays with his life for his devotion. Indeed, on the left wall as one enters the room, one can glimpse the dog running away, the leash trailing behind. And Sigune pays as well, as we know from *Parzival* and as we can also see in the image above the door leading to Room VII. Young people still play these courtship games, and the cost can still be as high, which of course calls the entire game into question. A harsh and painful reality threatens all players, and that reveals the hollow (and potentially tragic) fantasy of the ideal.

If we return to the text and the story of *Titurel*, we can see that the room illustrates the most important elements of the story: the dog who wears an extravagant collar and leash with a text on it and whom the viewer sees from a distance, as the dog is in the process of running away; a lance that is/was carried by Schionatulander and that does not remain whole, but rather it is broken in two pieces; the melody that one associates with the *Jüngerer Titurel*. This is offered in a display that invites visitors to take the mallet and attempt to play the melody themselves. Overhead, on the transparent collar-banner that extends from one side of the room to the other, hanging just below the ceiling, we find a brief summary of *Titurel*'s plot. As viewers, not unlike Sigune, we also want to look closer and to see what is written there. The movement of our eyes figuratively compels us to run after the dog and follow its path, much the way that Schionatulander did so that he could attempt to fulfill Sigune's wish to see more of the collar and its text. More questions arise, inviting us to compare our own situations with Sigune and Schionatulander. Are we also so eager to know and to read what is written on that banner? What would we do for love? The display insistently prompts us to confront that question. The room is designed to remind us of a hospital room or an emergency room, a place where we moderns sometimes end up as the consequence of rash actions often performed as part of the modern game of love. We often continue to break lances in dangerous games. This is the message that this room is trying to convey; arguably Wolfram wishes to convey this message as well.

The message of breaking lances is also echoed in the repetition of the forest metaphor from the earlier *Parzival* room: on the door leading into the *Titurel* room, there is a quotation from *Titurel* that refers to the forests being turned into lances (*Titurel* 31,1–4). These words are part of the rash promise that Schionatulander makes to Sigune when he promises to go off on his ill-fated search for the collar:

> My anxiety sleeps as long as your good fortune is awake. If the Black Forest were hereabouts, it would be all turned into spear-shafts for you![44]

The forest reference here underscores his devotion to Sigune with a love so great that only the most immense forest would be able to supply enough spears for him to break in her service. We know the conclusion of their story from *Parzival*. We see the couple in this room depicted above the door, in a tree, as they are when Parzival meets them for the first time in book V of *Parzival* after his own misadventure at the Grail castle. In the text that hangs from the ceiling, we read the story that Sigune and Schionatulander enact as we see the results of their actions; their fate illustrates the tragic consequences of courtly behavior and knightly pursuits for human life and happiness. As Wolfram expresses concern in both *Parzival* and *Titurel* with the consequences of the love game, this room takes unusual elements like the transparent banner and the stark lighting contrast to create a display that illustrates the depth of that concern.

Room VII: Tagelieder

From *Titurel*, the literary journey turns from verse romance to love poetry in the room devoted to Wolfram's *Tagelieder* (dawn songs); the harsh light of the *Titurel* room becomes the softer and warmer glow in a darkened chamber. The printed guide sets up the display by talking about how we need to see the two rooms in one as a representation of the way in which dawn songs straddle the transition from night to day as lovers must part to preserve their hidden relationship. We have "the room of night and love, the room of day and separation." Night comes first, the part of the room in which two lovers have spent their time together and are now awaiting the first rays of dawn. The material on the wall positioned directly across from the entrance is the comfortable material of a soft sofa cushion. From the couch/bed, the lovers will look up to the window and soon they will hear the call of the watchman. When one goes further into the room, around the corner of this wall, one sees the wall as though from the outside, where the rays of the rising sun stream into the window. This is the room of day. This story is not quite as immediately accessible perhaps as that of *Parzival* or *Titurel*; it is more personal but also more context-dependent. Thus on one of the room's walls (not the wall built to divide the room), amid the clouds painted on the wall, one can read the Middle High German text and one can also hear it through the available headphones; this is an excerpt from the beginning of the three-stanza poem "ez ist nu tac" (now it is day), which is reproduced on the wall in its entirety:

> Ez ist nu tac, daz ich wol mac mit wârheit jehen.
> ich will niht langer sîn.
> diu vinster nîht hat uns nu brâht ze leide mir
> den morgenlîchen schîn
> sol er von mir scheiden nuo,
> min friunt, diu sorge ist mir ze vruo.
> Now it is day, this I can say truly.
> I cannot stay longer.
> The dark night has brought us now to my sorrow
> the morning light.
> If my love must part from me now, the pain/sorrow is too sudden.[45]

In addition to the Middle High German text, there are notes next to each stanza, like this one beside the text cited above: "Day is like an animal. Its claws of light tear the lovers apart. The lightening rays of the morning are eyes."[46] Here, as in the previous room, we encounter artifact-like vestiges of medieval German culture in the music (the melody of *Titurel*) and in the language of the poetry (Middle High German) that we not only see on the walls but also hear as the poems are spoken aloud. All we need to do is pick up the "receiver" to hear and look around us to read. For this reason, says the museum guide, the texts appear in their own language in the clouds that decorate the walls of this room, with glosses in modern German. This room, unlike the others, devotes considerable space to presenting the language of the poems (Middle High German). The verses are depicted as one of those secrets that also must be interpreted like the secret love of a courtly lady and her knight, at least for the twentieth-century visitor who finds the now-obscure medieval German unfamiliar and difficult to understand. The guide suggests that "the language of the poems is dark," and we must all interpret that language as a secret for ourselves. Some secrets will also remain hidden; for that reason, we find the text of Wolfram's poems depicted as though appearing through the clouds.[47]

As a display, the room conveys a sense that the experience of the words is already far removed from the interpersonal experience (the relationship) that they describe. The spaces in this room, really two rooms in one, are meant to show aspects of that relationship: the velvet of a couch, the light of the sun, the brick of the wall. But those aspects, while visible, are fleeting and fragmentary—like the text in the cloud and the relationship of the lovers who can only meet at night.[48] We can feel the closeness of the room, the closeness perhaps of the lovers who must part at dawn. We are also prepared for this as we enter the room of the *Tagelieder*: above the door that we must pass through is the picture of Sigune with the dead Schionatulander in her arms. As we cross the threshold to the next room, we effectively pass under the tree in which she sits mourning her dead lover—and we are once again reminded of her tragedy. We hear a warning about the potentially disastrous consequences of the comfortable night that we may spend in the room with the couch. On the other hand, we may recall that Sigune never actually consummates her relationship with Schionatulander, since she promises herself as reward for successful retrieval of the leash. Schionatulander met his untimely end on that foolish quest. Perhaps more importantly, then, we bear witness to the disastrous consequences of what happens when the courtly ideal collides with reality.

Room VIII: Willehalm

The room devoted to *Willehalm* is perhaps the most visually stunning of them all. The light seems to flicker as the room, glowing with a fire-like mixture of oranges and reds and yellows and browns; the mood evokes the horror of war (**Figure 9**). The only missing piece might be the sound of clashing metal swords or loud battle cries, but one does not need to hear the soundtrack on the audio guide to feel the room's impact. Leaning against the wall are objects that could represent shields, albeit standing without their owners—perhaps these are already among the fallen.[49] These shields also could be remnants of shells or bombs, of which one still reads in the newspapers: unexploded bombs are still found beneath homes and cities in Germany and need to be deactivated even now, more than seventy years after the end of the Second World War. Or these could also be the bombs that have fallen since 1995 and that still fall on the numerous battlefields of our world today; we are prompted to think of Bosnia, Kosovo, Iraq, Afghanistan, Syria. Again, we are reminded of the dangers and the reality of knighthood and knightly pursuits. The museum guide describes the main themes of this room as follows: The reality of knighthood is not filled with glory, joy, and love. The reality is cruelty, suffering, and death. Shields, weapons, and grave markers show traces of the battle between Christians and heathens that Wolfram called "murder."[50] Indeed, the room has a kind of sensory and emotional impact that the other rooms do not have, as the designers try to connect our human experience in the present with the human experience Wolfram thematizes in *Willehalm*. The room's colors, its images, and its mood elicit not only a question ("what is this about?") but also an answer to that question ("it is about us/me").

On the wall facing the entrance, which leads from the room of the *Tagelieder*, we glimpse what we think may be summaries of *Willehalm* like those we found hanging from the tent poles in the first room about *Parzival*. The text is set off in white from the glowing orange-yellow background of the wall. Upon closer examination, however, we realize that this text offers us something completely different in style and tone:

> Provence. Invasion of the Unbelievers. Margrave beaten badly. [Provence] After a bitter battle, the vastly superior forces of the Unbelievers under the leadership of the great king Terramer were able to obliterate the weak defensive forces of the margrave Willehalm. Only by employing a military ruse could the margrave alone make his way to Orange.

Figure 9 Museum Wolfram von Eschenbach Room VIII: The battlefield of Willehalm, *author's own*.

I have translated here a portion of the text that can be seen behind the shields in Figure 9. We miss the well-crafted summaries on parchment from Room III, but this is clearly not the place for admiration or artistry or long heroic tales. We have entered a different world; we feel as though we have walked into a war zone. We read the clipped and precise language of reports from the battlefront. When we look down, we see more evidence of battle. Strewn across the floor, the plaques for the dead are an ingenious idea on the part of the museum team. They were trying to show the scope of the dead and somehow illustrate the randomness of war, and they hit upon a way to make the arrangement of the names truly random. Museum director Oskar Geidner, who was on the design team, admitted that the team had taken all of the names of the fallen in Willehalm and written them on index cards, which were then shuffled and thrown into the air. The plaques on the floor mark where the cards landed.[51] Heathens lie next to Christians, animals lie next to people, and those whose names are known lie next to those whose name remain unknown. As one of the texts on a nearby shield states, the combatants were very "generous with their lives."[52] Lives were lost, and war seems to be yet another game played out in one of Wolfram's texts (**Figure 8**). The plaques seem to resemble small cards, as if we were to be reminded of the cards the make up the mobile in the second *Parzival* room. They look as though they have fallen randomly on the floor; indeed, they had. These small plaques seem to ask if the dangerous game of a knight's life (the knightly code) is fundamentally different in this situation or in this context from the situation we find in *Parzival*. This is also a game of life and death. The plaques ("Totentafeln") scattered on the floor recall, in this battlefield setting, the cards and the game metaphor of the mobile in the family room. Yet again the game of knighthood and of courtly love reveals its dangerous and deadly reality. Once more, we are encouraged to understand Wolfram as a champion of human rights and human life:

> The tongues of many languages had much misery to bemoan and misfortune to report at home. Is it a sin, when one kills like cattle those who have never heard of baptism? I tell you it is a great sin. All is God's creation, all seventy-two peoples that he nurtures.[53] (*Willehalm* 450, 12–20)

Just as Parzival must learn that all human beings are related, so also must the audience learn the same lesson. And the depiction of Willehalm's battle, enhanced by the room's colors and texts, shows that it remains eerily relevant now. Not surprisingly, now in *Willehalm*, we have a third repetition of the forest metaphor that describes the tragic transformation of forests into weapons. We might hear a note of exasperation here: He's ruining entire forests. Imagine him as a forester. The Black Forest is doomed. ("Der versticht ganze Lanzenwälder. Stellt euch vor: Den als Förster! Der Schwarzwald ist hin!")[54] There are no brave knights or brave ladies in the passage from *Willehalm* about the destructive hand of Poydwiz; he would be a poor forester because entire swaths of the wood have been laid bare as a result of his jousts. The visitor is surrounded by similarly desolate images of the battle and of destruction: shields, weapons, suffering, cruelty. On the right-hand side of the room, one can see Rennewart's massive staff as it comes crashing down onto an opponent's shield. Rennewart is the brother of Willehalm's wife Gyburc, who has refused to become a knight and insists on carrying his great staff instead of a sword. Even so, Rennewart's staff, which Kugler describes here as nearly identical to a door lintel,[55] is also a deadly weapon that wields great power and can have devastating consequences. The tools may change but lessons of that power and those consequences seem to have changed little in the last 800 years.

Rooms IX and X

The last rooms bring the visitor out of Wolfram's texts, out of the realms of literary and historical creation, and into a kind of mausoleum. Room X houses an empty tomb (because there really is nothing to put there), and a series of square display windows that let the viewer look literally and figuratively into the reception of Wolfram's work through the centuries up to the present; here Wolfram himself becomes "the object of works of art" because his work has remained an object of fascination for all forms of cultural research.[56] As we seek to answer the question of where Wolfram's remains lie, we are encouraged to look around us in this room. Wolfram's remains, and his legacy, lie behind every window, which is inscribed with the text: "Hier ligt der streng ritter herr Wolffram von Eschenbach" ("Here lies the good knight Sir Wolffram von Eschenbach"). This is the inscription noted in a travel diary by Johann Wilhelm I. Kress von Kressenstein, who apparently visited the church of Obereschenbach (now Wolframs-Eschenbach) around 1608 and recorded this inscription on a tomb in the church. But that tomb also no longer exists. In effect, Wolfram is everywhere and nowhere in Wolframs-Eschenbach. Von Kressenstein's phrase is reproduced on each window of Room IX, as if to suggest that Wolfram lies nowhere and everywhere at the same time. For us as interpreters and recipients, Wolfram "lies" (and he lives on) in all of the later works that were based on his originals. Some of these later works can be found behind the windows of the mausoleum: the fictional Wartburgkrieg from the mid-thirteenth century, in which Wolfram allegedly participates; Albrecht's *Jüngerer Titurel* from 1270; Richard Wagner, who composed the operas *Tannhäuser, Lohengrin, and Parsifal*; information about tournaments in the late Middle Ages and the early modern era[57]; the editorial work of Karl Lachmann, who published the first critical edition of Wolfram in 1833; the advocacy of Johann Baptist Kurz, who ensured that Obereschenbach became Wolframs-Eschenbach in 1917. Finally, there is a list of fashionable names that are documented in the two centuries after Wolfram's death: Parzival Zenger (1400), Leutwinus Kahmured (Domherr zu Regensburg, 1311), Rennwart von Hautzenberg (1319). Bernhardin Stauffer zu Ernfels had a penchant for names from Parzival: his children (end of the fifteenth century) were apparently named Gramaflantz, Secundilla, and Ferafis. And finally there is a small representative library: "The library shows only a few books about Wolfram and his works. It would be nice if all of the literature about Wolfram could be collected in Wolframs-Eschenbach sometime."[58] This would, of course, require a huge library, but one can always dream. In the meantime, perhaps we will turn again to Wolfram's texts, echoing the reviewer in the national *Frankfurter Allgemeine Zeitung* from October 1994: This is the way that literature should be put on display: as an enticement to read. ("So läßt sich Literatur ausstellen, als Verführung zum Lesen.")[59] Arguably, this is what a literature museum should do.

Medieval literature and/as local history

And then we have arrived back at the entrance, left with our varied impressions of an amazingly creative and fairly compact museum.[60] The museum seems to have as many descriptors as there are visitors: for school students, from their comments on the museum bulletin board, it is a "cool" field trip; for tourists, it may offer a pleasant surprise and departure from the ordinary; for some critics, it is perhaps even a "Mini-Gesamtkunstwerk"; for students of medieval literature in general (and German medieval literature in particular), it is a fascinating visualization of medieval German literature and a unique case study in reception (*Mittelalterrezeption*). Author Hansen, tongue firmly in cheek, marvels that the museum designers resurrected Wolfram in these nine rooms. Were the museum designers just looking for the "real" Wolfram von Eschenbach? One would imagine that the local inhabitants of that city might want to have some connection to (and some sense of ownership of) the museum, its contents, and its representation of collective identity. One such connection is evident in the efforts of the museum designers to emphasize social themes in their interpretations of Wolfram's work. They repeatedly portray, for example, the phrase "Wälder zu Lanzen!" ("forests turning into lances"), to describe the destructive effects of war and of knightly activity on nature and on the people who inhabit it. Wolfram, who keenly observed the dangers of the courtly game, pairs forests and lances slightly more ambiguously, to impress his audience with the size of an army or the power of love—though the subtext of dangerous consequences is indeed present. The museum designers clearly understand art-making as social action, which also suggests that the art must then connect "to other things."[61] This connectedness means that "an artwork is not complete unless it earns a response from someone else" and it is the audience that "completes the utterance."[62] The Museum Wolfram von Eschenbach is an extremely dense "text"; since every detail has meaning, the museum has the potential to frustrate both the amateur as well as the specialist.[63] So the question inevitably must arise: Who is the audience who should complete the museum's "utterance" and how can that dialogue take place with such a hard text?

One answer is that the "Mini-Gesamtkunstwerk" (*Die Zeit*) becomes a playground ("Spielplatz") for interpretation and for our imagination, what Muschg terms "Menschenphantasien" (literally human fantasies). In the rooms of the museum, we encounter Wolfram the poet, but also Parzival the Grail seeker, Sigune the mourning lover, Rennewart the powerful warrior in a destructive conflict. The figures themselves tend to fade against the backdrop of the ideas and even the minute details of the museum; Kugler describes it as an ensemble of "imagination-spaces" or rooms for the imagination ("Ensemble von Imaginationsräumen").[64] Nevertheless, the museum offers the story of a poet whose stories still resonate with modern audiences: war, human relationships, growing up, becoming adult, family. Wolfram becomes a figure in his story, and in our story. This is a museum of literature, of ideas, and of the dialogic encounter between old and new. In other words, we have returned to the museum's initial question: Can one put literature on display? There are very few objects or artifacts that one can put on display because one simply does not have any—just the outline of a trace ("Abdruck einer Spur"), as Muschg notes. The museum, like Wolfram's texts, challenges us. But we want to accept and meet those challenges, because we do not want to be counted among the "tiumben liuten" (the slow-witted). Something new and curious, maybe interesting but not really relevant or just too much effort? Can we really put medieval literature on display in a museum? The museum, I think, wants us to answer this question unequivocally in the affirmative. As its audience, we hope the museum is not one of those winged examples that flies past us far too quickly. Coming as it does (and here I agree with the assessment of *Die Zeit*) from a spirit of 1968, it is appropriate to cite Hans Robert Jauss here about the process of reception as a process of "active understanding"—this is a continuous and continuing process in which the sense of a text is, over time, repeatedly made concrete in new and different ways ("immer wieder neu und anders konkretisiert").[65] As an interpretation of German Arthurian literature, at least with respect to the *Parzival*, the museum seems to affirm the comment of Müller and Wunderlich in their contribution on the modern reception of Arthurian literature in German-speaking areas in the volume *The Arthur of the Germans*, where they comment that "Arthurian figures and stories occur in the German-speaking countries more as metaphors for the failure of utopianism and for history's inability to achieve lasting peace, freedom and progress." Further, the German reception of Arthurian legend does not often "draw parallels between Arthur's world and

German history and German political ideology."⁶⁶ As we will see in the following chapter, the Nibelung museum makes those parallels very explicit at times, while the Museum Wolfram von Eschenbach does not. In fact, the Museum Wolfram von Eschenbach actually has no need to do so. With its innovative displays (the mobile in Room IV, the sterile hospital atmosphere of Room VI, the plaques in Room VIII), it offers a close reading of Wolfram's own medieval texts that speak eloquently to modern sensibilities in a way that makes the specifics of history and ideology irrelevant while emphasizing the immediate importance of general overarching lessons to be learned from them.⁶⁷

What response does the museum earn from its audience now? In the Museum Wolfram von Eschenbach, visitors continue to respond positively to its creative approach to literature and to the appealing presentation.⁶⁸ The museum and the town are still topics for weekend travel sections in area newspapers and tour guides of Franconia, like the *Nürnberger Nachrichten* or the *Mittelbayerische Zeitung* or the regional edition of the Munich-based *Süddeutsche Zeitung*. The general impression is that the town and the museum are well worth the extra effort to leave the more well-traveled tourist routes.⁶⁹ In general, reviews still marvel at the fact that the museum really has no artifacts to display. There was originally discussion of a more traditional kind of *Heimatmuseum* when the idea originated in 1989; indeed, according to one report from the *Nürnberger Nachrichten*, one very early proposal followed more traditional expectations, according to reports of a presentation in 1981, where the design would have included books in glass display cases and manuscript facsimiles on the wall.⁷⁰ In consulting with the faculty at the University of Erlangen and with a designer from Munich, however, the later concept developed much differently.⁷¹ The concept seems to have aged well, not least because the designers spared the world yet another museum with faded documents and old firehouse implements.⁷² The museum remains at least a curiosity twenty years on; it wins praise for its conceptually interesting and innovative display that impresses even without touchscreens or other technical gimmicks.⁷³ There is still very little actual text on display in the museum.⁷⁴ And there is also still very little, if anything, that one could actually connect to Wolfram von Eschenbach.⁷⁵ But the museum persists as an imaginative and elegant interpretation of Wolfram's works. In a sense, the Museum Wolfram von Eschenbach remains relevant and even cutting edge because it does not use the kind of technology that audiences have perhaps come to expect in the last twenty years, especially with the ubiquity of Smartphones and tablets among museum visitors now. The permanent exhibition in the museum can continue without revision because it deals specifically with Wolfram's texts and lays out its interpretation; text, for at least one reviewer, does not overpower the visitor as the museum invites visitors to embrace and experience Wolfram's texts with all of their senses.[76]

The museum's rooms still garner praise as optically impressive ("optisch beeindruckend" for Staffen-Quandt of the *Mittelbayerische Zeitung*), and they still burst with ideas ("sprüht von Ideen") that continue to inspire insight and open up a new world with each visit ("nach jedem Durchgang tut sich eine neue Welt auf"). And today the museum insists that there is something for everyone in the museum; it is not meant to be merely a display for experts and scholars ("Experten-Schau"). These are the words of volunteer museum director Oskar Geidner in conversation with Staffen-Quandt at the *Mittelbayerische Zeitung* in January 2015. I imagine the museum designers also had Gottfried von Strassburg's critique of Wolfram in mind; they did not wish to make the displays so opaque that a general public could not enjoy them. No assumptions are made about previous knowledge, for example. The permanent exhibition is designed to take most visitors from nothing ("bei null"), to give them interesting displays to ponder and relevant ideas to consider despite the apparently esoteric topic of medieval literature. This is the credo of the museum: no one has to know anything about the Middle Ages or Wolfram before they visit. On the other hand, the museum also offers scholars ("die Fachkundigen") a creative and unexpected tour of familiar intellectual terrain.[77]

From these recent comments, it would appear that the museum that has remained unchanged for over twenty years does not seem to have atrophied, nor has it lost relevance or otherwise suffered from a location that would limit expansion or inhibit change. All the same, one can always wish for more visitors. Speaking with the *Süddeutsche Zeitung* in August 2015, Claudia Eder from the tourist office ("Amt für Kultur und Tourismus") suggested that the number of visitors seems to be decreasing from year to year. In 2014, there were 1242 visitors, whereas at one point, there were as many as 4000, which is more than the population of the town itself.[78] The town hoped that putting its literary son and his medieval works on display would help it wake from its "Dornröschenschlaf" (Sleeping Beauty's deep sleep) following the Teutonic Order's loss of power in the wake of secularization and the establishment of more heavily trafficked routes that diverted travelers from the town. In 2017, the town enthusiastically celebrated 100 years since it adopted its identity as Wolframs-Eschenbach. This anniversary may perhaps entice more visitors to the town and to the museum in the future.

As a municipal institution and a tourist attraction, the museum must seek new audiences, continue to secure funds, and justify its existence. Thus, it shares many of the problems faced by other museums in the twenty-first century. On the other hand, as a museum, it succeeds in its mission to display medieval literature. I believe that the museum succeeds because it recognizes (and attempts to make use of) the distinct advantage offered by intentional dissonance, of alienation (*Verfremdung*) in a good Brechtian sense. As Adolf Muschg indicates in his remarks at the museum's opening, the museum designers and the people of Wolframs-Eschenbach have a good understanding of the place and the project, and they do have a sense of humor about this admittedly odd situation. Muschg describes the place (the museum and the town) as the "Abdruck einer Spur, die hier nicht gefunden, sondern geschaffen wurde" ("the outline of a trace, that wasn't found here but rather created").[79] Originating from a kind of "dream frame" that wants to create an origin where there is only the supposition of one,[80] the museum makes very concrete and very real connections between medieval literature and the present; if the actual town history is neglected, then one could perhaps say it is mirrored in the presence of the individuals who visit the museum.

In sum, the audience of the museum in Wolframs-Eschenbach is presented with a provocative visualization of medieval German literature. The idea of a text being constituted and reconstituted continuously as part of a process over time, a process that creates meaning, relates to the medieval concept of *memoria*. Memory makes the voices of the past part of the present and thereby creates space for both the past and the present. In this sense, the art of memory is definitely practiced in the museum of Wolframs-Eschenbach. Wolfram's voice becomes present, becomes audible and even visible—his texts are offered to modern visitors for discussion and the visitor is challenged to engage with the texts and their themes on several levels. The museum becomes, in effect, the actual historical record as missing documents are made unnecessary by the museum's interpretation of and display of Wolfram's texts.[81] Indeed, the museum issues its challenge to us in Wolfram's own words: Can we be different from those "unripe wits" lacking "the power to grasp" the story that "will wrench past them like a startled hare"? The museum encourages us to rise to that challenge. The engaged practice of memory is a practice we modern visitors share with Wolfram von Eschenbach and with the city of Wolframs-Eschenbach. This sharing is the work of a continuing and continually renewing medievalism. The museum participates in the scholarship of Wolfram's works, offering as detailed and nuanced an analysis of his texts as any scholarly article or book.

It participates in Wolfram's reception history as a holistic adaptation of his works, interpreted visually as a museal display form. This aspect might more appropriately correspond to the German term *Mittelalterrezeption*, as a more traditional reception of the Middle Ages. On the other hand, the medieval literature on display in the Museum Wolfram von Eschenbach also participates in the process of creating the Middle Ages. It "presences" the past by asking its central question (can one display literature?) and then by displaying each text in an interpretive exhibit that engages visitors on multiple levels but finally makes the connection between older literature and the modern world. In this way, the museum is a splendid example of medievalism as a vehicle for presencing the literary past. Indeed, I believe Wolframs-Eschenbach can provide us with a model to emulate in future dialogues generated at similar intersections, where the past and the present meet to create an understanding of the Middle Ages that can live and breathe for a modern audience.

4

The Machinery of Myth: The Nibelung Museum and the Interrogation of Cultural Memory

Der wunsch lac darunder, von golde ein rüetelîn.
der daz het erkunnet, der möhte meister sîn
wol in aller werld über ietslîchen man.
der Albrîches mâge kom vil mit Gêrnôte dan.[1]

(*Nibelungenlied*, 1121)

Over the centuries, I have seen what you, the living, have made of my story, and how you have interpreted it. I have seen it inspire entire generations within the spheres of image, music and film. You who enter here have certainly come across these images, and you may know that German schoolchildren have even recited my strophes. But perhaps neither you, nor they, knew of the vast collective edifice known as "The Nibelung Myth," which stood behind it all. Today, you are going to discover it, in sound and vision, for every element of this myth has been gathered here in this sceptre which looms before you.[2]

(*Das Buch des anonymen Dichters. Museumsführer*)

Out of the murmur in the background of the audio, a single voice emerges to greet the visitor adjusting her earphones as she approaches the monitor that displays exhibit one of the twelve in the museum's first tower: "Welcome to my new home ... Allow me to introduce myself. I am the author of *The Nibelungenlied*." The deep baritone continues, as the poet invites the visitor to enter his new abode. This introduction is both less and more ambiguous than the provocative introductory question in the Museum Wolfram von Eschenbach about whether literature can be displayed ("Kann man Literatur ausstellen?"). Whereas the Museum Wolfram von Eschenbach greets the visitor with an open-ended query, to which both the museum and the visitor may variously interpret the answer, the Nibelung Museum tells its story embedded in a fictional narrative of its own creation. Visitors are not left to their own devices to answer a question; in the Nibelung Museum, visitors need a guide, namely the poet. The fact that the poet of the medieval *Nibelungenlied* remains anonymous allows for considerable creative license here and gives the museum designers a creative platform for their agenda, because the poet has a very specific plan for his visitors.[3] In his opening statement, he acknowledges that visitors may know much about his story already, since it has inspired "entire generations" through "spheres of image, music, and film." Many visitors may recall their own time as schoolchildren in Germany where they recited his strophes. The poet intends to enlighten his audience, to reveal to them "the vast collective edifice" of the Nibelung Myth; he promises that "every element of this myth" has been gathered in the immense seventeen-meter-long structure hanging before us. Visitors will discover the entire story "in sound and vision," the poet promises us. Drawn into the poet's narrative, we wonder what awaits: what kind of museum is this, what does the myth entail, and how does this hanging structure fit. Those with some knowledge of the *Nibelungenlied* may wonder if the poet, who has remained anonymous for over 800 years, will be identified.[4] Thus, we enter a walkable audiobook ("ein begehbares Hörbuch"): the Nibelung Museum in Worms.

The Nibelung Museum opened its doors in 2001, six years after the Museum Wolfram von Eschenbach. Focusing primarily on the modern history of the *Nibelungenlied* text and the material of the Nibelung legend in the last 200 years, the Nibelung Museum highlights the wide-ranging proliferation of intertexts that have emerged from the story. The legend of the Nibelungs, the medieval *Nibelungenlied*, and their accumulated afterlives have grown into a nexus of intertexts that the museum wants to frame for the Worms community; the museum wants to deconstruct these intertexts in order to reconstruct the underlying narrative that they have buried in their accretion over time. By enumerating these intertexts in their various forms (visual, musical, textual), the museum dismantles the story that has become inextricably intertwined with modern German history and attempts to recontextualize it as a story within a more appropriate history, like the literary history of the *Nibelungenlied*. Throughout, the museum insists that the audience participate in a larger conversation about the machinery of myth (what the museum calls the "Mythenmaschine"), about its creative power, and about the audience's responsibility to deal knowledgeably with the stories it generates. Hutcheon's concept of "palimpsestic intertextuality" accommodates the museum's complex depictions of the nineteenth- and twentieth-century cultural history that situate and shape modern understandings of the older text. This chapter considers the Nibelungen Museum as a similar kind of interpretive "Spielplatz" (playground) and "Mini-Gesamtkunstwerk" that we encountered at the Museum Wolfram von Eschenbach. The displays in the Nibelung Museum offer interpretation of the literature that shows an equally distinctive but different process of adaptation and past presencing than that in Wolframs-Eschenbach.

Not only does the museum take us through adapted narratives, cultural memory, and local history; the museum was also built into the medieval city wall (**Figure 10**). Literally ensconced in the wall itself, physically located both in the past and in the present, the museum employs both its structure and its program to pull the story of the Nibelungs back into a material and three-dimensional space for its visitors. The architecture facilitates dialogue at first glance. Built into a section of the city's medieval wall, a fifteen-minute walk from the train station, the museum catches the eye of even a casual visitor, once one finds it. The medieval city wall and the towers that form the museum are on the periphery of the city center, as one would expect. That particular spot at the Bürgerturm was allegedly originally singled out because that spot best corresponded to people's perception of the Middle Ages.[5] Designed to coordinate with and to complement the medieval architecture, the museum's metal arches appear to emerge naturally from the wall even as they demand a second look; from the outside the building is unremarkable yet unusual, familiar yet alienating. The outward design seems to convey the impression that this museum is not what it may appear to be at first glance. Likewise, in an innovative and compelling way, the museum demands a second look at the history and story of the Nibelungs along with the history and story of the city of Worms. The museum designers see this "second look" as an integral part of their concept for the museum. Any new additions are definitely not intended as reconstructions; rather, they should be recognized as artistic conceptions that inspire fresh perspectives as older structures are seen from different angles.[6] The museum transforms the space at the wall into a contemporary place invested with a new story to make the past (the literary past, the remembered past, the conflict-ridden past) present for local, regional, and perhaps even national or global audiences. We will see that the Nibelung Museum presents us with another innovative example of Macdonald's past presencing in its display of medieval literature on a museal stage.

Figure 10 Nibelung Museum exterior, *Book of the Anonymous Poet*, pg. 23.

Medieval story and modern city

As the masthead of the city's homepage illustrates, the legend of the Nibelungs has become a cornerstone of the city's modern public image. Modern Worms proudly markets itself as the "Nibelungenstadt" (the city of the Nibelungs), wrapping the city's identity in the intertwining strands of history and narrative. Indeed, the modern city of Worms seems to have been as obsessed with the

Nibelungenlied as Kriemhild was with the treasure, with a passion that might threaten to overshadow other aspects of the city's rich heritage. In 2017, it was perhaps Martin Luther who had top billing in town as sites across Germany celebrated the 500th anniversary of the Reformation. This monument from 1856 commemorates Luther's appearance before the Reichstag in 1521, which culminated in his banishment and subsequent sojourn at the Wartburg, where he translated the New Testament. From the Lutherplatz, we glimpse the towers of the majestic twelfth-century cathedral that, along with its contemporaries in Mainz and Speyer, provides a magnificent example of German Romanesque architecture. Finally, Worms was long a center of Jewish learning, life, and culture. Sometimes called "Little Jerusalem" ("Klein-Jerusalem"), Worms was home to one of the oldest continually existing Jewish communities in Germany from the tenth century to the time of the Nazis.

All this to say that several pasts contribute to the layers that make up the present city of Worms; these layers are evident in documents, in archives, in buildings. The semantic field of the German word for history beautifully reflects the process of how stories become layered and evolve into tales that tellers may later categorize as fact and/or fiction. German is not the only language in which the word for story and the word for history are the same; the word for both is the feminine noun *Geschichte*. The semantic field for the word *Geschichte*, however, includes the related word for layer as well, and this association applies neatly to the discussion here. Both stories and histories reveal multiple layers (*Schichten*) of narratives that have become layered (*geschichtet*) over time. In sum, it is clear that several pasts contribute to the layers that make up the present city of Worms and that are evident all around. It should not surprise us, however, that the city has claimed the story of the *Nibelungenlied* as the cultural heritage that makes it stand out. For Volker Gallé, the identity that emerges from myth, legend, and story requires a particular kind of monument if it is to be put on display. This narrative as "monument" must be enacted—because there are few, if any, tangible artifacts of it to be had; no manuscripts, for example, are available for display.[7] Other pasts have established, and they maintain, a tangible foothold in the city landscape of Worms: the Jewish past, the Holy Roman imperial past, and the Reformation past. The medieval past enfolds these others, demarcating them with remnants of the city's medieval wall. For the Nibelungs, however, artifacts and visitable structures must therefore be found or created.

A renewed focus on the city's identity and its "brand" in the late 1980s and early 1990s coincided with the need for a fresh wind out of the tourist and economic doldrums; as one early planning report wryly commented, the state of the city had inspired a new term in the popular lexicon (the term "Verwormsung") to describe that sense of decline embodied by haphazard city projects and apparent lack of strategic planning.[8] The term, coined from the name of the city itself, connotes a decline of the kind only seen in the city of Worms. So, in 1998 the old Nibelung story gained another new stage, more conspicuous, more emphatic, more permanent. The city approved plans for the Nibelung Museum in the existing medieval wall, at the spot known as the citizens tower ("Bürgerturm"). This was a new and ambitious plan by the city to stage a modern encounter with the legend of the Nibelungs, to honor the insistent presence of the city's narrative past but also to show that the city of Worms was more than just the backdrop for a very famous story about a warrior, a lady, a treasure, and the downfall of kingdom. The head of the arts council, Gunter Heiland, gave one of the main justifications for the project as the fact that the construction of the wall and the composition of the *Nibelungenlied* are approximately contemporary. The location was chosen for two primary reasons: first, this location had the largest intact sections of the old city wall; second, the new construction was intended as a step toward revitalization of this neighborhood around the old fish market (Fischmarkt). City officials had also expressed a desire to find a way to keep some of the 250,000 yearly tourists in the city a bit longer.[9] With the museum, the city hoped to capitalize literally on the story, seeking an increased revenue stream from the museum. For that reason, despite vocal opposition in the six years of planning,[10] the Nibelung Museum in Worms opened its doors in August 2001 and it continues to reinvent itself within the cultural and museum landscape of Worms. The city's narrative legacy became fixed in the cityscape, taking actual physical shape in the museum, literally built into the material of the city's history.

The museum is not without its detractors, and criticism still surfaces. Calling the museum a "contested birthday child" around its tenth anniversary in August 2011, an article in the *Wormser Zeitung* noted that many misconceptions "have persistently remained, since the Nibelung Museum was proposed."[11] Calls to shut the museum doors recur intermittently in the city council. After more than seventeen years in existence, the museum almost certainly continues to raise questions about whether its economic and cultural impacts have met predicted expectations for the neighborhood and for the city. On the other hand, it remains. Why? I think the architecture offers an apt illustration of at least one answer. Here, the twenty-first-century museum emerges from the older stone that anchors it literally in city's medieval past; the city's most famous story now enjoys a materiality in the contemporary cityscape that it did not have before.[12] Its appearance also demonstrates how the museum intends to draw the narrative past into the present through the old stone arches and towers. The odd juxtaposition of new metal with old wall hints that the familiar story we expect in the Nibelung Museum may perhaps not be the one we know. Indeed, the museum's stage could aptly be described as Brechtian in its "Verfremdungseffekt." It draws the past into the present to alienate, to estrange, to disillusion, to provoke—to make the familiar unfamiliar.

The museum

When constructing its museum around the narrative of the *Nibelungenlied*, Worms encountered the same fundamental paradox faced by the town of Wolframs-Eschenbach: legends, literary texts, and their reception history offer few tangible artifacts around which to build a museum that should represent and display the city's cultural identity. And the Nibelung Museum was interested in the display of narrative on multiple levels—not just the story but the story of the story—in order to sort through the "confusion that, century after century, works to create myths."[13] The designers address this situation explicitly in their introduction to the museum guide, musing with the reader that this is a "strange museum" in which there are "no collections, no rare objects, no famous paintings and no jewelry." On the other hand, there is a treasure: "And what a treasure!"[14] The designers reveal their purpose for the museum: to recover the treasure of the Nibelungs. In the *Nibelungenlied*, the treasure arrives in Worms after the death of Siegfried, coming to the mourning widow Kriemhild in Worms as her dowry. It took twelve huge carts four days to collect it all, and each cart had to make three trips each day (stanzas 1122 and 1123). Perhaps most intriguing and mysterious of all is the golden scepter (*rüetelin*) that lies among those heaps of coin and precious jewels; this scepter holds such power that the person who wields it can rule the world (*Nibelungenlied*, 1124). The scepter receives no further mention in the *Nibelungenlied*. The image of the scepter and the treasure, however, inspired designers of the *Nibelungenmuseum* in Worms to try and succeed where fictional forbears could not.[15] Interpreting the treasure as the motor that drives the narrative, the designers imagine the scepter further as the motor of the treasure.[16]

Many reviews of the Nibelung Museum make comments similar to those made of the Museum Wolfram von Eschenbach, noting the irony of constructing a museum with literature as its subject and few tangible artifacts to display. The museum designers consciously play on the unusual aspect of a literary museum that has no collection, no original, no single trinket,[17] and yet the Nibelung treasure is real.[18] As the headline of the *Süddetusche Zeitung* indicates, the Nibelung Museum responds to its creative dilemma by bringing "a piece of world literature virtually to life"[19] through its use of technology. Without a single exhibit object, the museum places literature at its center; however, visitors explore one of the most famous myths of world literature, without bending over glass cases merely to read about it because there are no display cases.[20] The *Frankfurter Rundschau* reviewer described a treasure for eyes and ears in the virtual spectacle that the museum offered by presenting the *Nibelungenlied* and its story with a combination of fantasy and facts.[21] Reviewers generally agreed that the project was very impressive and even charming.[22] One important key to this charm lies in the emphasis on a much more directed and intentional engagement with the palimpsests that comprise the intertextual narrative of the *Nibelungenlied*'s reception history. The designers exploit the numerous intertexts at their disposal, piecing together and giving creative form to the Nibelung treasure that they describe as an imaginary "invisible monument" for the city of Worms.[23] In the remainder of this chapter, we will explore the machinery of myth, or the "Mythenmaschine," as the museum's poet-narrator-guide terms it. I will begin with a brief overview of the museum before turning to each section of the museum in greater detail.

Overview

To exhibit that story, the Nibelung Museum divides its display into three main sections: the *Sehturm* (the "tower of sight"), the *Hörturm* (the "listening tower"), and the *Mythenlabor* (the "myth laboratory"). The first tower shows us visual interpretations and images; its design centers literally on the concept of the scepter. The second tower, as one expects from the name, highlights the medieval *Nibelungenlied* (the oral origins and the written) text as well as its sources and later continuations. In both towers, the story of the medieval *Nibelungenlied* is presented chronologically in the context of the cultures and traditions that led to its production and subsequent reception in the Middle Ages and later. An audio guide provides background by narrating the "tale" of the *Nibelungen* through the fictional character of the *Nibelungenlied* poet. I should note here that the towers are connected by a passage along the medieval wall that takes the visitor from the mid-twentieth century "back" to the Middle Ages by means of a series of city maps showing the city of Worms in various stages of growth since the fifteenth century. The third section of the museum, the myth laboratory, is essentially a multipurpose seminar and meeting room. At times, the space will have interactive displays to provide visitors with additional opportunity to explore the broader context of medieval literatures and cultures in Worms and in Europe. This room serves as a center for various outreach activities. Throughout its displays, the museum asks the audience to participate in a larger conversation about the creative and generative power of myth, about our responsibility to deal knowledgeably with the legacy of our stories and to deal with the machinery of myth. The intertexts engage the visitors—they are part (an integral component) of the palimpsests of adaptation—and the figures in the mosaic "take apart" or dismantle the narratives that have become solidified into coherence over time. The museum lays them bare to the audience. This allows the openness of the texts to emerge—prompts the questions of the viewers, directs and allows the interrogation of the images and the words as well as the history.

Before we continue, I want to offer one note on the museum's design. Designed with the need for modern technology and the need to preserve the medieval city wall, the space is pleasant, though rather narrow and dimly lit; the architects had to leave the medieval city wall as it was.[24] The entrance price includes the audio guide (available in German, English, and French), without which one really would not have much from the museum; the original guides have been upgraded to iPods with one track for adults, one track for kids.[25] The designers did a great deal of work to set up their narrative through a very engaging and informative presentation on the audio guide, offering a continuous and unifying narrative that takes visitors through the entire museum, told by the anonymous poet of the *Nibelungenlied*.[26] The audio guide also has the advantage that it allows visitors to determine their own pace as they view the displays. In addition, the guide reflects the museum's reliance on technology, and this reliance continues to be received both as a creative innovation as well as a drawback for visitors.[27] While frustration can result when the technology does not work properly, the influence of technology carries through in the metaphor of the machinery of myth ("Mythenmaschine") and makes sense in the concept of the museum as a whole and particularly in the concept of the Sehturm.[28]

The *Sehturm*: Visual palimpsests from the romantics to the national socialists

The *Sehturm* brings the twenty-first-century audience into a visual confrontation with the history of the *Nibelungenlied* since 1800 (**Figure 11**). As noted above, the presentation here focuses on the reception history of the *Nibelungenlied*

Figure 11 Nibelung Museum Sehturm, *Book of the Anonymous Poet*, pg. 24.

through images. Video screens are set into the wall on landings placed in the turns of the spiral staircase. They are on the right as one ascends the tower. Clips of Fritz Lang's films serve as one iconic interpretation of the Nibelung story as the audio guide critically examines the bias and influence of Fritz Lang's interpretation.[29] Excerpts of the films at most of the twelve stations outline elements of the medieval *Nibelungenlied* with commentary that looks through Fritz Lang's cinematic lens at centuries of interpretation and misinterpretation. As one turns on the audio guide, one hears a murmuring in the background— could be the voices of the ages, the voices of all the poets of the past from which the one voice of the poet emerges. Throughout, the poet-character offers a humorous commentary for the visitor that supplements the information one might expect in those missing display cases; indeed, the authors of the script have a good bit of fun with the history of *Nibelungenlied* scholarship through the figure of the poet. He accompanies the listener through the tower, explaining the basic plot of the *Nibelungenlied* in each of the audio segments (numbered 1–12) while also offering commentary in additional sections (numbered 1+, 2+, etc.) on various related aspects of the text's reception: the mythological phenomenon of sleeping princesses, the story of the treasure and the "ring," the biography of Fritz Lang, the issue of the author's anonymity, the patriotic fervor embodied by the figure of Germania, the transformation of nineteenth-century patriotism into national socialist propaganda. The narrator-poet figure makes the journey through the *Sehturm* interesting and entertaining, rather like the jovial grandfather-like figure that the Germans might call a "Märchen-Onkel" (as some reviewers noted). The narrative is artfully done, weaving together a complex textual history in an engaging way.

The most imposing structure that dominates the *Sehturm*, however, is in the center of the spiral, extending the length of it. The *Sehturm* is further dominated by images arranged in a huge mosaic set into panels of a sleek, conical seventeen-meter-long structure suspended from the ceiling of the tower, encircled by the spiral staircase on which visitors ascend: this is the scepter, the aforementioned *rüetelin*, the magic object that would make the owner lord of all. In fact, many of the reviewers talk about the scepter/*rüetelin* as the actual treasure of the Nibelungen for Worms: it is the sum of history and reception and story, and it also points the way to the future as we interpret and reinterpret the stories we encounter here. The treasure is the veritable barrage of images that greets the visitor, as the scepter contains more than 400 picture collages comprised of a total of almost 1200 themes and motifs.[30] The collage on the scepter offers a collection of images with an amazingly wide range from nineteenth-century depictions of Germania and the Loreley along with images from Fritz Lang's films to posters of the *Dolchstoßlegende* (stabbed-in-the-back legend) from 1920s political propaganda to Disney's *Sleeping Beauty*, Luke Skywalker, and Romy Schneider's iconic Sissi. The images are arranged (and then subsequently rearranged) in concept groups around key words. The audio guide, with the poet as narrator and guide, supplies necessary explanation and background, as there is very little text that one can read as one moves from station to station (save for the displayed concept words). I would like to follow three sets of associations to demonstrate the intricacy of the conceptual networks (as it were); then we will examine two particular collages in detail to show how they variously untangle and reassemble the almost bewildering array of images. Indeed, this is an artful display of visual interlacing, creating a visual narrative that enacts the museum's medievalism. Organizing it all, the shape of the scepter (tapered at the points and broader in the middle) emphasizes the shape of the story, from "simple" legend to more complex associations from the beginnings to the narrow interpretations of the national socialists. In the analysis of the collages, I will structure these related sets of associations around three particular nodes: myth (*Mythos*), heroes (*Helden*), and Romanticism (*Romantik*).

We start, perhaps, at a "beginning." We are perhaps in the depths of the earth where dwarves and other fantasy figures dwell, perhaps in a cave where we stumble upon hidden treasure. These are the basics: the origins of the Nibelungs, mysterious folk who seem to be a dwarvish race. There is a bit of fun with the associations of: Nibel and Nebel (fog), gnomes and dwarves from folklore, like the *Heinzelmännchen* from Cologne, who appear mysteriously at night and do all manner of domestic tasks in addition to a bit of mischief, and contemporary lawn art (**Figure 12**). This is clearly a museum with a sense of humor, expressed in how it wishes to engage its visitors and in how it wishes to portray itself. Then we walk up the spiral staircase. The movement "up" and "down" through the museum's story of the Nibelungs is physical as well as intellectual.

Shrouded in those mists, waiting to be revealed, we encounter our first concept "node." The poet-narrator opens his introduction to the museum by reminding us that the "myth of the Nibelungs" is real, though we may not realize that the parts we perhaps already know (from school or from film) contribute to a larger whole/phenomenon. Not surprisingly, the word "myth" ("Mythos") has a complex web of associations that extends throughout the scepter. We do not encounter the word itself for awhile; rather, we start with the Nibelungs. Station two discusses the origin of the Nibelungs. Perhaps the name is related to the word "Nebel" or mist, such that the Nibelungs would be people of the mists "the dark, the underworld."[31] Perhaps this also meant they were dwarves who guarded an immense treasure of gold and precious stones, which also harbored "a golden wand, precursor of this golden scepter you see before you." Opposite the video screen that shows a clip from Lang's *Siegfried* in which the ghostly figures of the Nibelungs appear following his defeat of the dragon, the collage on

Figure 12 Nibelung Museum Sehturm collage, *author's own*.

the *rüetelin* augments the film excerpt with related images. The poet explains the connections visually represented on the scepter; images of golden crowns, fierce, bearded dwarf warriors, and even garden gnomes are grouped around key words such as "Nibel," "Zwerg," "Hort," and "Garten." The poet decries the proliferation of dwarf figures in later versions of his *Nibelungenlied*:

> Now for something more about those dwarves: the most gullible of my contemporaries firmly believed in their underground world and treasure. As for me, I wasn't crazy: I treated the subject quite circumspectly. As such there are no dwarves directly involved in my poem … But no matter what you do, there are still some dwarves about … I have been dead for centuries and they still keep sprouting up, in tales, in films and in gardens.[32]

The appearance of the *Gartenzwerge* seems incongruous amid images of Siegfried and the Nibelungs, like the visual reference to the folktale of the Heinzelmännchen.[33] However, the insertion of modern landscape decoration into a discussion of the origins of the Nibelungs visually underscores the breadth of connections that one can make (and many have made) over time. The incongruity of the juxtaposition makes the viewer pause and consider the connection, encourages us to make the connection explicit where we might not have done so before.

Other associative pathways lead from, and back to, the concept of myth. One could follow the path of the figures: from dwarves generally to one in particular called Alberich or perhaps Andvari. A creature of Scandinavian mythology, Andvari connects us to other members of the Norse pantheon: Odin, for example, and the trickster Loki. Loki not only represents the connection to northern Germanic myths but also highlights the spirit of play that undergirds both the installation and the narrative. In fact, the theme of the game will come back around again; the scepter is, after all, an object that we circle as we ascend the stairs. Andvari branches out into another path simultaneously, where the images seem to follow the theme of treasure. We have crossed one intersection, meeting the Nibelungs as dwarves who guard an immense hoard (*Hort*), a treasure (*Schatz*) of unimaginable worth. This is the treasure that Hagen eventually casts into the Rhine in the *Nibelungenlied*. The figure of Andvari, perhaps reimagined as Alberich, appears in mythical precursors to the *Nibelungenlied* as a dwarf who may have origins in Scandinavian myth and who watched over the treasure and its most valuable piece: a ring of great power. The image of the ring goes on to connect to German composer Richard Wagner and his rewriting of the Nibelung myth in the opera cycle *Der Ring des Nibelungen* and then by extension to the performances of the Nibelungen festival in Worms initiated by the National Socialists in 1939. Words such as "power"/*Macht* and "greed"/*Gier* accompany these images, the darker side of the game. Yet another path follows the work of director Fritz Lang, whose Nibelung films provide a parallel script for the viewer's journey through the Sehturm. Lang represents film as the new technology of storytelling in the early twentieth century; thus, in addition to the scenes from the Nibelung films, we see a Lang behind the camera, we see the iconic images from *Metropolis* (the clock and the golden robot/*Maschinenmensch*), and we juxtapose the face of Lang's wife Thea von Harbou with that of Kriemhild. In this web of associations, we are also meant to place Lang as a modern storyteller at the side of another influential adapter of older tales: Walt Disney. Disney seems quite a distance not only from the Nibelungs but from Worms and Wagner and Germanic mythology. Another important set of associations around from the *Mythos* node leads toward the theme of the hero (*Helden*). Here we find images of Siegfried, Saint George, the Archangel Michael, and Disney's Prince Philip—all slayers of dragons, if we stop to think about it. And the museum wants us to stop and think about it. The scepter shows us other motion picture heroes, such as James Bond and Luke Skywalker, whose swashbuckling feats we admire as they battle for good and triumph over evil. Heroes do not always win; Siegfried does not. Another unavoidable path on the scepter is the one that takes us by the *Dolchstoßlegende*—the "stabbed-in-the-back" legend that proliferated after the First World War, depicting Germany as the dying Siegfried stabbed in the back by the treacherous foe Hagen. We are compelled to recall that the word "Aryan" (*Arier*) resonates also with hero and power and myth, and that a perverted heroism became part of the national socialist ethos.

From dwarves, the exploration of German literature and culture takes a rather more serious turn. The general trajectory of the visual history in this display follows the cultural and literary contours of the nineteenth and twentieth centuries with a somewhat meandering but ever upward spiraling chronology. The third node centers on the term *Romantik*. We start with a group of images near the ground floor, for instance, that describe the legacy of German Romanticism with terms such as *Romantik, Germania, Loreley, Prinzessin*. Each term is literally surrounded by a mosaic of images related to it. One finds the portraits of the poets Heine and Brentano next to nineteenth-century Rhine landscapes opposite a figure of heroic Germania carrying a shield embossed with the Prussian eagle followed by a panel featuring two well-known princess figures immortalized as fairy tales (the one fictional and the other historical) in twentieth-century film: Disney's Briar Rose and Romy Schneider's Sissi. We could also call this collection of pathways "the paths of beautiful princesses and seductive dangerous women warriors." Germania is one of them, spirit of the German nation, embodiment of the newly emerging nationalism in the early nineteenth century. She leads us to Bismarck and German unification in 1871, to Wilhelm II and the First World War—and then we have an image of a group of women, attentively listening at a meeting that is probably taking place in the 1930s. This latter image is also labeled "Germania," prompting us perhaps to consider Nazi family policies that encouraged women to be warriors in the home? Germania connects, however, to two other pathways that are worth following here. Germania's reemergence in the nationalism of the German Romantic era brings her, as a female figure much depicted in the visual arts of the time, into association with other female figures—not war-like, perhaps, but also beautiful and inspiring, if not dangerous and threatening. These are the sirens (*Sirene*), the water sprites (*Nixen*). The most famous of these is the Loreley, who combed her golden hair, perched on the Rhine cliffs, and lured ships to their ruin. Placed next to an image of the shimmering Rhine, the Loreley leads us to Heine, whose poem is perhaps the most well-known and certainly most often sung—and, of course, we also know that the Rhine conceals the Nibelung treasure in its depths, dumped there by Hagen. The poet Heine is pictured with other giants of German Romantic poetry, notably Friedrich Hölderlin and Clemens Brentano; together, they laid an aesthetic foundation, the scepter seems to suggest, for what may come around the next turn on the staircase. We are meant to ask ourselves what qualities do perhaps the dangerous seductress (Loreley) and the patriotic muse (Germania) share with the other women whose images we encounter. There is the image of a saintly virginal Kriemhild, as we see her in the first part of Lang's film, whose face recalls that of Thea von Harbou—Lang's wife and collaborator, actress, fervent Nazi supporter (we are meant to conflate images of greed, desire, and power here). Beauty and treasure, like nationalism and power, seduce us.

The figure of Brünhild participates in these associations as well, embodiment of these old dichotomies, though leading in a slightly different direction. The warrior Germania evokes images of the fierce Brünhild, whom Gunther desires but cannot defeat (on the field or in the bedroom) without help from Siegfried. This resonates with the image of the Valkyrie, daughters of Odin who bring the heroic dead to Valhalla (and, yes, we are meant to hear Wagner's music here). Later the scepter will show us other modern warrior women whom we may know from action films (Jane Fonda in *Barbarella*, Grace Jones in James Bond, Brigitte Nielssen in *Red Sonya*). But, in an interesting interpretive twist here, we are also meant to connect Brünhild with the sleeping princesses of folklore and fairytales (recall the versions of the Siegfried myth where Brünhild sleeps under a spell surrounded by a ring of fire until the hero comes who can awaken her—this is, of course, a story that Wagner writes into his *Ring*). So the scepter takes us on an unexpected turn to other famous sleeping princesses like Sleeping Beauty or Snow White (no, we do not necessarily go into their reasons for sleeping—the fact that they are kissed awake is the common denominator). Indeed, we are to connect Brünhild with Dornröschen, Sissi perhaps also with Kriemhild to compare with an earlier photo of Thea von Harbou and the silhouette of Fritz Lang behind the camera (key word "Macht") not far from the images of a simple golden ring and a picture of Richard Wagner. These images are clustered around themes like love (*Liebe*), betrayal (*Verrat*), princess (*Prinzessin*). We are meant to recall that the Grimms were contemporaries of Brentano, Heine, and Hölderlin; when we are perhaps startled to find images from Disney's *Sleeping Beauty*, we are prompted to consider Disney as a direct cultural descendent of the Grimms.

We also find Disney's Prince Philip depicted here; as a slayer of dragons, he may descend not only from Siegfried but also (as perhaps Siegfried may at least in the Romantic imagination) from St. George and the Archangel Michael. That those figures appear in the collage of images around the terms *Gut* (good) and *Heiliger* (saint) would suggest that viewers are to make this connection. The association of *Dornröschen* and *Schneewittchen* with Brünhild as sleeping princesses seems as far-fetched as the association of Prince Philip with Siegfried. However, the scepter convincingly makes the case for Disney's Americanized fantasy middle ages as an outgrowth of German Romantic *Mittelalterrezeption* through its adaptations of Grimm's fairy tales.

This is, of course, a museum in Worms. A final set of associations can be found around the city of Worms itself. It is on the Rhine, which connects it back to the water nymphs and the Loreley. There is the Hagen monument that commemorates the sinking of the treasure in the river. At Worms, the river is spanned by a Nibelung bridge—which stands for several other bridges that carry the name, notably in Regenbsurg and Linz. The cathedral in Worms plays a central role in the *Nibelungenlied* itself; the north portal is where the quarrel (*Streit*) between the queens Kriemhild and Brünhild took place. Maps of the surrounding area show us places where other events of the story, such as Siegfried's murder, could perhaps have occurred. The scene of Siegfried's death (*Mordstelle*) is alleged to be somewhere in the Odenwald/Odenheim, now part of what is called the Nibelungenstraße for tourists. Siegfried's burial place (Ruhestätte) is alleged to be at Lorsch, not far from Worms, where Kriemhild mourned him for thirteen years before her marriage to Etzel. Real-world geography meets the imagined geography of the narrative, just like the ideals of Romantic poetry inspired the real politics of nineteenth-century Germany and like the received narrative of the Nibelungs fueled nationalist and patriotic sentiment through the two world wars. Worms has a history as an imperial city as well as a religious center. The seal of the city of Worms carries a dragon, which connects it to the dragon slayer Siegfried (and by extension dragon slayers of all kinds; there is a rather kitschy image of the dragon from Disney's *Sleeping Beauty* morphing into the dragon from the seal). Finally, there is the aspect of play and game in both positive and negative forms—Worms is now well established as the site of the Nibelung Festival (*Nibelungen Festspiele*). The festival was reinstituted at the end of the twentieth century, seeking to overcome its history as part of Nazi culture politics. In the scepter we actually see a poster advertising the event from 1939; this is part of the game we play with the machinery of myth at our disposal.

The collages also succeed in deconstructing the two most influential versions of the *Nibelungenlied* that emerged from, and contributed to, the story's evolution in the last century: the operas of Richard Wagner and the films of Fritz Lang. The intertexts engage the visitors—they are part (an integral component) of the palimpsests of adaptation—and the figures in the mosaic "take apart" or dismantle the narratives that have become solidified into coherence over time. The museum lays them bare to the audience. This allows the openness of the texts to emerge—prompts the questions of the viewers, directs and allows the interrogation of the images and the words as well as the history.

The museum pushes the envelope further, however (**Figure 13**). In one turn on the spiral staircase, one spies Sleeping Beauty's Prince Philip again—this is not surprising as the images recycle. But the collage is dominated unexpectedly by the figure of Roger Moore's James Bond. Moore, as Bond, stares intensely out of the picture, taking aim at an assailant with the revolver in his hand, pointing the weapon for all intents and purposes at the viewer. This collage of "Helden" features other heroes familiar from Hollywood films. Next to Bond stands Obi Wan Kenobi, and below Bond, directly under the pistol, is an image of Luke Skywalker. The combination seems bizarre, though the figures of Disney's Prince Philip and Fritz Lang's Siegfried place the Hollywood heroes clearly in a Nibelung context. Siegfried sits on horseback, looking back over his left shoulder in the scene where he leaves Mime and the forest. His posture imitates that of Prince Philip (or is his posture imitated by Philip? We are encouraged to ask, though the museum will not give us a definitive answer). The message is that we should consider their legacy as "hero prince" extending through the network of modern fairy-tale heroes like James Bond, Luke Skywalker, and Obi-Wan Kenobi. In this ensemble of images, the viewer cannot avoid looking at Siegfried in the shadow of Bond; similarly, one cannot focus on Prince Philip without having Luke Skywalker in the field of vision. My own response to the juxtaposition of images in this collage echoed my response as an American medievalist to the museum: surprise mixed with curiosity, delight in the cognitive dissonance generated by the visual display. Out of this dissonance, the museum hopes to offer the possibility of a new narrative for a modern audience: an epic tale of history and myth, of truth and untruth, of art and manipulation that reveals itself through the palimpsestic intertextual layers of narrative, of history, and of adaptation and interpretation. Elsewhere, Gallé comments on the power of the images: One can begin at any point, he says, and allow oneself to be guided by the figures that catch one's eye. The Nibelung Museum creates space not only for a more traditional museum visit but also for current ways of learning.[34] The visitor must take responsibility for that learning and for creating new narrative; there are no set answers. In a museum dedicated to a medieval narrative and its reception, in word and in image, Walt Disney fairy tales share the stage with modern fantasy myths and popular action heroes. In the process, the museum tries to dismantle the story that has become inextricably intertwined with modern German history

Figure 13 Nibelung Museum Sehturm collage, *author's own*.

and attempts to reposition it more appropriately in the twenty-first century, like the literary history of the *Nibelungenlied*.

The almost bewildering sea of images can appear random, though we have seen how it is not. Like our climb up the stairs, the museum's visual narrative does have direction. From the origin of the word "Nibelung," the poet manages to give the general outline of the *Nibelungenlied*'s plot by the time we arrive at the last station at the top of scepter. From the rediscovery and popularization of the myth by German romantics, with reference to its legacy in contemporary culture, the images document the transformation of the narrative from myth to propaganda between 1800 and 1939, "when the Minister of Culture, Herr Doctor Josef Goebbels, took it under his dark wing. What a wretched political reclamation."[35] The collages on the scepter simultaneously introduce and deconstruct the two most influential versions of the *Nibelungenlied* that emerged from, and contributed to, the story's evolution in the last century: the operas of Richard Wagner and the films of Fritz Lang. The viewing experience in the *Sehturm* also has a physical element: visitors must also climb the *Sehturm*'s spiral staircase and exert themselves physically in order to "get" the story. We must look, listen, walk; in that process, the images work into our imagination, encourage interpretation, prompt childhood memories, and transform the story we thought we knew. Similarly, the museum wants this kaleidoscope of images to work into our imagination, inviting embodiment and leading, perhaps more importantly, to not just reaction but action. In addition, because the tower has only one way up and one way down, visitors are physically compelled to follow the story of the images and the story of the museum narrative.[36]

As we approach the top of the scepter, we see a collage that represents the legacy of poets from the Middle Ages through modern times (from the anonymous *Nibelungenlied* poet to Fritz Lang)—a legacy of imagery and narrative from which we should learn better than others whose examples we have just witnessed. The emotional and visual trajectory of the images strongly implies that the modern interpreters of the medieval *Nibelungenlied* got it drastically wrong. With the poet, hoping to help the visitors see things clearly, the designers offer the *Sehturm* as a journey through the history of the Nibelungelied's modern reception and through the process of myth-making. The *Nibelungenlied* started with some basis in some history and became myth as different German eras needed to use the story differently for their own purposes. As the poet reiterates, the memory of the Nibelungs is alive. This living memory facilitates the transformation of history to story, becoming myth and then the basis later used to re-create a particular history for a particular group (e.g., by the National Socialists). The many versions of stories leave their own traces of the curse, as though there seems to be a real kind of curse of the kind symbolized by the ring in Wagner's *Ring der Nibelungen*.

Whatever the nature of the "curse," the scepter is clearly the key to the story and the story's enduring power; the guide notes that this reception story "appears to be woven into the golden wand as it serves as an enormous device that recycles all the different images and music inspired by the Nibelungs."[37] While the sheer number of fairly small images on the scepter, placed in close proximity, provides intense visual stimulation, the scepter offers a convincing example of the "machinery of myth" at work. The collages of images appear to vary endlessly on the scepter, leading to sometimes almost incongruous juxtapositions in the bewildering collection of images connecting to stories and interpretations throughout the history of the *Nibelungenlied*.[38] Bringing together myths like that of the sleeping princess awakened by a kiss (connecting Brünhild and Sleeping Beauty and Snow White) juxtaposed with images of seemingly invulnerable modern heroes (Siegfried, James Bond, Luke Skywalker), the collage is a puzzle of fragments that confront the twenty-first-century visitor with pieces of a cultural history that demand to be fit together over and over again.[39] As the mechanism that contains these images, the scepter is referred to as a machine with varying descriptors: "eine riesige Recyclingmaschine" (a giant recycling machine),[40] "eine Höllenmaschine" (a machine from hell),[41] "eine wahre Fälschungsmaschine" (a machine that manufactures deception),[42] a "Mythenmaschine" (a machine that generates myth), and finally a "Deutungsmaschine" (an interpretive machine).[43] All of these designations reflect the *Sehturm*'s (also the museum's) emphasis on the way in which the story of the Nibelungs took on a life and a dynamic of its own, depending on the interpreters who changed and manipulated the story in various contexts over time.

At the top of the *Sehturm*, we see the power of propaganda and fiction in one of the last images at the scepter's tip: a ruined Worms in the immediate aftermath of the Second World War. This final image resonates with the words of a speech by Joseph Goebbels we hear in the audio guide. The poet, however, insists that we not only acknowledge the machinery of myth but that we begin to counteract it. Taking humorous and witty offense at the variations and mutations of his story, the poet ends this first part of his tour with an outbreak of righteous indignation:

> I know that I have spoken at length, but justice had to be done. I have had to remain silent for eight hundred years, forced to endure the abuse, which has been hurled at me from all sides. The last two centuries have been the worst. Sitting here with jaw clenched, I have had to listen to warmongers use my *Nibelungenlied* to justify murder and assassination ... I only wish this demonization of my work would stop, as if the *Nibelungenlied* were responsible for the rise of German nationalism and everything that followed afterwards.[44]

The poet wants to frame a new perspective on history and on this story, since we cannot go further on this path. Literally, we have reached the end of the stairs, the top of the tower. We have to go back, literally and figuratively.

The Wehrgang: Time travel

This phenomenon of the Nibelungs began in the Middle Ages, of course, and by the time we have reached the top of the first tower, there is only one way to proceed: we can only descend and go further back into the past to explore the actual origins of the narrative. One must then follow the images back down to station 5, from which one exits onto the old city wall to walk to the next tower. The need to retrace one's steps offers an interesting and open opportunity to re-read the scepter images; one senses that the machinery of myth may be read forward or backward, going up the stairs or going down; this creates the same jumbled collection of images, all related thematically to the story of the *Nibelungenlied* and its history. There is only one way up the tower and one way down, so it is interesting to have to go down again, having heard the story and looked at the film clips as well as the images, and look again. And the placement of the scepter continuously draws the visitor's gaze, as it is in the middle of the staircase and one's eyes cannot avoid it. At station 5, a door leads out onto the outside wall to walk to the next tower. The towers are connected by a passage along the medieval wall that takes the visitor from the mid-twentieth century "back" in time by means of a series of city maps showing Worms in various stages of growth since the fifteenth century. The display starts with the image of a Worms in ruins in 1945, which is where we had ended our climb in the previous tower. There are reproductions of older city maps of Worms that symbolize the "walk back in time" from the modern era to the Middle Ages, from 1969 back to about 1550. As the visitor passes the map of 1945, air-raid sirens can be heard through the audio guide. In the year 1639, the city is on fire and one can hear the sounds of the city trying to deal with that emergency. In 1550, the town is rather sleepy and rural, as illustrated by the sounds of farm and pasture. The display brings us, along a more traditional linear timeline image by image through the city's history, back into the Middle Ages, where we meet our story again. By the time one reaches the door of the *Hörturm*, one is almost in the Middle Ages; one enters the thirteenth century, as it were, as one opens the door to the poet's study ("Schreibstube") in the *Hörturm*.

Hörturm: Medieval texts and intertexts

We enter the listening tower, the *Hörturm*, to the poet's second welcome: "Welcome to my workshop, my study!" ("Willkommen nun in meiner Werkstatt, meiner Schreibstube!"). The unifying element through the museum and through the narrative of the audio guide is the figure of the poet, who has taken up residence in the museum so that he can correct all of the misconceptions and misinterpretations caused by various audiences and partial understandings (compounded by political manipulations) over time. As the museum guide puts it: "May the anonymous poet—in his own home—succeed in reconciling you with his work and with his imaginary world."[45] And the poet takes this as his task for the audience of our present. He accompanies the listener first through the *Sehturm* and then, having left the visitors in the ruins of the Second World War with the shameful misuse of his text, he brings us back further to the "real" original found in his own "Werkstatt" or "Schreibstube" in the *Hörturm*.

The designers envisioned the *Hörturm* as a place to let the original text speak. The displays in this tower communicate a great deal of what one might consider more traditional museum-oriented information: visitors learn about medieval Germanic literature and medieval cultures in general. After a short introduction to medieval manuscript production, with a brief nod to the various versions of the *Nibelungenlied*, the poet gives an overview of the manuscript's discovery and reception in the eighteenth century and then invites us to listen. One can listen to the story of the *Nibelungenlied* along with information on medieval Germanic literature and medieval cultures in general. There are images from manuscripts, excerpts from the Middle High German text, discussions of themes that are culturally and historically related to the *aventiuren* from the *Nibelungenlied* that are the individual station's focus (courtly love, *Minnesang*, kingship, courtly culture). Chairs, resembling thrones, are placed at intervals in the tower for visitors to sit and listen to excerpts from the poem read aloud both in Middle High German and in modern German; this is the *Hörturm*, after all, and it only makes sense that the original textual language has an audible presence in this display. Indeed, the designers explicitly state their intention to give the poet "his" own voice back, where "he feels much more at home because he presents his own work."[46] The narrator takes up his verses in order to tell us about his sources, about medieval customs and literature, and about the audience of his time. And he need not concern himself, as he has in the previous tower, with what others have made of his poem.

Furthermore, the apparently empty thrones that invite us to sit in them also offer an indication that we also participate in that older culture as we listen to, and participate in, its stories (**Figure 14**). When it comes to medieval texts, modern listeners will lack the immediate recognition they experience when looking at a visual quote from Disney's *Sleeping Beauty* or the image of Luke Skywalker. Continuing to speak from his vantage point in the afterlife, the poet

Figure 14 Nibelung: The thrones of the Hörturm, *author's own*.

now takes the visitor through the work's textual history. As the name of the tower suggests, the emphasis is on what visitors can hear (and read); the emphasis on visual presentation is, by comparison, greatly reduced. The original text and its language have an audible presence in this display, as the visual presentation yields to the aural experience of the text. Straight-backed and high, the thrones might seem to convey a sense of the stiff and static nature of medieval culture as we moderns may tend to interpret it. Yet, when we sit down to listen to the excerpts of the *Nibelungenlied* read aloud, we move toward the story and it comes to us. While the thrones have wooden seats, the back and sides are transparent panels inscribed with the names of figures from the poem. The story becomes more transparent, as one can see through the sides; as one takes his or her seat, one literally becomes part of the story by taking a place among the names of the central characters.

After moving through the first twelve stations in the *Hörturm*, one arrives at the top floor of the tower with a beautiful panoramic view of Worms. At the midpoint of our journey, we are invited into the Nibelungenland, to look at the poet's world from each direction. On the table at the center of the room, we find the replica of a twelfth-century map; as one approaches it, the poet (in the audio guide) invites the visitor into the Nibelung's land, to look at the poet's world from each direction. The view to the east looks toward the land of Etzel and the Huns, to the north toward Island and Brünhild's home, toward the west to Worms. The map provides the designers with a comparatively simple mechanism (compared to the other technologies on display in the museum) for integrating the legend, its literary landscape, the historical medieval landscape, and the contemporary modern landscape as all have developed palimpsest-like over time and over one another. We have ascended the tower through the story of the *Nibelungenlied* in the context of medieval culture. We look out over the city of Worms to place the poem's geography on the contemporary landscape. And, finally, we come down through the story's medieval reception (in contrast to the reception of the nineteenth and twentieth centuries that we saw represented in the earlier tower). The stations here deal artfully and intelligently with the original medieval texts and the medieval literary context (in such works as *Parzival* or the Dietrichssaga) as well as the text's reception history in later works such as the *Rosengarten* or *Der Hürnen Seyfrid*. The Nibelung poet compares himself with Wolfram, suggesting that Wolfram draws on well-known sources for his *Parzival*, whereas he "had to deal with a narrative tradition at once rich, complex and full of pardox." He asserts, "It was I who turned it into a story and then into a great epic."[47] Originally, the display treated these topics in approximate chronological order, from the earliest sources of the Siegfried legend in the Edda and the saga of the Volsungs through its medieval variants.[48]

Here again the design of the museum is just as dense and "thick" as in the *Sehturm*; the Middle Ages also saw a proliferation of narrative adaptations and retellings that accumulated over time artistically packing layers of narrative together. The modern listener requires explanation or clarification, to bring these elements of the past into the present, to reveal the layers of these older and more unfamiliar palimpsests.[49] Thus, for those modern visitors who do not know the older texts, the poet tells the stories of related tales and contemporary works (like the Atli-Lied or *Parzival* or the Dietrich saga) and compares them to the *Nibelungenlied*. The layers of the "older" palimpsests become clear, as well as new treatment of them. The poet takes some offense at the poetic license, for example, with which both Adaptor C and Wolfram recast the figure of the cook Rumolt from the *Nibelungenlied*. The poet says that he depicted Rumolt, who attempts to dissuade the Burgundians from traveling to Hungary, as an administrator "highly placed in the court."[50] He complains about a subsequent adaptation by Adaptor C, who made "a joke in very poor taste." Adaptor C turned Rumolt from an administrator into a cook who tried to entice the Burgundians to stay by offering them a sumptuous meal. And then the poet expresses his frustration with Wolfram:

> And what did maestro Wolfram do? He quoted this, word for word, in his *Parzival*! Without wishing to spark off a diplomatic incident, I would just like to mention that this sort of error was very characteristic of Wolfram: he was always fond of saying stupid things.[51]

As in the *Sehturm*, the poet provides an entertaining commentary. He jokes about his life in the hereafter, for example, saying that he enjoyed reading the Old Icelandic sagas and he had no language issues at all. In the discussion of the saga of the Volsungs, the poet mentions images in wood carvings from Norway and ends up comparing them to modern comics like Mickey Mouse or Asterix. It is just that the words are missing from the story, he says, as we would expect to see in a comic today.[52] This aside is perhaps a nod to younger visitors, but it also addresses any visitors who grew up with Mickey Mouse and in any case are probably much more familiar with comics and cartoon figures than they are with thirteenth-century Norwegian woodcarvings. The comparison may appear naive at first glance; however, it is meant to be both amusing and thought-provoking as it connects the older narratives to an audience with cultural and historical experiences far removed from the Middle Ages. In general, the presentation in the audio guide for the *Hörturm* tends to play more on the personality of the poet as it attempts to make the chronologically distant time of the Middle Ages more accessible to a contemporary audience.

In 2015, the stations in the *Hörturm* were reorganized to make the experience more thematically coherent, not just an excursion through medieval literary history. The original sequence followed the manuscript history through the narrative and through the medieval adaptations ending with the map at the top of the tower. Now, the sequence leads up to and beyond the map, extending through the narrative to its imagined and real locations, and then bringing the visitor down through the reception history of the text back to the museum's final room. In other words, Stations 1–12 go through the *Nibelungenlied* in both Middle High German and New High German as well as in cultural-sociohistorical context. Station 13 is now the map, then the tour around the area with the maps, and then the text leads the viewer back down through the reception history of the material and its contemporary works in the Middle Ages. In the original version, which is still evident in the guidebook, the stations followed a strictly chronological and unidirectional format. Once one reached the map in the room at the top of the tower, the stations were at an end and visitors were directed to the last installation in the lowest level. In terms of structure and flow, the new arrangement should make the exhibit in the *Hörturm* more user-friendly to all. We encounter the text (which we have been waiting for since the *Sehturm*), we then place it in its geographical and cultural context, and finally we learn about its literary and literary-historical context.

The new organization does, however, highlight the museum's primary challenge: change. It is very difficult to make even small changes in displays, though that has not prevented the museum's administration team from attempting just that. The original plaques have the original numbering on them overlain now with the new numbers, the guide has the same order as well, and the electronic audio guide could simply be reorganized; the changes work. There is, however, little more that can be undertaken before upgrades or changes would completely distort the display. There is very little room for the museum towers to grow and change like a living museum should do, at least in their current constellation. However, as the reorganization of the *Hörturm* demonstrates, this seems to inspire creativity in the museum team. The next room, the *Mythenlabor*, shows this even more clearly in its evolution from its original configuration as a response to the community.

The *Mythenlabor*: Intertextual experiments

From the top of the tower and from a tour of the medieval world through contemporary eyes, the visitor must come back down into the present. And one must go through the present, especially as the final room of the museum (now called the *Mythenlabor*) is in the basement of the building.[53] The story of the final room itself reflects the larger story of the museum in its search for continued relevance and purpose in its community. Originally, the final exhibit was called the treasure chamber ("Schatzkammer"), the room in which visitors would encounter the treasure of the Nibelungs that Hagen had famously thrown to the bottom of the Rhein.[54] In fact, the museum guide published in 2001, and available for purchase in the museum shop, still describes the original installation as Room 42. Meant to reveal the true treasure hidden under the city of Worms, namely the legacy of the story and the people of the city who continue to contribute to it, this was a technologically sophisticated display of sound and image that invited visitors to view individual mosaic "tiles" from the scepter as free-floating images from a room ostensibly located beneath the city. These images were to represent the way in which the story and its reception became the real treasure of the city of Worms, particularly as the images could be dismantled from the scepter and reworked into new configurations and new stories that might release the present from the shackles of the past.[55]

Unveiled for the first time at the Goethe Institutes in Paris and in Boston in spring 2001, this particular display was intended to be one of the showpieces of the museum, in addition to the scepter in the Sehturm. Part of the Boston CyberArts festival in April 2001, the *Schatzkammer* was described by the *Boston Digital Industry* review as "an interactive multimedia artwork" that offered a "high-tech, cutting-edge" interpretation of the *Nibelungenlied*. The Boston reviewer suggests that the "scaled down version at the Goethe Institut was impressive enough" and so the project's "final embodiment at the Nibelungen Museum should be nothing short of awesome."[56] Following the museum's opening in August 2001, initial reviews seemed to confirm that prediction. The installation offered a virtual surfeit of images with soundscape in a computer-animated "Chill-out-Room,"[57] where all images and sounds from both the towers combined for a dramatic finale in a composition of image, music, text, and the dynamic of continual movement that highlights the museum's exhibits with an imaginative conclusion unfettered by history or pedagogy.[58] The installation did, however, have its detractors from the beginning; the reviewer for the *Neue Zürcher Zeitung* identified the main issues when he commented on the subterranean treasury that presented a technically even less convincing video installation in its attempt to represent the myth of the buried Nibelung hoard virtually.

Such responses eventually led to a reconfiguration of the display and transformation into the current laboratory ("Mythenlabor"). The original installation had three main problems. One was its location in the basement of the museum, physically separated from the main exhibit towers and conceptually abstracted from them. In addition, the technology inevitably needed adjustment. Finally, the installation was too abstract. Visitors seemed to find the display disappointing and anticlimactic after going through the rest of the museum for ninety minutes. In 2008, the museum took two steps that signaled a new direction in its focus and outreach. First, the museum hired a museum studies expert to help ensure into the future that visitors should not just visit but experience the museum in a way that differed qualitatively from the way knowledge is communicated through a book or through over-reliance on text.[59] Second, the original *Schatzkammer* installation was removed and the space was completely redesigned.[60] The installation was sent to the Zentrum für Kunst und Medientechnologie (ZKM) in Karlsruhe; the space in the Nibelung Museum was transformed into what they called a "Mythenlabor" or "myth laboratory." The city spent approximately 80,000 Euros on the renovation, and the laboratory opened in October 2008. Since the museum had been planned from the start as a multimedia museum, the new laboratory was a step in that direction.[61] The room could also be used for special exhibitions or events such as performances, which had not been possible with the previous installation.[62] Plans for the *Mythenlabor* also had the effect of providing the opportunity for naysayers opposed to the museum to raise their voices again, with little avail.[63] The laboratory tries to put the myths and legends behind and around the *Nibelungenlied* into perspective, just as the museum does as well. School classes are welcome, which shows the museum's attempt to win new audiences and find new purpose.[64] The assessment going into the following year (2009) was that the laboratory was a good idea, with more work planned in the area of outreach.[65]

If the original *Schatzkammer* was a dynamic composition of image and text and music in continuous movement, then the *Mythenlabor* unequivocally puts the didactic (and the participatory) back into the presentation. The change corresponds, however, to what one can see as a realistic and apparently successful shift in audience focus for the museum. The article in the local paper introducing the new features in July 2007 suggested that the museum laboratory aimed to capture the interest of younger visitors; the *Nibelungenlied* will be present in the exhibits, of course, but it will be situated among other world myths and legends from the ancient stories of gods and heroes to the *Lord of the Rings* and *Harry Potter*.[66] In addition, the laboratory offers the opportunity for museum visitors to explore the more "local" but still broader context of medieval literatures and cultures in Worms and in Europe. One can see longer (three-to-five-minute) video clips on a variety of topics and one can also sit at several interactive stations around the room to explore myths, archetypes, popular culture, and film or the entire catalog of images in the Sehturm. All of the main topics are related to the culture of the twelfth and thirteenth centuries that produced the *Nibelungenlied*, embedded in material that also places the text in the context of the history of Worms and of Germany. Clearly the museum is interested in creating a suitable environment not only for tourists but for school groups as well as for presentations and guest lectures; the renovation also aimed to make the display user-friendly for both younger and older visitors. The room is not large, however; it can still only seat around fifty people at a time. It has five screens, all of which can be in use simultaneously, and various competing audio texts can become distracting if not overwhelming at times. But, despite their proximity and the intermittent sound interference, the displays enable the laboratory format to offer space for special exhibits.

On the most recent level of the museum's narrative, then, we have the re-created story of the poet who wants to reclaim his text for the modern audience, rescuing it from the manipulations and misuses of the recent nineteenth- and twentieth-century past. This is the story the museum designers seek to tell, configuring the poet as a bridge to the past, as a frustrated author who desires to take back his own story and set it to rights. On another narrative level, the Nibelung Museum tells the story of that original story, charting its reception through numerous images and multiple media: clips of Fritz Lang's *Nibelungen* films, nineteenth-century depictions of Germania and the Loreley, photographs of Worms during the Nazi period, images of iconic movie heroes and heroines (such as Romy Schneider's Sissi and or Roger Moore's James Bond) who reveal aspects of the familiar story in unexpected form. As poets and artists have interpreted the *Nibelungenlied* over time, they have sought to represent the narrative's historical, pseudohistorical, or mythical elements as they reflected the interests of their times. These representations can also be found in adaptations and related narratives that belong to the text's reception in the Middle Ages—from the sagas through the later medieval adaptations of Siegfried's story. Thus, the museum tells a story assembled from palimpsests: the *Nibelungenlied*, the poet's "story," the myths and their afterlives, and the ever-accumulating adaptations that are recycled as images through the museum's vision of the scepter or myth-machine. Viewed in its totality, the museum also offers itself as a new and unique artistic creation. The designers urge that it should be judged on its own merits as a contribution to the reception history of the *Nibelungenlied*, taking its place in the extensive library of works that have told the Nibelung myth over time.

As a whole, the Nibelung Museum compels the attention of, and demands thoughtful response from, its visitors. The museum leaves up to visitors what they will make of this treasure, says the *Frankfurter Rundschau*, because there are no prepackaged answers; on the other hand, the museum offers a great deal of stimulation for the eyes and the ears. And, above all, it provides food for thought. In a very concrete way, the museum positions itself as another text in the reception of the *Nibelungenlied*. The museum designers address this explicitly in their introduction to the museum guide: The Nibelung Museum is not a conventional museum, rather, it is an artistic creation in itself; it can be read and visited as a museum, but it also wants to be evaluated as museum. The museum offers an overview of the legend and its interpretations over time; at the same time, it presents itself enthusiastically and self-reflexively as yet another one of those interpretations in a continuing process. The museum becomes thereby part of the myth-making process.

Literature, history, and heritage: The machinery of myth

This brings us back to the literal and figurative image of the "myth machine" (*Mythenmaschine*), a machinery in which the museum self-consciously participates and which audiences cannot stop.[67] As the Nibelung Museum takes up the themes of the Middle High German *Nibelungenlied* (love, death, loyalty, betrayal, honor), it illustrates how the text extends far beyond its origins and the framework of medieval courtly society, showing the history not just of a text but of a narrative of a story consistently reframed over time through mechanisms such as politics, nationalism, myth, and media. This is also, then, the history of a metanarrative that resonates through contemporary experience; it epitomizes the entanglements of text that give rise to Bakhtin's dialogic imagination. Visually and aurally, the museum demonstrates the process of remaking a "story" whose history was refracted and distorted through the cultural lenses of the nineteenth and twentieth centuries. The multisensory and multidimensional texts provided for the visitor facilitate this engagement as the museum itself becomes yet another text in the reception of the *Nibelungenlied*, part of a "Mythenmaschine" in which successive audiences participate. Finally, the museum emphasizes a need to reclaim the text of the medieval *Nibelungenlied* in a positive way for the modern city and for the future, creating in the process a new narrative to tell a new audience. Thus, we also participate in an activity that resembles the medieval work of memory, as we re-member and re-create these texts for ourselves. The fictional poet-narrator of the museum's guide, voiced by actor Mario Adorf, greets the visitor at the entrance with a jovial "Willkommen in meiner neuen Bleibe!" (Welcome to my new home). In its "new" home at the "medieval" Bürgerturm, the Nibelung Museum presences the past through its display of literature in general and the *Nibelungenlied* in particular in its reception from the Middle Ages to the present day.

Literature, connected to place and to a community, is what we might call intangible heritage, "rooted in the locality in real as well as in figurative terms."[68] The museum allows the narrative past, firmly embedded in the old wall, to become physically real and tangibly present for modern Worms. The materiality and the physicality of the place, compensating for a lack of textual materiality, invite visitors to meet the past by crossing its threshold, moving through the spaces (physical and ideological) that the past inhabits in our present. The museum's architectural blend of medieval and modern enhances its overall intent to make the modern appear as though it emerges from the medieval. Thus, the city seeks to cultivate the role of the *Nibelungenlied* and its legend as an even more active participant in the community's heritage and life. If heritage is a sign of modernity, as Kirshenblatt-Gimblett suggests, it provides an appealing opportunity for a city like Worms, trying to revitalize a flagging economy and enhance its identity in the new memorylands of a global Germany and a global Europe.[69] When we visit Worms now, I think we find a creative site of reflection and critique as visitors consider the past made present and ponder a future. The museum literally wants to place us within the story, just as the map and the window compel us to view the city of 2018 around, because of, and despite, the letters that form the names that create the story that has brought us to that very spot to begin with. Told in verse, entangled in narrative, visualized in images, embodied in sculpture, digitized in film, anchored in history and geography, the *Nibelungenlied* inhabits multiple spaces where the (re)imagined past and the real present resonantly comingle.

5

Presencing the Narrative Past: Old Structures, New Stories?

[A] mini-Gesamtkunstwerk ... a magic booth and a reading chamber ... a unique literary museum.[1]

(Tobias Gohlis, "Der Ritter mit der Leier")

Museums are not only about the collections they house—they are also about the sense of the past they represent. Museums symbolise culture, identity and heritage.[2]

(Elizabeth Crooke, *Museums and Community*)

[P]laces possess a marked capacity for triggering acts of self-reflection inspiring thoughts about who one presently is, or memories of who one used to be or musings on who one might become.[3] (Keith Basso, *Wisdom Sits in Places*)

When the Museum Wolfram von Eschenbach opened in January 1995, author Adolf Muschg hailed the museum a "Spielplatz für Menschenphantasien" ("a playground for human fantasies").[4] The review in *Die Zeit* called the museum a "Mini-Gesamtkunstwerk"; the museum designers had created "einen spirituellen Erlebnisraum, eine Zauberbude und Lesekammer, bestem 68er Geist entsprungen, ein Literaturmuseum eigener Art" ("a spiritual experience, a magical booth and reading chamber created from the best spirit of 68, a unique literary museum").[5] In Chapters 3 and 4, I suggest that both the Museum Wolfram von Eschenbach and the Nibelungen Museum in Worms offer examples of such an interpretive "Spielplatz" as the museums navigate layers of entangled narrative and history that have proliferated over time with the *Nibelungenlied* and the works of Wolfram von Eschenbach. In their interpretation and display of medieval German literature, the museums offer a kind of temporal archive of ideas made visible in the displays.[6]

In their visualizations of medieval German literature, both the Museum Wolfram von Eschenbach and the Nibelung Museum attempt to untangle narratives that have become enmeshed and intertwined since the thirteenth century; they reveal manifold layers of interpretation and reception over time. Each museum itself also adds to the layers of intertext in the ever-growing and expanding palimpsest of the narratives that are its subject. In their displays, and as exhibits themselves, the museums enact a medievalism that exemplifies Hutcheon's concept of adaptation both as product and as process; indeed, though Hutcheon does not necessarily consider museums adaptations, I would argue that the Nibelung Museum and the Museum Wolfram von Eschenbach are striking examples of her idea of "palimpsestuous intertextuality." Both museums embrace and extend the concatenation of intertexts that have emerged from the reception of the thirteenth-century narratives, attempting to reposition the fiction with respect to history and vice versa. I would be tempted to call this adaptive reception, adding to the four models of medieval reception articulated by Gentry and Müller.[7] As adaptive palimpsests, the museums encourage modern audiences to find their way, to find our way, back to stories that have been deconstructed and reconstructed over time.

Each museum does this in keeping with its own local environment and history, attempting to offer a close reading appropriate to the texts and their reception history (more or less) in those environments. In the following, I will offer a comparative analysis of both museums: their interpretations of medieval narratives and subsequent afterlives, their roles in the community as repositories of local history, their function as monuments and heritage. Both museums, for example, have been built into the existing historical cityscapes of their respective towns. The Museum Wolfram von Eschenbach replaced the former local museum ("Heimatmuseum") in the old city hall ("Altes Rathaus") of Wolframs-Eschenbach; the Nibelung Museum was built into the medieval city wall of Worms. The latter is now a modern structure literally ensconced in the older medieval wall. Physically located both in the past and in the present, each museum seems to pull an immaterial story back into a material and three-dimensional space. In their practice of medievalism, through the display of their respective texts, the museums transform the older structures of each town into new narratives for modern communities.

Medieval narratives and their afterlives

How can you display a poet and his work, asks Horst Brunner in his introduction to the Wolfram museum in 2010, when you have nothing to display—no manuscript, no quill, no drinking glass, no house, no article of clothing, nothing?

It is possible, Brunner answers his own question, if one has the courage to do something unusual.⁸ Such courage is, I would concur with Brunner, definitely palpable in the Museum Wolfram von Eschenbach just as the museum expresses the same kind of playful humor that pervades Wolfram's own works. The museum designers in Worms also had courage in abundance.⁹ The displays in the Nibelung Museum offer interpretation of the literature that show an equally distinctive but different process of adaptation and past presencing than that in Wolframs-Eschenbach.

In Wolframs-Eschenbach, literature takes center stage from the start with its question: "Kann man Literatur ausstellen?" The purpose is to take the older texts, to (re)introduce visitors to them, to give them a taste of the language, to navigate the "alien" nature of the Middle Ages as well as its alterity. The museum seeks, in a sense, to overcome the differences by highlighting the similarities between then and now. As they were then, human beings are human beings now; we have similar concerns now as we did then, and Wolfram's works arc over the intervening 800 years to share those concerns: compassion (*Parzival* and the Grail quest), the dangers of young love (*Titurel*), the randomness of war (*Willehalm*). The museum takes care to offer an educational frame as an introduction to the texts and to the main themes, rising to the challenge of putting literature on display. Some visitors, notably German medievalists, might miss a more focused or more traditional treatment of Wolfram's works. However, the museum endeavors to lead the visitors back to the text through its displays; appreciation of and return to the text, after all, are goals that a literary museum ("Literaturmuseum") often strives to achieve.

In Worms, by contrast, reception gets put on display. The later Nibelung Museum does not imitate the concept from Wolframs-Eschenbach, as Brunner believes; rather, the Nibelung Museum offers a provocatively complementary display. The reception of the Nibelung myth seems just as convoluted and complex as Wolfram's texts themselves. Reviewers noted, as we have seen, that the actual *Nibelungenlied* itself does not seem to have the central presence in the museum that some expect, along with its source texts and continuations. In fact, this is one of the main criticisms expressed by the Siegfried Museum in Xanten as it positions itself with respect to the Nibelung Museum and it states unequivocally that it wants to bring the text back into the discussion. The Siegfried Museum in Xanten does seem to focus more on the actual narrative of the *Nibelungenlied*, and it does indeed have more vitrines with traditional displays in the form of artifacts, posters, costumes, and books. None of these can be found in the Nibelung Museum, which relies much more on technology and multimedia installations for effect. The Nibelung Museum not only seems to want to show that (and how) audiences can interact with medieval texts through technology; it has a very clear mission to set right the multiple errors that its designers believe have occurred in the reception and interpretation of the *Nibelungenlied* since 1800. Indeed, the accruing palimpsests had all but erased the story, threatening to obscure it to the point where we barely recognize it. Like the Museum Wolfram von Eschenbach, the Nibelung Museum sets up to lead us back to the text, at the very least to an original medieval narrative. It may fall short of its mark—but, like the Museum Wolfram von Eschenbach, it knows its place in a world where reading suffers, where awareness of the Middle Ages struggles, where the past is just a sometimes questionably accurate Google search away. Both museums want to connect their texts to their place, to connect place to identity. Finally, they suggest that, if we really want to know who we are, we should revisit and re-read these texts, because they still speak to us if we know to listen.

Dangerous games: A common theme

The museums differ in their approach to the literature they display. However, they do take up a similar general theme of dangerous games, played with and played within the medieval stories that each museum will put on display. The Museum Wolfram von Eschenbach makes much of the game of chivalry; Parzival, Schionlatulander, Willehalm, and the knight-lover of the dawn-song all participate in that game with mixed results. Parzival must search for the Grail for almost five years because, while he could successfully joust, he did not have the empathy necessary to bring healing to his uncle. Schionatulander and the knight-lover wish to please their ladies, whether that means risking discovery in a forbidden bedchamber or chasing after a dog's leash—either path potentially leads, and for Schionatulander does lead, to disaster. Willehalm's game is war against the invading Saracens, a conflict which should seem straightforward but is not. The museum complicates the game, even as it constructs its displays with considerable humor of its own. The message is unambiguous: Now the game is not just knighthood. Rather, it is the game of human activity and folly. Implicit in Wolframs-Eschenbach are the aspects of the game over time that the Nibelung Museum makes more explicit: politics, nationalism, myth, and media. In its focus on the modern history of the *Nibelungenlied* text and the Nibelung material in the last 200 years, the Nibelung Museum highlights the proliferating number of narratives, adaptations, and intertexts that have emerged from the palimpsests revealed through the medieval text, the nineteenth-century re-creations, and the modern adaptations. In the words of the reviewer from the *Süddeutsche Zeitung*, the Nibelung Museum releases the legend from the shackles of history into the realm of science fiction and fantasy, and any ideological concerns that one might have with respect to the museum dissipate elegantly in the sea of images.

The museum insists on a new narrative to tell a modern audience; it tells an epic tale of its own: a tale of history and myth, of truth and untruth, of art and manipulation that reveals itself through the palimpsestic intertextual layers of narrative and history, of adaptation and interpretation. If the process of transformation in Wolframs-Eschenbach involves making "history" from story, the process in Worms has more to do with remaking a "story" whose history was refracted (and distorted) through the cultural lenses of the nineteenth and twentieth centuries. We have seen that the works of Wolfram von Eschenbach did not lend themselves to discussions of national identity as the *Nibelungenlied* has done. Although the history of the Nibelungs is about as "real" and verifiable as that of Wolfram von Eschenbach, the Nibelung Museum can tie itself not only to the history of the city of Worms but also to more extensive textual history of the *Nibelungenlied* over time, with its uses and misuses. Subsequent generations wrote the familiar narrative in their own way, interpreting the story and reshaping it to suit their own images and cultural aspirations.

Before we continue, there is another ongoing aspect of the "dangerous game" that needs to be mentioned here. The displays in the Museum Wolfram von Eschenbach and the images on the scepter in the Nibelung Museum have not changed since the museums opened in 1995 and 2001 respectively, but the world around the museums certainly has—in Germany, in Europe, in the global community. When we look at the visual displays now, for example, we need to ask: Do the images confound or clarify? And whose story are we meant to read in them? The decision to put this medieval literature on display should intrigue us as visitors, but it should also perhaps give us pause. Yes, the Nibelung Museum wants to correct for us the story of a misunderstood narrative. The museum works very hard to recover the *Nibelungenlied* from the clutches of the "myth machine." But visitors now bring with us other almost endlessly recycling associations of the Middle Ages,[10] as we enter the museum coming in from a contemporary world fraught with violence, with persecution of minorities, with rising populism and extremism. We have to acknowledge that the museum's intertexts, from the Romantics through Germania to the National Socialists, participate in a larger set of entanglements that involve medievalism, race, cultural memory, and heritage. We have to admit that the German Middle Ages of the nineteenth century intended to create a community that was homogenous, German(ic), European. And the medieval world of Wolfram von Eschenbach, though the museum offers meticulously constructed intricate displays to reflect that world's complexity, does not take up these entangled modern metanarratives either. But there would be ample opportunity and good reason to do so. One could connect to the quote on the Wolfram monument that refers to the baptism of Parzival's half-brother Feirefiz, who was black and white. In 1861, that reference was certainly meant to serve as an affirmation of unity recalling those homogenous Christian Middle Ages for nineteenth-century Bavaria. One could complicate that monument's clear message with a different twenty-first-century response like Lisa Lampert's reading of Feirefiz as part of her exploration of medieval constructions of race and the role of the medieval and medievalisms "in the construction, representation, and perpetuation of modern racisms."[11] Both museums demonstrate a keen sense of social justice that would serve them well in confronting these issues in a more explicit way. The overtones of chivalry's dangerous game reverberate with the games of other ideologies and their consequences (e.g., racism, nationalism) that our ideas of the Middle Ages still perpetuate.

Literature and text

One must acknowledge that the text as object is missing from the both museums; this is a fact that each museum celebrates, as they display no manuscripts or facsimiles. On the other hand, while the physical texts may seem absent, their stories permeate the museum displays—as subjects of literary interpretation, as generators of ideas, as products of adaptation, as partners in dialogue. The narratives remain ever-present; furthermore, both museums do attempt to integrate linguistic aspects of Middle High German as well as literary and cultural aspects of the medieval period in Germany. Arguably, the Nibelung Museum has perhaps the easier task of keeping its focus on one particular story—the story of a story, which is that of the Nibelungs, the dragon-slayer Siegfried, and the city of Worms. The Museum Wolfram von Eschenbach aims to display Wolfram's oeuvre in its entirety. At first glance, the creative design at the museum in Wolframs-Eschenbach can seem to obscure what visitors might expect to see of Wolfram's physical texts. I think this depends on what one understands as "text"—certainly, Wolfram's major works are present in their explication. The written word and the spoken word are also still present; though scholars may perceive their familiar texts one or two steps removed from the displays, the displays allow space for language and text. The biography room pairs Wolfram's own words with explanatory notes about his relationships to women, his understanding of family, his attitudes about knighthood. The verses of the dawn song peek out at us from the clouds in the room of the *Minnesang*, inviting us to read and to listen to what they have to tell us. Each room is a specific, image-rich, and sometimes intellectually crowded encounter with the Wolfram's texts, his words, and his ideas. With Muschg, I would have to agree that the museum knows very well that it is a place full of humor because it acknowledges its very nature as a place built on a fiction; it is the outline of a trace that is a self-conscious creation.[12] As the museum designers understand the poet Wolfram and his texts, they represent in each display the same playfulness and the same jocular wit that they find throughout his works.

Textual interpretation of the *Nibelungenlied*, on the other hand, is not the emphasis in Worms; rather, it is the reception of texts over time that is on display. There, too, the text of the *Nibelungenlied* can be lost, particularly in the formidable visual display of the *Sehturm*. Of course, the historical narrative does maintain a presence through the script of the museum's audioguide— though that is also a fiction, since the narrator is a creation of the designers in the persona of a poet who has remained anonymous since the Middle Ages. And the text itself, with a more narrow display focus on its reception history, returns in the second tower—where we have the opportunity to hear it; we hear Middle High German similarly rendered in the room of the dawn songs in Wolframs-Eschenbach. In a sense, however, the relative openness of the textual interpretation in each museum ultimately determines the engagement on the part of the audience. Because of the nature of the display, and the interpretations of the respectively museum designers, the audience participation is arguably more active in Wolframs-Eschenbach and perhaps more passive in Worms. The museum in Worms has 200 years of palimpsests and intertexts to address, including various historical/literary/political misappropriations—the museum feels a responsibility to make all of the connections as clear as possible. In a sense, the Nibelung Museum wants to dismantle the layers of false interpretation in the reception history of the *Nibelungenlied* in the nineteenth and twentieth centuries so that we can find our way back to the original narrative again. One last point of comparison that bears on the nature of literature and text in the museums has to do with the arrangement of the displays. On the one hand, the displays in each museum are structured based on very practical factors, as the layout of each museum is determined by the constraints of the physical space it has available. The spatial arrangements of respective installations, as well as the visitors' movement through those spaces, reflect the literary interpretations as well: the vertical up-and-down movement in the towers of the Nibelung Museum seems to reflect the Nibelung material caught in the thematic vicissitudes of history over time, whereas the primarily horizontal movement in Wolframs-Eschenbach offers a less strenuous but equally thought-provoking walk through Wolfram's narrative world.

In sum, both museums strive to place the literature, its reception and their interpretations in the context of their local communities, connecting through the literature to the broader history in which all participate. They are rather bold experiments. Critics continue to the use of media in the Nibelung Museum distracting and even limiting, for example. As a museum and not just an example of cultural/literary interpretation, however, it serves as a site of commentary, prompting us to reflect not only on the content in the media on display but on the media themselves. Thus the use of media is not just a distraction but perhaps also a chance "to reflect upon the differing affordances and implications of the media themselves."[13] This is reflected in the constant references in the Nibelung Museum to the machinery of myth. Through the scepter, the *Sehturm* offers an elegant and provocative display of an "old" premodern story that is projected onto and appropriated by the postmodern virtual world. The scepter images also insist on a continuing dialogue with the story beyond ideological issues that, for example, would have the *Niblungenlied* remain a part of a "stuffy" manuscript tradition. As the viewer encounters and seeks to make sense of these multiple and simultaneous images, impressed with their power and their variety, one realizes that there is no single perspective. The museum in Wolframs-Eschenbach does not make extensive use of technology; instead, the designers there innovate differently in their creative interpretations of the literary texts.[14] In effect, though, the Museum Wolfram von Eschenbach similarly displays Wolfram's works, insisting on their continued relevance for new generations. Both museums present their literary source material as stories with local roots that extend back to the Middle Ages.

Repositories of local history?

Worms proudly claims the title of Nibelung-City ("Nibelungenstadt"), just as Wolframs-Eschenbach advertises itself as the "Stadt des Parzivaldichters" and the "Heimatort des Dichters Wolfram von Eschenbach." And both towns want these museums to bring the communities out of relative obscurity, to rescue the cities from their perceived unimportance or relative oblivion, to give a literary past a historically significant anchor in the present—and last but not least to stimulate tourism. Having looked at the museums as with respect to the display of literature, I want to turn for a moment to an examination of each museum in its local and regional contexts. As we have seen, Wolframs-Eschenbach is the town that settles into a pastoral provinciality, nestled in an idyllic landscape, visited by the occasional tourist—which the town hopes will be eventually more than occasional. The change of name in 1917 from Eschenbach to Wolframs-Eschenbach may have offered the town a way to get "back on the map," as it were, and the museum offered yet another means of promoting the town by constructing its public identity around the famed medieval poet of *Parzival* and his texts. Worms also hoped to attract more than the occasional tourist. As a larger and more central city, Worms has its history punctuated by moments of glory with a comparatively wider reach than Wolframs-Eschenbach: Luther's appearance before the Imperial Diet, for example, attracts a steady stream of Protestant pilgrims to Worms. The cathedral is a religious and cultural magnet as well. Both communities want to make their literary heritage real. The museum landscapes are also unique as well, though each museum stands out in its region as something experimental, unusual, and innovative. The landscapes appear very different because of the different environments and cityscapes. But the issues of the museums are the same—in other words, in the same radius of approximately ten miles in both places, one finds the same kinds of museums. And, therefore, each of these literary museums stands out similarly from its respective landscape. In the following, I wish to compare and describe the land- and cityscapes of Worms and Wolframs-Eschenbach as a way of looking at how the museums function in their respective environments as repositories of local history. As a comparison, we will look at the immediate environment around the Nibelung Museum in Worms.

Wolframs-Eschenbach: Museum landscape

As we noted in the introduction, the town of Wolframs-Eschenbach lies just north of what is known as the Franconian lake district. The region is known for tourism and agriculture, literally and figuratively cultivating its history and its land; indeed, the area has a stunning number of local museums that celebrate various aspects of the collective regional history. And the town of Wolframs-Eschenbach, its monument, and its museum would seem to be no exception.

However, when the town decided to update the local museum and renovate the old city hall in the late 1980s, it followed a decidedly nontraditional path.

Three museum collections (Ansbach, Gunzenhausen, Merkendorf) in the near vicinity of Wolframs-Eschenbach offer a revealing point of comparison for any discussion of the Museum Wolfram von Eschenbach in terms of how these communities understand their history and how they present themselves to the outside world?[15] Although these three towns, like Wolframs-Eschenbach, have constructed museums with the clear objective to share and celebrate local history, their collections are much more traditional. We can place them in the category of Heimat museum, of a type that proliferated rapidly in the late nineteenth and early twentieth centuries; in fact, according to historian Alon Confino, at least 371 Heimat museums were founded in Germany between 1890 and 1918 as part of this "mania" for museum building.[16] Heimat museums displayed local identity and peculiarities, says Alon Confino, but they did so in a "language of similitudes." The exhibitions followed similar patterns, in that they represent "the identity of a community of people who shared a past and a present." The Heimat museum became, at least between 1871 and 1918, a powerful "integrative social force" for the German bourgeoisie.[17]

The message of social integration, or at least celebration of shared past, continues in the present. Arguably this need for connection, for memory, and for integration with the past is what Macdonald sees as a contributing factor to the "memoryland" in response to the anxiety of cultural amnesia gripping Europe today. The museums seem to convey a message of stability in heritage that, although it is clearly "global in scope" in the twentieth century, it is "experienced and most often expressed at the local level." [18] Indeed, we see this social force and stability of *Heimat* typified in the museums in the immediate proximity of Wolframs-Eschenbach, regardless of the museum's name (*Heimatmuseum* in Merkendorf, *Markgrafen Museum* in Ansbach, *Stadtmuseum* in Gunzenhausen). The Markgrafen Museum in Ansbach, which is the county seat and the historic administrative center of the region, focuses primarily on the story of the margraves of Ansbach, their families and activities, and their times, from the fifteenth through the early nineteenth century. Visitors find what they would expect: cabinets and display cases with weapons, tools, jewelry, and similar objects from the city's past and from the estates of the former margraves of Brandenburg. The museum also dedicates several rooms to its own famous son Kaspar Hauser. In general, the exhibits display traditional objects (portraits, furniture, weaponry), though the objects are arranged in creative and inviting ways; the museum organizers have also recently (within the last several years) developed an interactive display in the Kaspar Hauser exhibit. In a conscious attempt to unite the old and the new, the Ansbach museum also incorporates one of the oldest portions of the medieval city wall as part of a passageway to a second building where there are rotating exhibits of local artists.

The ancient and the new are highlighted in the city museum of Gunzenhausen, as well. Located approximately twenty-five kilometers to the south of Ansbach, Gunzenhausen was built on the site of a Roman fort that was part of the *limes* extending through the Germanic territories in the fourth century. In addition to its replica of the Roman fortifications, complete with part of the excavated foundation, the museum in Gunzenhausen offers its visitors a chronological tour through several centuries of life in the region and displays on its five floors many of the same kinds of artifacts one would expect, from linens to hunting weapons and parlor furniture. Clearly this museum understands itself as a repository of information (and objects) about the city and its past. The same holds true for the museum in the tiny hamlet of Merkendorf, population approximately 1,000, about three kilometers from Wolframs-Eschenbach. Opened in 1993, the Merkendorf museum is housed in the "Alte Scheune" (the old barn); the building, where tithes were collected in the early twentieth century, had served as the Rathaus until 1991.[19] The old barn seems more like a communal attic than a museum. Nevertheless, the existence of the museum testifies to the pride of the local people in their town's past; these artifacts are important pieces of a common history.

These three collections represent aspects of the collective regional history that central Franconia and its many museums wish to celebrate and cultivate for the modern public.[20] As the history of the city is presented to the outside world, these local museums have a number of functions and purposes. Clearly, one primary function is that of collective memory for the community: the museums take the objects of the past—that that have been deemed "important" as communal goods for any respective community—and they categorize these objects in certain ways. Each museum offers an expression of the story its community wishes to tell about itself, generally framing the community's identity within a traditional history that is emphasized more through the standard collection of traditional artifacts on display. These museums would be part of what Macdonald calls the "musealization of everyday life."[21] As a result, the region and its towns would not necessarily seem to represent a cultural avant-garde.

The town of Wolframs-Eschenbach and its museum would seem to be no exception. In its promotional materials, readily available at the city hall and in other locations frequented by tourists, Wolframs-Eschenbach markets its public self as part of this region and as part of this shared historical and cultural landscape. The museum could resemble those in Merkendorf or Gunzenhausen; however, Wolframs-Eschenbach took another path entirely. Rejecting more traditional approaches, the Museum Wolfram von Eschenbach attempts to engage visitors with its twofold question: Can one exhibit not just literature in general but the literature of the Middle Ages (represented by the town's namesake Wolfram von Eschenbach)?[22]

Worms: Museum landscape

In Worms, the Nibelung Museum took its place in a museum landscape that still, like the museums in the region around Wolframs-Eschenbach, offers the public fairly traditional displays. The Worms City Museum (Stadtmuseum Worms) in the St. Andreasstift has a more traditional focus. Two floors follow the history of the region around Worms and then the city after the Romans. In the museum, visitors find reconstructed archaeological digs, since many burial sites have yielded artifacts that show what an active settlement area this was in the Bronze Age and before. The museum is right next to the Andreasstift, which is the oldest church in Worms, and was, at the time of my visit in the winter of 2015, receiving badly needed renovations. The museum is filled with well-crafted display cases that carefully and accurately exhibit objects from various historical epochs. There is an emphasis on the considerable evidence collected through archaeological work done in the immediate vicinity of Worms, its suburbs, its region. The cases are thoughtfully placed and arranged, though relatively modest; they are not interactive per se and not technologically sophisticated. On the other hand, they do not require technological sophistication for their visitors to admire the artifacts they contain. The same holds true for the Jewish Museum (*Jüdisches Museum*). The Jewish Museum pays tribute to the thriving Jewish culture in Worms from the Middle Ages to the present. In addition to the display of artifacts from both daily and religious life in the Jewish community throughout the history of Worms, the museum also confronts the visitor with the responsibilities of the present in a wonderful series of videos that includes survivor accounts from Jews who left Worms (for example) for the United States after the Kristallnacht pogrom in November 1938. The purpose of both museums, similar to the museums in the region around Wolframs-Eschenbach, is to purvey information, to inform, to keep the past present for their visitors by telling them about it and by exhibiting material remnants of that past in photographs or objects or documents.

The city of Worms memorializes the Nibelung legend and the text literally everywhere. From marketing and signage to public art installations and street names, contemporary Worms wraps the city's identity in the intertwining strands of history and narrative, The *Wormser Nibelungen Lexikon* by Jörg Koch lists numerous references to the Nibelung saga in and around the city of Worms, from the ubiquitous multicolored dragons to the smokers' pub "Zum Siegfriedsbrunnen" located in the Hagenstrasse.[23] Performances at the *Nibelungenfestpiele*, revived in 2002, occur yearly in July on an outdoor stage by the cathedral. Tourists can also venture out into the surrounding countryside to drive or hike along the *Nibelungenstraße-Siegfriedstraße*, established in 1989.[24] The route features scenes from the *Nibelungenlied* depicted in a series of sculpture installations entitled "Die Nibelungen" completed between 2002 and 2005 in iron by artist Jens Nettlich. Scenes of the *Nibelungenlied* also dot the Worms cityscape itself; the city invites visitors to come to experience mythology and the world of legends up close ("Mythologie und Sagenwelt hautnah erleben").[25] An earlier installation by Jens Nettlich, from 2000, shows the quarrel between Brunhild and Kriemhild (the *Königinnenstreit*) by the front portal of the cathedral. Across the Neumarkt, a stone Siegfried atop the Siegfried fountain (*Siegfriedbrunnen*) faces the quarreling queens. Work on the Siegfried fountain was started in the early twentieth century but not completed until after the First World War (in 1921) with the help of Worms businessman and entrepreneur Cornelius Heyl. Heyl also commissioned the Hagen monument in 1905/1906 to be placed in one of the more centrally located city parks; however, the bronze monument was moved in 1932 to its current location on the banks of the Rhein for a perhaps more imaginatively authentic effect. Now, for all who pass by, Hagen stands permanently "caught" in the act of throwing the Nibelung's treasure into the water.

Like the Wolfram Monument in Wolframs-Eschenbach, I would argue, all of these examples illustrate Macdonald's concept of past presencing at work. As identities are performed, place becomes even more significant as it resonates with the story that has come to be associated with it. Places, for Keith Basso, facilitate an experience that becomes "reciprocal" as well as "dynamic."[26] In his book in *Wisdom Sits in Places*, Basso focuses on the ways in which, among the western Apache, the landscape holds the stories that tell the people's history. Memory pervades the landscape, even as the landscape provides the contours of memory.[27] To know and belong to a place is also to identify with its story. In such an environment, place-making is a way of doing history, where the landscape also informs the social fabric of the community. Places inspire self-reflection, causing us to consider who we are now even as we remember also who we were or ponder who we might be come. In this way, the stories of places can become a kind of moral compass.

This is admittedly a rather far stretch from the western Apache in the United States to Germany in the 1990s. But the idea of place-making intersects with Nora's sites of memory. Basso describes a people who have their archive in the places that surround them, a perfect union of interior and exterior memories/histories, in contrast to the relative impoverishment of modern European memory. In Worms and Wolframs-Eschenbach we feel the pull of place, the need to invest place with meaning. For the museums, place is of paramount importance; furthermore, the communities are also part of the display. The old structures that enclose the new shapes of the old stories are part of each respective cityscape, each city landscape. We are not talking so much about the natural landscape, as the Apache do. We are talking about the remnants of an older built landscape—remnants of an older time—and, in a way, these physical connections to previous generations of townsfolk provide the same attraction as the physical landforms that hold the stories of the Apache in Basso's study. Place is actually very significant for these museums and the communities that built them, that continue to support and promote them. The museums would not have come about without the firm anchor in place: in the buildings they inhabit, in the towns that they call home. They also have a very firm anchor in a time (the Middle Ages) that each community wants to celebrate; they want to promote the medieval past, and the literary past, as "pasts" and as "memories" that can be claimed by all because they are not actually controversial in the ideas and themes they promote—rather, for the Nibelung Museum, it was the themes promoted in the nineteenth and twentieth centuries that turned out to be the wrong ones. In short, the museums offer a new way to remember, to recover, and to refashion memory. Edward Said sees the need for a recoverable past as "a specially freighted" phenomenon of the late twentieth century arising at a time of "bewildering change" and "competing nationalisms" along with dissolving social or religious bonds that previously seemed secure. He suggests that people "now look to this refashioned memory, especially in its collective forms, to give themselves a coherent identity, a national narrative, a place in the world…."[28] With this time of change, of anxiety, Said refers specifically to the situation in Israel/Palestine. But the ideas could also apply to the state of mind in Germany in the late 1980s and 1990s, as political and social change seemed to occur at unanticipated speed and the future felt uncertain at best.

In Chapter 1, I suggested that the museums can be seen as part of the museum boom of the late twentieth century. The trend toward musealization reveals an underlying cultural need for "temporal anchoring in the face of loss of tradition and unsettlement" brought about by the increasing speed "of technological and related change."[29] For Macdonald, the "museal … offers a distinctive experience in a changing media landscape, and is capable of incorporating other media (such as film or computerised exhibits) as part of its specific offer." This is how she explains the proliferation of museums and "other three-dimensional representations of the past," as a "quest for differential experiences" compounded rather than suppressed by the expansion of other forms of media.[30] This quest for different experiences now, the need to incorporate new ideas and new media and technology, inspires a look back to look forward. Both museums grow out of the 1980s boom not only in the heritage industry generally but also in the need to engage and display objects or history in museums or museum-like environments. This phenomenon of "musealization" offers a response "to a pervasive, altered sense of temporality" in late-twentieth-century society that "manifested in part through an ever-faster atrophying of traditional practices and objects." This atrophy and this response reveal the collective cultural anxiety (not to mention political and social) underlying the gradual thaw of the Cold War and precipitous end in the fall of the Berlin Wall. As they fell out of use, traditional practices and objects because subject to preservation in historically novel ways, markedly expanding the boundaries of what museums could collect and show. In these years, seemingly "uncollectable" phenomena rapidly became germane topics for exhibition and made it appear that, in postmodern culture, nothing seemed to escape the museum.[31] Even literature. Musealization plays a critical role in "refracting the memories of present-pasts to create (imaginary) present-futures"[32]—as McIsaac and Mueller note, this is past presencing at work as a way to imagine the future or futures.[33]

Monuments and heritage

Both museums strive to place the literature, its reception and their interpretations in the context of their local communities, connecting through the literature to the broader history in which all participate.[34] Wolframs-Eschenbach is immediately associated with its alleged native son by name; on the other hand, the town has no choice but to embrace the literature as heritage because that is all it has. Worms chose to embrace the conflicted and historically burdened past of its most famous narrative, because of the associations made for it throughout its history in the last two centuries. The museal display of medieval literature reveals the various layers of intertextual palimpsests that have accumulated over time, as we saw them in the Wolfram monument we discussed earlier. The museum in Worms tells the story of the *Nibelungenlied*, but in doing so, it also asks its visitors to find themselves in the story of the Nibelungs in its numerous variations over time, simultaneously navigating through German history and literature and film. To do so, visitors must first sort through images from the last two centuries that recall the politics of German nationalism in the nineteenth century, the nostalgic beauty of German Romanticism, the rise of National Socialism, the literary and cultural foundations of myth and fairy tales. The narrative and history of the *Nibelungenlied* forms a common thread tying all of these recollections together. Similarly, Wolframs-Eschenbach urges visitors not only to become acquainted with the work and biography (albeit reconstructed) of Wolfram von Eschenbach but to connect twentieth-century experience of war and mass destruction with *Willehalm*, to hear in *Parzival* a message of compassion and coexistence in a world concerned with sustainability and climate change. These museums strive to place the literature and its reception, its adaptation and interpretation, in the context of local communities, connecting through the literature to the broader history in which all can participate. Visitors literally step into the narratives; they walk into and through the story that has been reassembled for them and displayed in multimedial formats. Use of technology and new media is part of this attempt to connect to the modern (postmodern) public in the Nibelung Museum, for example. New media have become a fixture of twenty-first-century experience, for example. Thus the museums see media and technology as a means to bridge the ever-widening chasm between alterity and modernity, between older literature and the present.

Museums communicate values; they tell patrons how to understand and use the art or artifacts they contain, and they offer a "legitimating history" of cultural expression.[35] "Museums symbolise culture, identity and heritage," asserts Elizabeth Crooke. Museums are not only about the collections they house or about the objects they have or do not have; Crooke reminds us that "they are also about the sense of the past they represent."[36] In the case of Worms and Wolframs-Eschenbach, I would argue, communities are organizing their identity around literary texts that they have invested themselves in. The museums are examples of memory culture—heritage, monuments, collections, shared experience—living with the ideas of the past and finding a way to create artifacts to put them on display, presencing the past in a very unique way. They offer an unusual example of displays of heritage at/as sites of literary, cultural, and historical memory. Literature has great power to express and shape that heritage, providing a visual and indeed a physical locus for memory. And, if done creatively and smartly, the Nibelung Museum suggests that the literature need no longer be as controversial as politics or history. In fact, as the Nibelung Museum takes great care to show, the literature has been much abused and distorted by history. Perhaps the message is also that in the literature, we can find ways to move forward when politics fail. The message in Wolframs-Eschenbach resonates here as well.

In their display of literature, we can see both museums addressing not only the issues of community identity but also the function of museums in general. Museums today seem to be experiencing a crisis of purpose or identity according to some; Diepeveen and van Laar describe museums now as "uncertain about their role in contemporary culture ... feeling alienated from the impulses upon which they were founded."[37] Diepeveen and Van Laar offer a series of questions that get at the heart of this crisis. These questions address the artifacts and displays of traditional collections (what does it mean to collect? who decides what is worth collecting? what kinds of things are collected?); they address audience and outreach (who is a museum for? how can a museum attract a broad range of people?); and they address purpose (what is the place of a museum in the technological age? is the museum obsolete?). To this list, we could also add the question of whether museums still need objects.[38]

To the last two questions about whether the museum is obsolete and whether museums still need objects, the museums in this study offer an emphatic "no!" as answer. They have no objects or artifacts in the traditional sense; in fact, these museums seem to insist that ideas suffice. Thus, literature "as object" seems to have come at an opportune moment for cities seeking new ways to express identity and for institutions (museums) at a crossroad. The literature has become part of the history of the places that display it. And the places believe that literature embodies the history they would like to project out into the wider world. Or at least this is what the museums indicate. In Wolframs-Eschenbach, the town displays the literature in a space that would normally have housed a *Heimatmuseum*; this is the point of comparison with other local museums in its area. The literature takes the place (and the space) of the town's history. In Worms, the museum also displays some of the city's history and German history as well as the text's history in its exhibits. Both museums in Worms and in Wolframs-Eschenbach want to address larger issues, make their visitors think, and unsettle commonly and perhaps deeply held stereotypes: about the Middle Ages, about the German Middle Ages, about literature, about medieval literature, about German history, about war, about peace.

Looking forward

There are three major issues that face the Nibelung Museum into the future. The first is space. Older architectural structures require funds for upgrade and renovation and restoration; this is a constant issue in a city like Worms. The larger issue, however, has to do with wiring and other infrastructure that one might want to upgrade for technology, for example. The demands of modern and rapidly changing technology present great difficulty for a structure like the Nibelung museum, which was built into the medieval city wall with a design specifically conceived to fit that space. On the other hand, in a kind of catch-22, the museum depends very heavily on that technology for the displays that comprise it. Space internal to the museum is also an issue because the museum was built as a creative *Gesamtkunstwerk*, and not necessarily as a living museum with a growth plan. The museum has few options, with the exception of the *Mythenlabor*, for changing or updating its displays. The architecture also cannot be changed because of its fixture in the city wall. Finally, the museum is on the periphery of the city center. Like the city museum in the Andreasstift, the Nibelung Museum is on the city wall, which means that by definition, both museums are on the periphery of the central city.

The second issue facing the museum has to do, oddly enough, with its original concept. The original concept, while interesting and even fascinating and innovative, comes with its own potential handicap: the museum installation was intended as a totality, and therefore it all forms an externally and internally cohesive unit. When the unit functions, all is well. But, as with the space, upgrades and improvements present a challenge. The original audioguides at the technical cutting edge in 2001, though still revealed as problematic, were eventually replaced with iPods because they were too difficult to keep up, even though they lasted for ten years. The technology maintenance presents huge challenges because of the need to make cutting-edge electronics work in a setting that has limited options and where one always has to contend with the proximity of the medieval wall and pretechnological conditions. The practical need for upkeep and upgrade in electronic infrastructure goes hand in hand with the spatial constrictions of the museum's location and architecture. The problem of space exacerbates the conceptual constraints of the display that is firmly embedded in the architecture (of the museum and of the medieval city) and deeply integrated by the audio script throughout the entire museum.

Issues with the museum's concept and its space, exacerbated by technology and location, lead to the third major challenge facing the museum: audience. The perennial question for museums is one of relevance and of connection to community. This is most basically related to museum design and part of the concerns shared by a number of critics in letters to the editor and other news forums. A museum focused on virtual texts, image, and narrative might attract a younger generation interested in media, but more traditional design might also attract a greater audience share. This is clearly a concern that the citizens of Worms have raised intermittently throughout the museum's short history. However, the museum continues to integrate itself into the museum landscape of Worms with innovative outreach programs and collaborative projects. And the inevitable question does remain about financial viability and the role of the museum plays in the cultural landscape of Worms, though the development of the laboratory (*Mythenlabor*) demonstrates how the museum administration has responded to audience critique. Attempts to infuse the technologically interesting but dated original displays from 2001 with new content have presented a challenge; it is also difficult to find ways to create "space" for temporary special exhibitions. The lab is a draw for people, one that can be updated and revised according to feedback and interest. Visitors can create their own content or watch media presentations. The lab also offers options for creative approaches to the Nibelung material, myths and legends as well as the history of Worms; the flexible space allows opportunity to create special exhibits like the one for the year-long celebration of the Staufer dynasty in 2010–2011 or to participate in the popular *Nibelungenfestspiele* by offering a showing of the film *Jud Süss* to coincide with a performance of the play of the same name at the festival. At one point, there was a searchable database of all images found in the *Sehturm*. The museum website indicates numerous mechanisms for engagement, feedback, and audience participation that would inspire changes or additions to the offerings in the laboratory (*Mythenlabor*). Initial reviews indicated that the museum would have needed approximately 42,000 visitors per year in order to make enough money to cover its costs. Over a decade later, the museum averaged about 20,000 visitors a year, occasioning another round of discussion about the benefit of the museum and even drawing suggestions to close the museum—critics took the occasion of the museum's tenth anniversary to raise the specter of closure again.[39] While some residents of Worms, at least the ones who expressed their opinions in public forums, articulated their frustration with the museum and its drain on other financial resources for the city, the city itself seemed then—and seems now—content to support it. The recent Wagner exhibit suggests a new direction for a museum that seems to be reaching out for collaborative opportunities. In November 2015, the museum unveiled a new exhibit of props from the 2012–2013 production of Wagner's *Ring* by Achim Freyer at the Mannheim Nationaltheater. The still-existing exhibit greatly enhances the reach of the museum by connecting the legend and the *Nibelungenlied* more explicitly with Wagner's operas.[40]

In general, the same holds true with the museum in Wolframs-Eschenbach, although that small town does not need to invest as much perhaps in its *Stadtmuseum* as Worms would need to. The museum in Wolframs-Eschenbach is also conceptually more complex, though it is put together much more simply on technological terms. It does not have the same reliance on media. It can easily be kept up and kept up to date. Furthermore, it is based on literature that has relevance to modern or popular culture, but it does not depend on that relevance and each display can be understood independently. The Nibelung Museum is context- and environment-dependent in a way that Wolframs-Eschenbach is not. One reason for this is perhaps that the Museum Wolfram von Eschenbach ask its central question "Kann man Literatur ausstellen?," answers with a firm "yes," and then resolutely says to any visitor "now watch us do it!" The Nibelung Museum is still searching for its question. What story does the museum tell now? It does not tell the story of Worms entirely, though it does in part as it tells the story of the *Nibelungenlied*. It does not entirely tell the story of the *Nibelungenlied* though it does through its various lenses that bend our gaze on various other stories: the story of Romanticism, the story of German unification in 1871, and Fritz Lang's version of the *Nibelungenlied*, Wagner's version of the legend, the story of the legend through the First World War and the rise of the National Socialists leading into the story of the Second World War. In those stories, one also finds the story of the city of Worms. One wonders if the museum, with its ambitions to tell the story of a story by means of a myth machine (*Mythenmaschine*), almost forgets to tell its *own* story. In both cases, the medievalism of the museums needs to examine further the museums as medievalism.

Conclusion

Wolframs-Eschenbach and Worms appear completely different with respect to size, history, geographical location, cultural activity, regional role. The city of Worms played a much more prominent role on the stage of German history than the town of Eschenbach in any incarnation. In addition, Worms already had multiple legacies to sort through, all intersecting and most still showing visible traces in its modern identity: the pre-Roman and Roman legacy, the Jewish legacy, the medieval imperial legacy, the Reformation legacy, the National Socialist legacy, the legacy of legend. It was, however, the legacy of the *Nibelungenlied* narrative that offered a compelling way to focus and organize these legacies.[41] We want to reclaim our (German) history and our (city) legacy, the Nibelung Museum in Worms seems to say, so that we can affirm and celebrate both on our own terms—or at least on different terms than we have previously had. Both Wolframs-Eschenbach and Worms imagine their communities anew through these museal adaptations of medieval German literature. As entangled as they are in numerous intertexts of their own, the medieval narratives become part of yet one more intertext, yet another adaptation that entices contemporary audiences to imagine as integral and relevant not just to their immediate surroundings but also to the global community. Both museums navigate heritage that is both tangible and intangible, using narrative (the works of Wolfram von Eschenbach, the *Nibelungenlied*, the legend of the Nibelungs) as both an object and vehicle of display, in an elaborate and multivalent example of medievalism.

These museums are adaptations in their own right. Hutcheon considers museum exhibits generally as adaptation that does not go far enough. The fact that a museum exhibit takes material objects, most often from the past, and "recontextualizes them within a historical narrative" fits with other ways in which she has defined adaptations, as an "extended interpretive and creative engagement" with history and with the past. Hutcheon questions, however, whether the audience experiences this engagement with past history as such, in "a palimpsestic way" actively contrasting with the present. A true adaptation, for Hutcheon, relies on this palimpsestic experience or (as she puts it) on "the oscillation between a past image and a present one." In other words, the dialogic interaction between audience and exhibit is an essential component of successful adaptation.

Hutcheon may miss in more traditional museums the "connected interplay of expectation and surprise" that for Julie Sanders inspires the characteristic oscillation between older story and new.[42] The case studies presented in Chapters 3 and 4 are, however, not traditional museums; indeed, they are not even traditional literary museums. They are displays of medieval literature that build on historical, cultural, and literary intertexts to create new narratives for the communities around them. The museums may shock their audiences a bit because they seem to lack an expected "comfort of ritual and recognition" to combine with "the delight of surprise and novelty." But novelty abounds; adaptation involves "persistence and variation" as well as "memory and change."[43] The process of memory is the process of adaptation, as we reconstitute stories, and the product of that activity (done collectively) the adaptation. If "cultural memory rests on narrative processes,"[44] then we can see the museums as an attempt to cultivate new memory for Worms and for Wolframs-Eschenbach—and for modern Germany. Palimpsests, as manuscripts that have been reused and overwritten, stimulate in us as readers and viewers an oscillation between the older story and the new, between the literary allusions and the visual representation on the wall. We have in each case study, the Museum Wolfram von Eschenbach and the Nibelung Museum, an interpretive doubling between what we know and what we experience as viewers. This conceptual flipping back and forth is also part of the virtual reality that we step into when we enter the displays to take our part in the process. In this way, we move perhaps from adaptation to appropriation, to the creation of a "wholly new cultural product"—in the museum and in ourselves.[45]

In this, the museums exemplify the process of medievalism in the service of imagining community as medieval literature becomes a vehicle for presencing the past and for shaping a future. Not only do the museums make a statement about the role of the medieval in the modern world; they are also simultaneously making a statement about the role of literature. Medieval memory aimed to mold moral character in new generations through memory of those who have come before. Literature can do this too; we recall Bhabha's impassioned statement on the power of literature and art to facilitate the chance for audience members to become part of a community in shared experience, potentially fulfilling a desire for solidarity. Solidarity and shared experience involve memory; the practice of memory is part of the process of adaptation. As memory displaces, it also replaces, reassembles, re-members; the join emerges in this creative (also imaginative) space. Memory facilitates the join that enables the process and practice of medievalism, the presencing of the medieval past. The cities seem to express a hope that the texts, their themes, and their history become more visible and more firmly established as part of the respective community's heritage; this will happen both on a local and on a national level. Here, we have medieval German literature placed prominently at a dynamic cultural intersection. The museal exhibitions and visualizations of medieval literature demonstrate what Stephanie Trigg has noticed in recent scholarship on medievalism; we find a "more mobile and fluid understanding of temporal, cultural, and intellectual heterogeneity both within the middle ages and in modernity's construction of that concept."[46] The museums visualize and enact that mobile and more fluid understanding; in their installations, the medieval goes global.

6

The Future of the Past: Medieval Literature on Display

What happens when longing remains with nothing left to cling to, like the Cheshire cat's smile after the cat has gone? Perhaps one comes to a point where there is nothing left to lose and different possibilities open up.[1]

(Helen Dell, "Nostalgia and Medievalism")

Significance ... is no atemporal, basic element which is always already given; rather, it is the never-completed result of a process of progressive and enriching interpretation which concretizes-in an ever new and different manner-the textually immanent potential for meaning in the change of horizons of historical life-worlds.[2]

(Hans Robert Jauß, *Alterität und Modernität*)

In the previous chapters, *Medieval Literature on Display* has sought to use close study of the active processes of applying medievalism in a museum context to shed new light on use of the medieval in the modern world. Like the Museum Wolfram von Eschenbach, the Nibelung Museum compels us to engage the older literature it so creatively displays. Like the designers in Wolframs-Eschenbach museum, they are well aware of the paradox that confronts them in their attempt to display text and culture with few tradition artifacts. Wolframs-Eschenbach asks: Can one display literature? Worms asks: Can one display reception and untangle a convoluted history? As in Wolframs-Eschenbach, the answer here is also an enthusiastic and resounding "yes!" In her introduction, Dell actually phrases this another way, or at least this is how I choose to see her allusion to the Cheshire cat, when she asks what happens when the longing loses (or loses sight of) its object, when nothing remains to cling to. Dell's answer is an expression of hope born of that sense of loss; when one has no more to lose, when one cannot hold on to that opinion or that history or that memento any longer, then hitherto-unlooked-for opportunities may present themselves. A door closes … and a museum opens. Thinking of the Cheshire cat, I am tempted to see the museums in Worms and in Wolframs-Eschenbach as a defiant insistence on recovery of something, of something significant, of narrative with firm intent to create an object where there is none. There are ideas, of course, there is literature, there is story, but there is nothing concrete to which one can physically attach that longing. When there seems to be nothing left to cling to, like the Cheshire cat's smile after the cat is gone, we create a pet—perhaps not the cat that we imagine we cannot see, but rather the pet that we imagine we would like to have. We create, to adapt Augustine here, a kind of "present of things imagined." This image of the Cheshire cat recalls the installation in the Museum Wolfram von Eschenbach of Wolfram's empty tomb: a plain transparent glass plate commemorating a poet whose life we only know through his works and through the reception history that has made him even more real with every successive adaptation over time. The intersections of pleasure and desire and longing that Dell associates with the Cheshire cat materialize in the museums: each community connects its medieval texts with a past that it wishes to make copresent, to integrate into the experience of a now even though that past is past and remains so. There is a doubled (palimpsestic) vision that persists here, a vision of the past as past along with the present as present but also a vision of the present that also includes the past as part of its immediate experience. This is the kind of creative vision that Dinshaw attributes to what she discusses as "amateur readings" of medieval texts: "Amateur readings, participating in nonmodern ways of apprehending time, can help us to contemplate different ways of being, knowing, and world-making."[3] This is not to suggest that the designers, creators, and directors of the museums in Wolframs-Eschenbach and Worms were amateurs of their respective crafts; they most certainly were not. However, following Dinshaw's use of the word, the readings of medieval narrative in the museums are infused with the same kind of passion, conviction, and sheer delight that amateurs have long practiced and traditional medieval studies has long tended to dismiss. By way of conclusion, having looked at our case studies in detail, I want to return to the key concepts outlined in Chapters 1 and 2 in a kind of interlaced sequence that will situate the museums in today's Germany. Ultimately, I want to move from adaptation and memory to heritage and musealization via medievalism and nostalgia.

Adaptation and memory

As I noted at the conclusion of the previous chapter, Linda Hutcheon addresses museums as adaptation at the end of *A Theory of Adaptation*. A traditional museum exhibit takes material objects, most often from the past, and recontextualizes them within a historical narrative. This fits with other ways in which she has defined adaptations, as extended interpretive and creative engagement with history and with the past. However, she questions whether the audience experiences this engagement with past history, in what she calls "a palimpsestic way." A true adaptation, for Hutcheon, relies on this palimpsestic experience or (as she puts it) on "the oscillation between a past image and a present one." The "interpretive doubling" that is so integral to the process of understanding the palimpsest must always be present.[4] I argue that both museums exemplify Hutcheon's understanding of adaptation as "double vision"[5] though sometimes one can experience that vision not just as double but as multiple in bewildering complexity. Furthermore, they represent a mode of adaptation that does not merely show or tell—it enacts. They illustrate how adaptation involves "both memory and change, persistence and variation."[6] The process of memory is the process of adaptation, as we re-constitute stories, and the product of that activity (done collectively) is the adaptation. Adaptation as product is the product of memory.

In the museums, medieval literature is the source of the adaptations that have driven and continue to drive memory. The reception and adaptation of the texts over time, including the museum displays we have encountered, demonstrate literature as an engine of cultural memory, as an "ongoing process, characterized by a dynamic interplay between text and context, the individual and the collective, the social and the medial."[7] Erll suggests that the "world of cultural memory is a world of narrative."[8] Memories and narratives can be difficult, traumatic, or challenging on individual or collective levels. In the Nibelung Museum and in the Museum Wolfram von Eschenbach, the older narratives on display offer a way to counter standard narratives with different ones. In the museums, the displays create that new narrative through a process of remediation; they transcribe their stories into the new medium of display. The Nibelung museum also examines the history of media transcription for its text, as it moved over time from saga, to poem, to opera, to film. Remediation is made possible by the cultural resonance of certain images and narratives that have circulated widely and "may even converge into sites of memory."[9] The museums are just such sites. Macdonald says of "difficult heritage" that "places may find themselves being interpreted and evaluated—not always as they might wish—in relation to how they present their pasts."[10] The museums, both implicitly (Wolframs-Eschenbach) and explicitly (Worms), insist on the opportunity to find different ways to present the past, particularly if places (cities, towns, regions) find themselves wishing to change how they are perceived by visitors and tourists and outside populations in general.

Memory and medievalism

The museums untangle older narratives for modern audiences, reveal the intertextual palimpsests, so that they can adapt and remediate the medieval stories in creative explorations of cultural memory and local history—so that they can forge different narratives. This is how the medieval literature on display, and through it the medieval past, invite contemporary (global) audiences to join their dialogue. This invitation succeeds on one level because the museums interpret not *the* German Middle Ages but *a* German medieval past for audiences of the present. The past changes from present to present, changing for us and with us. It is thus a good example of what we call medievalism at work. The playful presentations in the museums capture the spirit of recent scholarship that continues to ponder why the Middle Ages will not quit, referencing Groebner's book once again. In the words of Pugh and Aronstein, the Middle Ages are "endlessly protean" and "endlessly malleable."[11] Not only do the Middle Ages seem malleable. They offer ample opportunity for experimentation in the broader cultural landscape. As a medievalist, I am interested in the museum as a space where medieval literature meets modern experience. Each museum stages a twenty-first-century encounter with the Middle Ages, expanding the afterlives of German medieval literature as they potentially resonate in popular culture on both sides of the Atlantic.[12] Such afterlives are responsive, changeable, complex. This is the "New Middle Ages" Weisl finds in popular culture "where we live"; it allows us "to respond in all the immediacy of the present."[13] Both museums demonstrate how medieval literature and the Middle Ages—regardless of national origin—can be relevant in (post)modern communities. They both enact what Pugh and Weisl call the "magic" of the Middle Ages that is "continually reborn in new stories, new media, new histories."[14] Further, each museum offers an intermedial environment, where medieval literature meets modern experience in an encounter thrumming with creative and cognitive dissonance: modern technology and medieval literature, visual and written text, collage and pastische, thirteenth-century architecture and twentieth-century surroundings, comics and Romantic poets, and manuscript illustrations and photographs.[15] Both the "medieval" and the "recent" share similar characteristics that distinguish them from the modern; the medieval and the recent are visual, collective, achronic (as opposed to printed, individual, and linear).[16] In the museums here, new media and creative display try to have it both ways, as they remediate older texts and reposition them for their viewers in a modern world. First, the museums actually strive for a harmony of structure and display, not unlike the stereotypical cathedral we associate with that "age of cathedrals" we read about in medieval history. Time is also suspended in the museum; we oscillate (to use Hutcheon's term) between past and present, between literature and display. In the Nibelung museum, visual and aural media bombard us—images both static and dynamic, photo and video. Yet each museum strives to reconnect us with the older literature from an earlier time, highlighting historical differences and human commonalities to break the illusion of unidirectional linearity.

In this process, the Museum Wolfram von Eschenbach in Wolframs-Eschenbach and the *Nibelungenmuseum* in Worms exploit the performative and imaginative qualities of medieval literature to presence the past and transform medieval texts for their new audiences. Both museums involve contemporary audiences/visitors in a very medieval task of memory/of remembering, an act of bringing disparate or separated impressions together. This act remains very evident in the museum displays today, where the "medieval" becomes a place where the work of memory is to navigate within texts and between texts. The "medieval" and the Middle Ages, as "nonorigin and origin," provide a vehicle for multiple layers of enactment among texts and audiences; this is the perfect material for "a dream frame for popular culture, ... that can be read as either the present or the future."[17] The displays at the Museum Wolfram von Eschenbach and the Nibelung Museum show how the Middle Ages can be refracted through familiar figures and inscribed in changing narratives. As the museums work at presencing the medieval past, as they enact with us the process of remembering and re-membering older texts, the Middle Ages becomes a more active locus of imaginative memory. The Middle Ages then becomes a place where communities can seek a solidarity with their past, find affinities in the present, and perhaps imagine themselves into a future. This collateral benefit, namely community building, makes the medievalism much deeper and, I would suggest, more meaningful, more effective, and more sustainable. Further, as we presence the medieval past, we also bridge the gulf between alterity and modernity in other interrogations of local and regional history against the backdrop of national and global events.

Medievalism and heritage

This interrogation happens on a local level, in Worms or in Wolframs-Eschenbach, but also in a broader context. In the museums, the process of medievalism becomes the vehicle by which the communities of Worms and Wolframs-Eschenbach utilize place and space in their museums to make various pasts become present: the literary past, the remembered past, the conflict-ridden and difficult past. As they participate in this active "past presencing," the Nibelung Museum in Worms and the Museum Wolfram von Eschenbach are also involved in an ongoing process of creating heritage. The museums thus clearly demonstrate Barbara Kirshenblatt-Gimblett's concept of display as "an interface that mediates and therefore transforms what is shown into heritage."[18] Thus, medievalism shapes encounters with heritage in tangible and intangible form.

For Svetlana Boym, the development of local or national heritage in the nineteenth century is an "institutionalized response," a modernity that is fundamentally nostalgic. Boym sees the institutionalization of nostalgia through provincial and national museums as well as urban memorials, through the kinds of memorials for which Nora coined the term "sites of memory" (*lieux de memoire*).[19] Institutionalized nostalgia is, comments Boym, a paradox: "the stronger the loss, the more it is overcompensated with commemorations, the starker the distance from the past, and more it is prone to idealizations."[20] This paradox is evident in the particular kind of dilemma that medievalist tourism must negotiate. It is not possible to possess again the very things we long for in the medieval past; yet, twenty-first-century tourists demand to do just that experientially. In her discussion of the Jorvik Viking Center, D'Arcens addresses "the abiding prominence of the Middle Ages as a site of nostalgic projection"[21] in the context of contemporary heritage tourism and modern nostalgia that cannot be ignored when one considers the case of medievalist tourism. With similar perspicuity, in her essay "Walking through Cathedrals," Stephanie Trigg turns a critical lens on the mediation of English religious sites as tourist attractions and national heritage.[22] Both D'Arcens and Trigg show the paradox and pitfalls of medievalist tourism that seeks "to make the Middle Ages present to its clientele in the form of 'living history.'"[23] Of course, the museums in this study do not aim to offer living history as such. They are a qualitatively different kind of tourism, to say nothing of a unique brand of medieval tourism. On the other hand, the museums exploit both the elasticity of medieval time as well as the modern longing for the medieval past—perhaps also longings of other times for that medieval past as well, as we may see in the Nibelung Museum. They seem to echo Trigg's eloquent affirmation of how we can acknowledge and embrace the unavoidable temporal dissonance of then and now, finding space to appreciate both Canterbury Cathedral and the Canterbury Visitor Attraction Center. As we presence the past, whether we walk through a Gothic cathedral or a twentieth-century museum, we create a present for things past that are both the product and the process of a continuing medievalism.

In recent examinations of *Sound of Music* tourism and the performative construction of places, Gundolf Graml posits that enacting the *Sound of Music* is a display of tourism that negotiates a "desire for belonging and wholeness with the demands of a globalized world in which identity construction must be performed anew day by day."[24] Graml suggests further that a display of identity in such a tourist experience involves a "snapshot that captures a particular moment in a never-ending series of social interactions and performances" in its relation to economy, travel, and media.[25] In this example, what Salzburg is or what Austria is relies on the constant interactions of visitors, media, imagination, history, and place. This particular aspect of Salzburg tourism and its relative authenticity illustrates the point I do want to make with respect to the Nibelung Museum and the Museum Wolfram von Eschenbach: as identities are performed, place becomes even more significant as it resonates with the story that has come to be associated with it. Place generates story; story shapes place. Fiction mingles with fact; imagined story intersects with actual history. I bring up Graml's nexus of tourism and media, place and identity, history and heritage because this example describes not only what happens when tourists come to see Austria through the *Sound of Music*. It applies to Trigg's description of modern Canterbury, with its Canterbury Tales Visitor Attraction in the shadow of Canterbury cathedral. It can also apply, perhaps on a globally smaller but locally no less important scale, to Worms and Wolframs-Eschenbach and their museums. In the landscape of new European memorylands, the museums enable the past to become present these modern communities at the intersections of heritage and identity and memory.

In the introduction to *How Soon Is Now?*, Dinshaw insists that time is lived: "it is full of attachments and desires, histories and futures; it is not a hollow form … that is the same always."[26] I would like to substitute narrative for "time" here to describe the representations of medieval German literature on these museal stages: Narrative is not a hollow form that is the same always; it is lived, it is alive, and it is capable of change. It allows us to continue participating what we might see as a quintessentially medieval activity: the performative process of memory, the presencing of individual and communal pasts. The idea of change beautifully ties the thirteenth-century *Iwein* murals at Rodenegg, as well as the narratives of the *Nibelungenlied* and of Wolfram's works to the twentieth-century museums. The asynchronous collision of times and places and images is the physical (emotional, intellectual) situation of the medievalist who is both the scholar and the amateur, navigating the complex but fascinating interconnections from which medievalism emerges. Wolframs-Eschenbach and Worms firmly place their older narratives, along with numerous entangled adaptations from the thirteenth century through the twentieth, on display for modern audiences in a powerful encounter with alterity: asynchronous, simultaneous, heterogeneous. The question of how this encounter shapes or becomes heritage, tangible, or intangible, is our task to address if the past is to shape our future.

Heritage and musealization

Both the Nibelung Museum and the Museum Wolfram von Eschenbach, in their display of ideas and of literature (also of literary interpretation), participate in the display of intangible heritage. It is not the same perhaps as folklore or other types of intangible heritage that UNESCO deals with. But perhaps we can understand the term literally—the ideas on display in Worms or in Wolframs-Eschenbach are not tangible and there are no artifacts other than idea-related images in the exhibits. The museums are an attempt to reinvigorate cultural heritage. This is also evident in the buildings renovated to house the museums—the old city hall ("Altes Rathaus") in Wolframs-Eschenbach and the medieval city tower ("Bürgerturm") in Worms—as well as to create living heritage for the contemporary community. The hope is to make the literary past live and breathe and become part of new stories and narratives. The most stunning aspect of all remains this choice of each museum; they each provide a fascinating lens into "what is deemed worthy of such effort, and how the past is articulated, at particular times and in particular places."[27] And it is literature that is deemed worthy; it is story at work here. Basso's work among the Apache of the American southwest echoes here: knowledge has place, place has story, story connects people, and people connect the past and the present. While there are these initiatives to unsettle and to engage with difficult history and challenging stories, there is also simply a need to assert place, to assert those stories, to create a new story, to stage the city's story.

The museums in *Medieval Literature on Display* literally reposition and rewrite older narratives for communities that seek to reclaim those older stories not only for themselves but for new audiences—local regional, national, global. The process is reflected in the trend toward musealization, particularly in Europe. Macdonald explains the proliferation of museums and "other three-dimensional representations of the past," as a "quest for differential experiences" compounded rather than suppressed by the expansion of other forms of media: "The museal ... offers a distinctive experience in a changing media landscape, and is capable of incorporating other media (such as film or computerised exhibits) as part of its specific offer."[28] Memory becomes institutionalized in museums or in monuments (Nora's *lieux de memoire*) such that it becomes constitutive of communal identity.[29]

In this sense, heritage turns the past into The Past that represents the community's origins.[30] The issue of heritage is complicated: it is negotiated and negotiable, untidy, sticky, difficult. The trend toward musealization in Europe also reveals an underlying cultural need for "temporal anchoring in the face of loss of tradition and unsettlement" brought about by the increasing speed of change.[31] It is also literature meant not only to be revived for visitors but also designed to provoke and to unsettle. Macdonald compares uses of heritage in the United States and in Europe, commenting that the European perspective views patriotism and consumerism and nationalism with "a good deal more ambivalence." Furthermore, "heritage in Europe is increasingly being used to *unsettle*—to dislodge us from our comfort zones ... to provide a dutiful cold shower in what are otherwise at risk of being overly consumerist and unreflective lives."[32] The emphasis on *unsettle* is in the original. A distance, or a dissonance, is created through the differences we can perceive in a story on display such that we enter into critical dialogue with a text that has perhaps entrapped us in the past; Gustafson speaks of entrapment by familiar stories that have become too much a part of our habits—we have to be able to extricate ourselves from the familiar.[33] We need provocations that challenge established beliefs, where the reframing of established knowledge affects previous knowledge and creates conditions for a boundary-crossing learning process. In order for us to become aware of our prejudices and stereotypical assumptions, to cross boundaries, our established beliefs need to be disrupted. This can be achieved through stories that are often suppressed and marginalized: stories that surprise and unsettle, or (in Brechtian terms) alienate.

Unique in Worms and in Wolframs-Eschenbach, however, is the fact that literature and ideas provide the anchor without any other concrete items for exhibition. Worms chose to embrace the conflicted and historically burdened past of its most famous narrative in order to reclaim it from the associations that accumulated in the last two centuries. At the top of the *Sehturm*, at the midpoint of the museum's tour, the fictional poet rails at the injustice done his verses since the rediscovery of the *Nibelungenlied* in the mid-eighteenth century:

> I have had to remain silent for eight hundred years, forced to endure the abuse, which has been hurled at me from all sides. The last two centuries have been the worst. Sitting here with jaw clenched, I have had to listen to the warmongers use my *Nibelungenlied* to justify murder and assassination. Sometimes, I believed it was cursed, just as the ring of Andvari and the treasure was. My work will bear the stigma of their curse forever more. But to ignore it, to discard it, would be futile, and I have no intention of doing so. I only wish this relentless demonisation of my works would stop, as if the *Nibelungenlied* were responsible for the rise of German nationalism and everything that followed afterwards. No, the living should see things clearly.[34]

The Nibelung Museum asks its visitors to consider the warmongers of yesterday and today, to sort through the images of popular culture and of politics, and to take responsibility for molding the older story into a new one. The Museum Wolfram von Eschenbach similarly urges responsibility and tolerance. In the room that portrays the family relationships, for example, the museum display offers a short gloss on *Parzival*'s prologue:

> Where would we find people who are entirely black or entirely white? Wolfram does not want noble heroes and dastardly villains. His people are always both, they are good and bad, and they are not always in control of their actions. Even good becomes bad sometimes, and vice versa. The story and its message do not always run in a straight line.[35]

Even in this simplified and condensed form, integrated into a more nuanced display (the mobile), the image of the magpie resonates powerfully.

In their displays of medieval German literature, both museums seek to show their literature as an active participant in heritage and in the life of the community around it; the museum display becomes a site of reflection and critique. And heritage is a sign of modernity—this appeals particularly to a city like Worms that is trying to revitalize a flagging economy. More importantly, I think we can see that both communities in Worms and in Wolframs-Eschenbach have consciously sought to enhance their identity in the new and developing memorylands of a global Germany—a global Europe. Needing to create the displays around ideas in the absence of artifacts, the museum gives visual form to the central themes of those narratives, interpreting and making use of the older literature to tell the community's story. Here, we have medieval German literature placed prominently at a dynamic cultural intersection with transhistorical and transnational implications. From my vantage point, I see that the museums make the past present with potentially global resonance, which is particularly important for an understanding of the Middle Ages and medieval literature today. The medieval past becomes a creative and engaging, while also entertaining, vehicle for global audiences to engage the present.

"Sticky" heritage is difficult. It clings, it is hard to disengage, and it binds the members of a community together whether they will or no. The difficult heritage of Germany in the twentieth century functions as a kind of inverse adhesive—not the positive mementos and commemorations, but rather the negative ones. Germany's problematic past was "a lurking presence—a virus in the system—" that had to be confronted after 1945. It needed to be addressed and "mastered" because otherwise there was a danger that it would do the "mastering" and would infect subsequent life and generations.[36] But Germany seems to have turned it into an opportunity for self-reflections toward a different kind of coming to terms with the past (*Vergangenheitsbewältigung*) characteristic of the 1960s. Reunification occasioned a different collision with the past and perhaps a renewed conviction to confront the dangers of the past when Germany had been unified before. Macdonald describes the German situation thus:

> In Germany, this idea gained major political traction in the face of unification. Clearly, looking back with pride to the last time that the divided Germany had been whole was not possible. Moreover, it was vital to ensure that the difference from when Germany was last a single nation was clearly signaled both internally and to the wider world. As such, developing initiatives to address difficult heritage was also a means of showing unequivocally that the Nazi past had not been forgotten and that Germany was facing up to its crimes.[37]

Also significant for the two museums here is the moral responsibility to reflect on the past that seems to characterize them both. This is a significant element of each museum's message. Macdonald sees this as typical of how Germans generally understood their responsibility to deal with the past: "What this meant was that, increasingly, any non-acknowledgement of the Nazi past—any unwillingness to confront it—was regarded not just as non-action but as a moral failing."[38] The museums both participate in this endeavor to acknowledge, to be morally responsible, to confront. They are part of what Macdonald calls the "turn to difficult heritage," which also includes a kind of "past-oriented omnivorousness" that tries to offer more nuanced explorations of the past.[39] A story on display should provoke, should prompt us to interrogate that past, uncomfortable or unsettling though it may seem.

What is unique in the museums of Wolframs-Eschenbach and Worms is their appeal to heritage with a global scope and a local focus through the ideas expressed in the medieval literature produced in those areas. The museums clearly express heritage as a "product of a self-conscious kindling and celebration of the past."[40] In these instances, the display of the past appears even more self-conscious, with the focus on literature as a vehicle for attempting to grasp the remains of the past. With their displays that address a range of topics from medieval to modern, the museums are an example of how heritage seems old, as it focuses in these cases on the presentation of literature that most of the audience does not know (or know well) yet also highlights the connections between the older texts, their ideas, and the contemporary world.[41] We produce heritage through objects, images, events, and representations, since "the original experiences of the past are irretrievable" and we can therefore "only grasp them through their remains."[42] Heritage is where memory becomes a looking back and a longing for the past, a nostalgia, that desires to re-create an authentic past experience in the present to be remembered into the future as constitutive of identity. Like the Middle Ages, heritage here is both found and made.

A future for the past

After 1989 and a subsequent reawakening of history, to use Aleida Assmann's term, the desire for heritage and the construction of identity gained a renewed urgency. This is evident, for example, in Michaela Fenske's study of the small town of Werben in rural Saxony Anhalt.[43] Located northwest of Berlin in the former East Germany, Werben experienced a downturn after the *Wende* like many towns of similar size. Not unlike Worms, but in much more isolated surroundings, the town of Werben sought a way to invigorate an economy that had suffered after an exodus of young people following the reunification of 1989.[44] Werben saw promise in its well-preserved homes from the early nineteenth century and chose, on the model of Colonial Williamsburg, to "stage time travel." In an interesting development, the locals have taken ownership of the market and the reenactments in ways that even seem to surprise the original organizers—or at least the social and community benefits of the time travel were not necessarily considered in the original discussions of historical authenticity, for instance. The market becomes a kind of enchanted zone to offer "special spheres of activity," where people can step "outside of their everyday lives" to experience the time of the Biedermeier.[45] As Fenske puts it, the tangible outcome may be unclear, if we want to gauge how staged history can enable social renewal, "but the evolving practices are intriguing."[46] These evolving practices, a veritable "time travel phenomenon," bring us back to the Middle Ages, too. With the increasing popularity of medieval reenactments since the 1980s, particularly around the turn of the twenty-first century, Krug-Richter explores the appeal is of the Middle Ages for hobbyists, students, and tourists—exploring not the reception of the medieval but rather what the enthusiasm for the medieval says about the twenty-first-century enthusiasts and about their present time.[47] History becomes opportunity for creative exploration that can result in something that is genuinely new and culturally unique. This kind of play with the Middle Ages can be understood as a process that takes the medieval and adapts it, putting the pieces together with new applications. Krug-Richter comments on the effect that this enthusiasm for medieval reenactments has on museum displays but she does not really pursue that further—it is also not the point of her article.[48] The public interest in historical reenactment or staging ("Inszenierung") here certainly confirms the Middle Ages as an endless source of fascination and emulations and creativity.[49] It also suggests that the public, as with the Jorvik museum or the Werben reenactments, invests these exhibits with a kind of authenticity in its desire to be part of its past both made and found. The museums display the medieval literature located historically and narratively in each place (Worms and Wolframs-Eschenbach) as sources of collective memory, not only for each local community but also for modern Germany; the museums take the present of literary things past and refract these memories of now-present pasts "to create (imaginary) present futures."[50] The museums establish authenticity by encouraging active remembering, self-critical and analytical contemplation.[51] Indeed, the museums become a prism through which to view the future of the past. They can, I think, provide a new link in the relations between literature and history, between the Middle Ages and the present, between each community and its visitors. The work of memory has only increased since 1989 and the dramatic changes in Europe since the reunification of Germany and the collapse of the former Soviet Union. I contend that the museums position medieval literature at the intersections of memory, heritage, and history for their respective communities as a way of making the past continually present and relevant.

Both museums enact the process of medievalism through a local practice of past presencing with global resonance, as they frame explorations of medieval German literature, adapted narratives, cultural memory, and local history. As they reconstruct and transform medieval narratives for the contemporary audience, the museums offer a thought-provoking response to the question of how literature—regardless of national origin and period—can assert its relevance for modern communities. The exhibits in the museums of Worms and Wolframs-Eschenbach form a new kind of "mnemonic horizon."[52] Through these museal palimpsests, at the intersections of narrative and image and three-dimensional space, we have witnessed how cultural identity emerges through the reception of seminal German medieval texts as that reception refracts through political, social, cultural experiences over time.

As they transform the premodern texts, the modern museums facilitate an interactive encounter between the texts and modern audiences, as the displays continue to engage and provoke twenty-first-century audiences. The museums also seek to capitalize on the ubiquity of the Middle Ages in popular culture, where it builds fantasies across genres and media and frames a variety of narratives. They place themselves squarely between alterity and modernity by taking up and engaging the question of whether it is possible to exhibit not just any literature but medieval literature. They exemplify the dialogic process that constantly generates meaning in progressive interpretations over time that Jauß describes in *Alterität and Modernität der mittelalterlichen Literatur*: the result of an ongoing, always open process of continuing and ever-accumulating interpretation. As their medieval origins become incorporated into later iterations, the medieval narratives of Wolfram von Eschenbach and the *Nibelungenlied* mediate between alterity and modernity; the intertexts, incorporated into multiple palimpsests, give tangible and concrete form to the potential for meaning ("Sinnpotential") of older texts for changing audiences whose worlds ("Lebenswelten") continually take, and often demand, new shape (**Figure 15**).

Over time, this process of creating meaning and framing narrative becomes part of the practice of memory, the practice of creating identity, the practice of imagining community. As they aspire to express community and community heritage through the display of medieval literature, the museums show yet again that the Middle Ages, "whether surviving in artefacts or existing in fantasy form, has long provided a reservoir of images and ideas which, in expressing modern ideas about the past, are in fact closely engaged in defining what it is to be modern."[53] The museums in Worms and Wolframs-Eschenbach support interactions of place and memory that drive the presencing of the past in their

Figure 15 Museum Wolfram von Eschenbach Museum sign visible from the town's central square, *author's own.*

communities. When we visit Wolframs-Eschenbach or Worms now, we find medieval literature firmly ensconced in the cityscapes. Each museum makes a unique contribution to the European memory complex by literally placing literature at the center of its display in a creation of new-old heritage.

This nexus of medieval literature, cultural memory, and local history stages a captivating encounter with the past that resonates in the present that we, collectively and individually, inhabit. The museums want the public to come and visit, to enjoy the installations, to reflect on a larger message. They also urge us to respond. Indeed, in the future, I hope that in the future, they do more to confront and to unsettle and to challenge their visitors. I think the museums clearly intend (as Macdonald suggests of heritage in Europe generally) "to *unsettle*—to dislodge us from our comfort zones" as we confront the heritage of the narrative past.[54] The materiality of heritage, on this local level, may indeed become that "potentially compelling" dimension of cultural policy that will assist in cultivating an educated citizenry.[55] Whether the municipal or museum administrators aim that high, I believe that these "local" museums do achieve a global resonance in their presentation and interpretation of older narratives for contemporary audiences; the medieval narrative past becomes living present. The medievalism of the museums in Worms and Wolframs-Eschenbach therefore not only provides a model for other communities to participate in the European memory complex. The museums, like medievalism, allow us to imagine new directions as we continue to explore a future for the past.

Notes

Preface

1 "Can one display literature?" Oskar Geidner, Hartmut Beck, Karl Bertau, and Dietmar Peschel-Rentsch (eds.), *Museum Wolfram von Eschenbach* (Wolframs-Eschenbach, 1994).
2 Pierre Nora, "Between Memory and History: Les Lieux de Mémoire," *Representations*. No. 26 Special Issue: Memory and Counter-Memory (Spring 1989): 7–24, p. 9.
3 Eric Hansen, *Die Nibelungenreise. Mit dem VW Bus durchs Mittelalter. Aus dem Amerikanischen übersetzt von Astrid Ule und Cornelia Stoll. Deutsche Bearbeitung von Astrid Ule* (München: Piper, 2004), p. 342. Translation mine.
4 Nora, "Between Memory and History," p. 9.
5 Sharon Macdonald, *Memorylands. Heritage and Identity in Europe Today* (London and New York: Routledge, 2013), p. 1.

Introduction

1 Eric Hansen, *Die Nibelungenreise. Mit dem VW Bus durchs Mittelalter. Aus dem Amerikanischen übersetzt von Astrid Ule und Cornelia Stoll. Deutsche Bearbeitung von Astrid Ule* (München: Piper, 2004), p. 342. Translation mine.
2 Sharon Macdonald, *Memorylands. Heritage and Identity in Europe Today* (London and New York: Routledge, 2013), p. 16.
3 It is *we* who have a need of an occasion, a place, a date, in order to see signs of life—not just those signs that come from habit or supposed tradition but also those from festivity or from our capacity to remember the Other, to remember ourselves. Adolf Muschg, "Abdruck einer Spur. Rede für Wolframs Eschenbach," *Literatur in Bayern* 39 (1995): 2–5, p. 3 (Translation mine).
4 Hansen, *Die Nibelungenreise,* pp. 341–342. Translation mine.
5 In summer 2017, the banner proudly proclaimed the 100th anniversary of the city's renaming.
6 This is prominent on the city's homepage, https://www.wolframs-eschenbach.de/ (accessed January 29, 2019). Wolframs-Eschenbach remains historically significant

as a city of the Teutonic Knights. However, this history was deemed secondary to the less tangible but more culturally significant literary legacy.
7 Macdonald, *Memorylands*, p. 16.
8 Richard Wagner's opera Tannhäuser was first performed in 1849, treating the material of the song contest.
9 "By water trees are sapped. Water fruits all those creatures acknowledged as Creation. By water man has sight. Water gives many a soul such sheen that the angels need be no brighter." Wolfram von Eschenbach, *Parzival and Titurel*, Cyril Edwards (trans.) (Oxford: Oxford University Press, 2006), p. 342. All further translations will appear in the text.
10 A certain Emmanuel Geibel, well known in Munich literary circles, was tasked with finding a suitable passage from Wolfram to go along with the royal dedication. Hartmut Kugler, "Lokale und regionale Wolfram-Verehrung," in Joachim Heinzle (ed.), *Wolfram von Eschenbach: ein Handbuch* (Berlin: de Gruyter, 2011), 818–834, p. 823.
11 Erwin Seitz and Oskar Geidner, *Wolframs-Eschenbach. Der Deutsche Orden baut eine Stadt* (Verlagsdruckerei Schmidt GmbH: Neustadt an der Aisch, 1997).
12 As Seitz and Geidner put it, the town became "ein x-beliebiges bayrisches Provinzstädtchen." Seitz and Geidner, p. 124.
13 In terms of Wolfram's actual connection to the town of Eschenbach, there is also no hard evidence. Jakob Püterich von Reichertshausen references Wolfram's grave in the church in a letter of 1462. There is note by Johann Wilhelm Kress von Kressenstein in 1608. But these reports can only be considered as what they are: reports. What visitors to Eschenbach saw could very well have been a later installation, rather than something original to the burial of Wolfram, if indeed that burial took place in that church.
14 Kugler, "Lokale und regionale Verehrung," p. 822.
15 Ibid., p. 825.
16 See the recent essay by Jakob Norberg, "German Literary Studies and the Nation," *The German Quarterly* 91.1 (2018): 1–17.
17 Kugler, "Lokale und regionale Verehrung," p. 822.
18 The essay was entitled "Über Wolfram von Eschenbach, des altdeutschen Dichters Heimat, Grab und Wappen" and appeared in *Abhandlungen der philosophisch-philologischen Classe der Königlichen Bayerischen Akademie der Wissenschaft* in 1837. Cited in Seitz/Geidner, p. 127 and n. 198 p. 145–146.
19 Kugler, "Lokale und regionale Wolfram-Verehrung," p. 823.
20 Seitz and Geidner, *Wolframs-Eschenbach*, p. 127.
21 I am adapting here Bakhtin's suggestion that "any concrete discourse (utterance) finds the object at which it was directed already as it were overlain with qualifications, open to dispute, charged with value, already enveloped in an obscuring mist—or, on the contrary, by the 'light' of alien words that have already

been spoken about it." M. M. Bakhtin, *The Dialogic Imagination, Four Essays*, Michael Holquist (ed.), Caryl Emerson and Michael Holquist (trans.) (Austin and London: University of Texas Press, 1981), p. 276.
22 Linda Hutcheon with Siobhan O'Flynn, *A Theory of Adaptation*, 2nd ed. (London, Routledge, 2013), p. 6.
23 Interestingly, *Tannhäuser* (originally 1845; final version 1860) and *Lohengrin* (1848) emerged from the same creative period of Wagner's life.
24 From Wolfram von Eschenbach, *Parzival*, Karl Lachmann (ed.) (Berlin: de Gruyter, 1965). See n. 9 above for the translation of these lines by Cyril Edwards.
25 Macdonald, "Presencing Europe's Pasts," in Ulrich Kockel, et al. (eds.), *Companion to the Anthropology of Europe* (Oxford: Wiley-Blackwell, 2012), 233–253, p. 244.
26 Ibid., pp. 234–235.
27 *Das Nibelungenlied. Mittelhochdeutsch. Neuhochdeutsch*, Ursula Schulze (ed.), Siegfried Grosse (trans.) (Stuttgart: Reclam, 2010). The translation is from *The Nibelungenlied: The Lay of the Nibelungs: The Lay of the Nibelungs*, Cyril Edwards (ed. and trans.) (Oxford: Oxford University Press, 2010), p. 7. All other references will appear in the text.
28 In the text, Worms is also one of the three courts that can be compared; the other two are found in Island (Brunhild) and in Hungary (Etzel).
29 More familiar to modern audiences perhaps, the Hagen of Wagner's *Ring des Nibelungen* fares no better as he drowns in the raging waters of the Rhine in the concluding scene of the final opera in the cycle.
30 "Wenn das Alleinstellungsmerkmal einer Stadt im kulturellen Bereich liegt und kein Gebäude, sondern eine Erzählung ist, ergibt sich daraus die Notwendigkeit, diesen Text zu inszenieren." (translation mine). Volker Gallé, "Wenn Städte sich erzählen," in Jörg Koch (ed.), *Wormser Nibelungen-Lexikon* (Worms: Worms Verlag, 2014), p. 6.
31 Muschg, p. 4. Muschg says, "der Name für eine Gelegenheit, bei der einmal viel los war und, wenn wir ihrer gedenken, bei uns viel los sein, los werden kann" (English translation mine).
32 Homi Bhabha, *Location of Culture* (London and New York: Routledge, 1994), pp. 26–27.
33 Macdonald, *Memorylands*, p. 94. Macdonald continues: "In heritage it is through place—and its specific physical elements, such as buildings or natural features—that the past is made present." Past presencing occurs through narrative but it also has material, affective, and embodied aspect. (Macdonald, "Presencing Europe's Pasts," p. 244.)
34 The implication is that the Bavarian roots of cultural authority go deeper than those of Goethe and Schiller, whose statue in front of the Weimar national theater inspired Maximilian's commissions of the monuments to Walther and Wolfram.

35 Aleida Assmann, *Der lange Schatten der Vergangenheit. Erinnerungskultur und Geschichtspolitik*, 2nd ed. (Munich: C.H. Beck, 2014), p. 17.
36 Ibid., p. 260.
37 Rudy Koshar, *From Monuments to Traces: Artifacts of German Memory, 1870–1990* (Berkeley: University of California Press, 2000), p. 301.
38 This is one of the main arguments of Barbara Kirshenblatt-Gimblett, *Destination Culture: Tourism, Museums, and Heritage* (Berkeley: University of California Press, 1998).
39 Macdonald focuses particularly on the party conference grounds in Nuremberg in her 2008 article "Museum Europe," but we should also understand the materiality of place (as well as the stickyness of difficult histories) from the Middle Ages to the present. See Sharon Macdonald, "Museum Europe: Negotiating Heritage," *Anthropological Journal of European Cultures* 17.2 (2008): 47–65, p. 60.

Chapter 1

1 Augustine, *Confessions*, Vernon J. Bourke (trans.) (Washington: Catholic University of America Press, 1966), p. 350.
2 Umberto Eco, "The Return of the Middle Ages," in *Travels in Hyperreality* (Harvest New York: Harvest, 1986), p. 61.
3 Augustine, *Confessions*, p. 348.
4 Ibid., p. 350.
5 See Mary Carruthers, *The Book of Memory: A Study of Memory in Medieval Culture* (Cambridge: Cambridge University Press, 1990).
6 Nibelungenlied, *Mittelhochdeutsch*. English translation from *The Nibelungenlied: The Lay of the Nibelungs*, Cyril Edwards (trans. and ed.) (Oxford: Oxford University Press, 2010). Further references will be in the text.
7 Jan-Dirk Müller, *Episches Erzählen. Erzählformen früher volkssprachiger Schriftlichkeit* (Berlin: Erich Schmidt, 2017), pp. 146–147.
8 Klaus von See, "*Das Nibelungenlied*—ein Nationalepos?" in Joachim Heinzle and Anneliese Waldschmidt (eds.), *Die Nibelungen. Ein deutscher Wahn, ein deutscher Alptraum. Studien und Dokumente zur Rezeption des Nibelungenstoffs im 19. und 20. Jahrhundert* (Frankfurt: Suhrkamp, 1991), 43–110, pp. 56–58.
9 The film does not take up, nor do the museums really address explicity, the role of medieval narratives, such as the *Nibelungenlied*, in supporting problematic ethnic nationalisms now. The film from 1990 shows its age; the museums work on consciousness raising. But they subordinate contemporary politics to literature and its history.

10 This concert, as far as I and others can recall, took place during the meeting of the Medieval Academy of America at the University of Wisconsin in the spring of 1989.
11 Jan Assmann, *Religion and Cultural Memory*, Rodney Livingstone (trans.) (Stanford: Stanford University Press, 2006), p. 11.
12 Astrid Erll, *Memory in Culture*, Sara B. Young (trans.) (New York and Basingstoke: Palgrave Macmillan, 2011).
13 Koshar, *From Monuments to Traces*, p. 9.
14 Ibid., p. 13.
15 Macdonald, "Presencing Europe's Pasts," 233–252, p. 235.
16 Bruce Holsinger, "Analytical Survey 6: Medieval Literature and Cultures of Performance," *New Medieval Literatures* 6 (2003): 271–311, p. 284.
17 Amy G. Remensnyder, *Remembering Kings Past. Monastic Foundation Legends in Medieval Southern France* (Ithaca and London: Cornell University Press, 1995), p. 1. See also Remensnyder's essay "Topographies of Memory," in Gerd Althoff, Johannes Fried, and Patrick Geary (eds.), *Medieval Concepts of the Past: Ritual, Memory, Historiography* (Washington DC: Cambridge University Press, 2002), 193–215, p. 195.
18 Ibid., pp. 2–4.
19 Linda Hutcheon, with Siobhan O'Flynn, *A Theory of Adaptation*, 2nd ed. (London and New York: Routledge, 2012), p. 121.
20 Hartmann von Aue, *Iwein. Text und Übersetzung*. Text der siebenten Ausgabe von G. F. Benecke, K. Lachmann und L. Wolff. Übersetzung und Nachwort von Thomas Cramer (Berlin: De Gruyter, 2001). English translation from *Arthurian Romances, Tales and Lyric Poetry. The Complete Works of Hartmann von Aue*, Frank Tobin, Kim Vivian, Richard Lawson (trans.) (University Park, PA: The Pennsylvania University Press, 2001), p. 237.
21 For this reason, Macdonald advocates for the "present" as an analytical starting point that is "not privileged as inherently more worthwhile to study than 'the past' itself." Macdonald, "Presencing Europe's Pasts," pp. 233–234.
22 Tison Pugh and Angela Jane Weisl, *Medievalisms. Making the Past in the Present* (London and New York: Routledge, 2013), p. 1. Indeed, as the title of the book and the first chapter show, the authors emphatically argue that medievalisms can actually only be understood in the plural.
23 Ibid., p. 1.
24 Leslie Workman and Kathleen Verduin (eds.), *Medievalism in Europe II. Studies in Medievalism VIII* (Cambridge: DS Brewer, 1996), p. 1.
25 See David Matthews, *Medievalism: A Critical History* (Cambridge: D.S. Brewer, 2015); Richard Utz, *Medievalism: A Manifesto* (Leeds, UK: Arc Humanities Press, 2017); and Louise D'Arcens (ed.), *Cambridge Companion to Medievalism* (Cambridge: Cambridge University Press, 2016).
26 Hutcheon, *A Theory of Adaptation*, pp. 7–8.

27 "medievalism, n." *OED Online*, Oxford University Press, January 2018, www.oed.com/view/Entry/115639 (accessed February 22, 2018).
28 The earliest reference is 1844, according to Matthews, *Medievalism*, p. 117.
29 Elizabeth Emery and Richard Utz, "Making Medievalism: A Critical Overview," in Elizabeth Emery and Richard Utz (eds.), *Medievalism: Key Critical Terms* (Cambridge: Boydell and Brewer, 2014), 1–10, p. 2. Emery and Utz offer a brief current summary of definitions, starting with the term "medievalism" itself and then giving an overview of what has come to be known as medievalism studies.
30 Dinshaw eloquently lays this out in her introduction in Carolyn Dinshaw, *How Soon Is Now? Medieval Texts, Amateur Readers, and the Queerness of Time* (Durham and London: Duke University Press, 2012). See also Richard Utz, "A Panel Discussion," in Roger Dahoud (ed.), *The Future of the Middle Ages and the Renaissance. Problems, Trends, and Opportunities for Research* (Turnhour: Brepols, 1998), 3–19, pp. 9–13.
31 Tom Shippey, "Medievalisms and Why They Matter," *Studies in Medievalism* 17 (2009): 45–54, p. 45.
32 Pugh and Weisl, *Medievalisms*, p. 1.
33 Matthews, *Medievalism*, pp. 37–38.
34 Erll, *Memory in Culture*, p. 141.
35 Elizabeth Emery, "Medievalism and the Middle Ages," *Studies in Medievalism* 17 (2009): 77–85, p. 83.
36 Shippey sees medievalism with a mission that resonates with the work of many in medievalism studies. Scholars have a duty to "trace connections" as well as to "expose errors" and to "make their voices heard" so that medievalism is not co-opted by nationalism as it once was in the nineteenth century (Shippey, "Medievalisms and why they matter," p. 52).
37 Emery, "Medievalism and the Middle Ages," p. 78.
38 Ibid., p. 85.
39 For an articulation of the main differences and an overview of the scholarship, see Richard Utz, "Resistance to (the New) Medievalism? Comparative Deliberations on (National) Philology, Mediävalismus, and Mittelalter-Rezeption in Germany and North America," in Roger Dahood (ed.), *The Future of the Middle Ages and the Renaissance: Problems, Trends, and Opportunities in Research* (Turnhout: Brepols, 1998), pp. 151–170.
40 D'Arcens, *Companion*, p. 1. Perhaps the clearest indication of medievalism's firm place in the academy as a recognized discipline in its own right is the publication of this *Cambridge Companion to Medievalism*, which serves both as survey and summary of medievalism to date.
41 We see this, for example, in the contributions of Volker Mertens, Ulrich Müller, and Peter Wapnewski in the *Wagner Handbook*, Ulrich Müller and Peter Wapnewski (eds.), John Deathridge (trans.) (Boston: Harvard University Press, 1992).

42 Matthews sees common developments in scholarship in the 1980s on both sides of the Atlantic, suggesting that "the parent discipline, medieval studies, had arrived at a particular juncture, even a crisis" (Matthews, *Medievalism,* p. 7). A good example of this "arrival" is the six-volume series edited by Ulrich Müller and Werner Wunderlich on *Mittelalter-Mythen* for medievalism from the German-speaking disciplines (UVK Verlagsgesellschaft, 1998–2008).

43 Herweg and Keppler-Tasaki also use the term "topoi of cultural memory and identity" to describe these sites of memory or "Erinnerungsorte." See Mathias Herweg and Stefan Keppler-Tasaki (eds.), *Rezeptionskulturen. Fünfhundert Jahre literarischer Mittelalterrezeption zwischen Kanon und Populärkultur* (Berlin: de Gruyter, 2012), p. 6. See also Etienne François and Hagen Schulze (eds.), *Deutsche Erinnerungsorte.* Vol. I (Munich: C.H. Beck, 2001).

44 Mathias Herweg and Stefan Keppler-Tasaki (eds.), *Das Mittelalter des Historismus. Formen und Funktionen in Literatur und Kunst, Film und Technik* (Würzburg: Königshausen und Neumann, 2015), p. 4.

45 Groebner argues for a long tradition of medievalism, on the one hand; he also attempts to address the still problematic and traditional focus he notices particularly among German historians of the Middle Ages. Valentin Groebner, *Das Mittelalter hört nicht auf. Über historisches Erzählen* (Munich: C.H. Beck, 2008), p. 165.

46 Pugh and Weisl, *Medievalisms,* p. 10.

47 Macdonald, *Memorylands,* p. 94.

48 Svetlana Boym, *The Future of Nostalgia* (New York: Basic Books, 2008), p. 44.

49 Ibid., p. 351.

50 Louise D'Arcens, "Presentism," in Elizabeth Emery and Richard Utz (eds.), *Medievalism: Key Critical Terms* (Cambridge: Boydell and Brewer, 2014), 181–189, p. 185.

51 Weisl places nostalgia in the context of spectacle and performance, where we see "both a longing for the past and a longing to make it present, a desire to make the fantasy of the spectacle into a kind of reality, just as that image retreats again into the imaginary." Angela Jane Weisl, "Spectacle," in Elizabeth Emery and Richard Utz (eds.), *Medievalism: Key Critical Terms* (Cambridge: Boydell and Brewer, 2014), 231–239, p. 234.

52 Dinshaw, *How Soon Is Now?* p. 36.

53 Stephanie Trigg, "Medievalism and Theories of Temporality," in Louise D'Arcens (ed.), *The Cambridge Companion to Medievalism* (Cambridge: Cambridge University Press, 2016), pp. 196–210.

54 Dinshaw, *How Soon Is Now?* p. 37.

55 Helen Dell, "Nostalgia and Medievalism: Conversations, Contradictions, Impasses," *Postmedieval: A Journal of Medieval Cultural Studies* 2 (2011): 115–126, p. 119.

56 Ibid., p. 121.

57 Eileen Joy and Craig Dionne, "Before the trains of thought have been laid down so firmly: The premodern post/human," *postmedieval: a journal of medieval cultural studies* 1.1/2 (2010): 1–9, p. 3.
58 Joy and Dionne, "Before the Trains of Thought Have Been Laid Down so Firmly," p. 6.
59 Gail Ashton and Daniel Kline (eds.), *Medieval Afterlives in Popular Culture* (Basingstoke, New York: Palgrave Macmillan, 2012), p. 5. The predecessors in this particular instance include Umberto Eco and his well-known reconfigurations of the middle ages from his 1986 volume of essays entitled *Travels in Hyperreality*.
60 Macdonald, *Memorylands*, p. 99.
61 Ibid., p. 108.
62 Ibid., p. 94.
63 They reflect, for Nora, the reliance of modern memory "entirely on the materiality of the trace, the immediacy of the recording, the visibility of the image." See Pierre Nora, "Between Memory and History: Les Lieux de Mémoire," *Representations*. No. 26 Special Issue: Memory and Counter-Memory (Spring 1989): 7–24, p. 13.
64 Macdonald, *Memorylands*, p. 138.
65 Koshar suggests that this continuity of metaphor, if one will, provides a connecting thread for Germans from 1870 to 1990, the period of his study. In this time, there were two world wars, the Holocaust, the Cold War, and six different governments and yet Germany was unified at the beginning of the time period covered by the study and at the end. Koshar is careful not to see this as a "Hollywood happy end" but it is really quite amazing to consider the impact and significance that monuments and memory have in this phenomenon. Koshar, *From Monuments to Traces*, pp. 11–12.
66 The museum also asks questions like: What is literature? What can literature do? What remains of literature when we look for it in the archives from 1899–2001? http://www.dla-marbach.de/museen/literaturmuseum-der-moderne/ (accessed January 29, 2019).
67 https://www.onb.ac.at/museen/literaturmuseum/ and http://strauhof.ch/ (accessed January 29, 2019).
68 Georf Renöckl, "Glücksfall und Wurf," *Neue Zürcher Zeitung*, 06.05.2015, https://www.nzz.ch/feuilleton/buecher/gluecksfall-und-wurf-1.18536078 (accessed January 29, 2019).
69 Bernhard Fetz, "Ein Museum für österreichische Literatur," in Bernard Fetz (ed.), *Das Literaturmuseum. 101 Objekte und Geschichten* (Salzburg and Vienna: Jung, 2015), 14–22, p. 22.
70 "Das Literaturmuseum Strauhof wird fortgeführt," *Neue Zürcher Zeitung*, 30.11.2017.
71 https://www.srf.ch/kultur/literatur/der-verein-literaturmuseum-zuerich-fuehrt-kuenftig-den-strauhof (accessed February 19, 2018).

72 http://www.schloss-neuenbuerg.de/museum/ (accessed September 7, 2019).
73 *Schloss Neuenbürg. Ein Führer durch das Nordschwarzwaldmuseum. Zweigmuseum des Badischen Landesmuseums* (Karlsruhe: Badisches Landesmusem, 2011), pp. 7–8.
74 See the museum's homepage at www.grimmwelt.de/ (accessed January 29, 2019).
75 "Das Ärschlein, Verbrechen und ein 'C,'" *Frankfurter Allgemeine Zeitung*, 21.08.2013, Nr. 193, S. 46, https://www.genios.de/document/RMO__FDA201308213981726 (accessed January 18, 2016).
76 "Gäste kommen von überall her" *Frankfurter Allegmeine Zeitung*, 29.12.2015. Nr. 301, S. 41, https://www.genios.de/document/RMO__FDA201512294749141 (accessed January 18, 2016).
77 https://www.theguardian.com/travel/2015/dec/21/10-best-new-museums-new-york-venice-germany (accessed September 7, 2019).
78 See the museum's homepage here, http://www.siegfriedmuseum-xanten.de/(accessed January 29, 2019).
79 Ralph Trost, *Vom Umgan mit Helden. Das Museum Nibelungen(h)ort Xanten* (Frankfurt: Peter Lang, 2012), p. 95.
80 Ibid., p. 83.
81 Ibid., p. 11.
82 Ibid., p. 96.
83 Bhabha, *Location of Culture*, pp. 26–27.
84 Ibid., p. 27.
85 Bhabha, "The World and the Home," *Social Text* (1992): 141–153, p. 152.
86 "I am want to join she whispers to me she whispers I reach for her chewing and swallowing she touches me she knows I want to join she chews and swallows me I am gone now I am her face my own face has left me I see me swim away a hot thing I see the bottoms of my feet I am alone I want to be the two of us I want the join." Toni Morrison, *Beloved* (New York: Penguin, 1987), p. 213.

Chapter 2

1 mîn hêr Hartmann von Ouwe,
   frou Ginovêr iwer frouwe
   und iwer hêrre der künc Artûs
   den kumt ein mîn gast ze hûs. Wolfram von Eschenbach *Parzival* (Berlin: de Gruyter, 1964), 143, pp. 21–24; Wolfram von Eschenbach, *Parzival and Titurel*, Cyril Edwards (trans.) (Oxford: Oxford University Press, 2006), p. 61.
2 Linda Hutcheon with Siobhan O'Flynn, *A Theory of Adaptation*, 2nd ed. (New York and London: Routledge, 2012), p. 116.

3   For a recent overview of Arthurian intertextuality, see Marjolein Hogenbirk, "Intertextuality," in Leah Tether and Johnny McFadyen (eds.), *Handbook of Arthurian Romance. King Arthur's Court in Medieval European Literature* (Berlin: de Gruyter, 2017), pp. 183–198. Also Tobias Bulang, "Intertextualität und Interfiguralität des 'Wartburgkriegs,'" in Gert Hübner and Dorothea Klein (eds.), *Sangspruchdichtung um 1300. Akten der Tagung in Basel vom 7. Bis 9. November 2013* (Hildesheim: Weidmann, 2015), pp. 127–146.
4   *The Book of the Anonymous Poet. Guide of the Nibelungen Museum* (Worms: A+H/Nibelungenmuseum, 2001), p. 82.
5   Evelyn Birge Vitz, *Orality and Performance in Early French Romance* (Cambridge: D.S. Brewer, 1999), p. 275.
6   Ibid., pp. 281–282.
7   Whitaker enumerates many other painted chambers in Chapter 5 ("Painted Chambers") in *The Legends of King Arthur in Art* (Woodbridge, Suffolk/Rochester, NY: D.S. Brewer, 1990).
8   This must be Hartmann, because Chrétien's romance does not name the lord of the castle who dies at Iwein's hand.
9   James Rushing, *Images of Adventure. Ywain in the Visual Arts* (Princeton, NJ: Princeton University Press, 1995).
10 Susanne Hafner has noted that this creates an effect of simultaneity that allows the viewer to be surrounded by the story, its people, its court, and its courtliness. For a modern visitor, the effect here is actually not unlike the effort required at the Nibelung Museum or at the Museum Wolfram von Eschenbach; understanding demands that effort. Susanne Hafner, "Erzählen im Raum. Der Schmalkaldener Iwein," in Horst Wenzel and C. Stephen Jaeger (eds.), *Visualiserungsstrategien in mittelalterlichen Bildern und Texten* (Berlin: Erich Schmidt, 2006), 90–98, p. 97.
11 Michael Curschmann, *Vom Wandel im bildlichen Umgang mit literarischen Gegenständen: Rodenegg, Wildenstein und das Flaarsche Haus in Stein am Rhein* (Freiburg, Schweiz: Universitätsverlag, 1997), p. 584.
12 Haiko Wandhoff, "Jenseits der Gutenberg-Galaxis. Das Mittelalter und die Medientheorie," in Volker Mertens and Carmen Stange (eds.), *Bilder vom Mittelalter. Eine Berliner Ringvorlesung* (Göttingen: V&R unipress, 2007), p. 33.
13 Horst Wenzel and Christina Lechtermann, "Repräsentation und Kinästhetik," *Theorien des Performativen. Paragrana*. Bd. 10. Heft 1 (2001): 191–214, pp. 193–195.
14 Hutcheon, *A Theory of Adaptation*, p. 6. The process of lamination overlays one material with another through which the first remains visible. A palimpsest functions similarly.
15 Ibid., p. 8.
16 Ibid., p. 21.
17 Ibid., p. 33.

18 Ibid., p. 116.
19 Ibid., p. 139.
20 Ibid., p. 173.
21 While the museums in Worms and Wolframs-Eschenbach are products of the twentieth and twenty-first centuries, I would argue that they draw on the imaginative memory (the way Remensnyder defines it) of medieval thought by virtue of the fact that medieval literature is the subject of their exhibitions. I would also submit that the thirteenth-century murals in Rodenegg suggest a kind of interpretive doubling for modern viewers now. We cannot know how the medieval audience reacted to them or lived with them. On the other hand, the murals do indicate a critical process at work as a visual interpretation and adaptation of Hartmann's verses.
22 Wolfram von Eschenbach, *Parzival*, 420, 25–30. The cook stays home in Worms and survives.
23 Winder McConnell (ed.), *A Companion to the Nibelungenlied* (Columbia, SC: Camden House, 1998); Francis G. Gentry, Winder McConnell, et al. (eds.), *The Nibelungen Tradition: An Encyclopedia* (New York and London: Routledge, 2002). Otfried Ehrismann's *Nibelungenlied. Epoche-Werk Wirkung* (Munich: C.H. Beck, 2002) is in its second edition.
24 Andersson calls it "bold literary experiment." Theodore Andersson, *A Preface to the Nibelungenlied* (Stanford: Stanford University Press, 1987), p. 3.
25 Andreas Heusler, Nibelungensage und Nibelungenlied. Die Stoffgeschichte des deutschen Heldenepos (Darmstadt: Wissenschaftliche Buchgesellschaft, 1973), p. 50.
26 Theodore Andersson, *A Preface to the Nibelungenlied* (Stanford: Stanford University Press, 1987), p. 81. The poet of the *Nibelungenlied* is both a recipient of and a critic of romance.
27 Joachim Heinzle, *Das Nibelungenlied. Eine Einführung* (Fischer Taschenbuch: Frankfurt a. M. 1994), p. 89.
28 See Francis Gentry, "Key Concepts in the *Nibelungenlied*," in Winder McConnell (ed.), *A Companion to the Nibelungenlied* (Rochester: Camden House, 1998), pp. 66–79.
29 Edward Haymes, *The Nibelungenlied. History and Interpretation* (Urbana and Chicago: University of Illinois Press, 1986), p. 113.
30 For Ehrismann this puts the Nibelungenlied in third place behind Parzival and Willehalm. See Ehrismann, *Nibelungenlied*, p. 40. See also Heinzle, "The Manuscripts of the Nibelungenlied," in Winder McConnell (ed.), *A Companion to the Nibelungenlied* (Rochester: Camden House, 1998), pp. 104–123.
31 One of the newest editions Middle High German/Modern German uses as its basis for the B manuscript. Ursula Schulze and Siegfried Grosse, *Das Nibelungenlied. Mittelhochdeutsch. Neuhochdeutsch* (Reclam: Stuttgart, 2011), p. 907. The guide for the Nibelung Museum (*Book of the Anonymous Poet*) briefly addresses the editorial

history (pp. 59–60) to give an idea of the story's variability/instability as well as to introduce the concept of manuscript transmission.
32 Schulze, *Das Nibelungenlied*, p. 907.
33 Gentry, et al. (eds.), *The Nibelungen Tradition. An Encyclopedia*, pp. 11–12.
34 Ibid., pp. 43–46.
35 Ibid., pp. 41–43.
36 Another indication of Parzival's popularity is the fact that of those sixteen manuscripts, six of them are illustrated, including the printed version from 1477. See Bernd Schirok, "Die Bilderhandschriften und Bildzeugnisse," in Joachim Heinzle (ed.), *Wolfram von Eschenbach. Ein Handbuch. Bd. 1 Autor, Werk, Wirkung* (Berlin: de Gruyter, 2011), 335–365, p. 337.
37 Bernd Schirok, "Wolfram und seine Werke im Mittelalter," in Joachim Heinzle (ed.), *Wolfram von Eschenbach. Ein Handbuch. Bd. 1–2 Autor, Werk, Wirkung* (Berlin: de Gruyter, 2011), pp. 1–81.
38 Schirok, "Wolfram und seine Werke," p. 8.
39 Will Hasty (ed.), *A Companion to Parzival* (Columbia, SC: Camden House, 1999).
40 Joachim Bumke, *Wolfram von Eschenbach*, 8th ed. (Metzler: Stuttgart, 2004), pp. 407–414. Heinzle, *Wolfram von Eschenbach. Ein Handbuch*, pp. 443–445.
41 For one of the most recent full-length studies of *Titurel*, see Alexander Sager, *Minne von maeren: on Wolfram's* Titurel (Göttingen: V&R Unipress, 2006).
42 Bumke, *Wolfram von Eschenbach*, pp. 276–320. Heinzle, "*Willehalm*. Abriß der Handlung," *Wolfram von Eschenbach. Ein Handbuch*, pp. 525–543.
43 De Boor notices a courtly "humanizing" of the heathen ("höfische Humanisierung des Heiden"), which more recent studies have begun to complicate, notably Frakes, *Vernacular and Latin Literary Discourses of the Muslim Other in Medieval Germany* (New York: Palgrave Macmillan, 2011). Helmut de Boor, *Die höfische Literatur: Vorbereitung, Blüte, Ausklang 1170–1250* (Munich: C.H. Beck, 1974), p. 115.
44 de Boor, *Die höfische Literatur*, p. 116.
45 Karl Bertau, *Deutsche Literatur im europäischen Mittelalter. Bd. II 1195–1220* (Munich: C.H. Beck, 1973), p. 1169.
46 See Kathryn Starkey, *Reading the Medieval Book. Word, Image, and Performance in Wolfram von Eschenbach's* Willehalm (Notre Dame, IN: University of Notre Dame Press, 2012).
47 de Boor, *Die höfische Literatur*, p. 43.
48 Joachim Heinzle, *Das Nibelungenlied. Eine Einführung* (Fischer Taschenbuch: Frankfurt a. M., 1994), p. 91.
49 *Nibelungen Tradition*, p. 9.
50 Andersson, *A Preface to the Nibelungenlied*, p. 166.
51 Joachim Bumke, *Höfische Kultur: Literatur und Gesellschaft im hohen Mittelalter* (Deutscher Taschenbuch Verlag, 1990), pp. 268–269.

52 The essay by Bernd Schirok, "Wolfram und seine Werke," pp. 49–63 offers a comprehensive list of works from the thirteenth century through the seventeenth century that mentions Wolfram or figures from his works.
53 Marion Gibbs, "Fragment and Expansion: Wolfram von Eschenbach, *Titurel*, and Albrecht, *Jüngerer Titurel*," in W.H. Jackson and Silvia Ranawake (eds.), *The Arthur of the Germans. The Arthurian Legend in Medieval German and Dutch Literature* (Cardiff: University of Wales Press, 2000), 69–80, p. 78.
54 Also deserving of mention are Ulrich von dem Türlin's *Arabel* (a prequel to Willehalm) and the continuation in Ulrich von Türheim's *Rennewart*.
55 Matthias Meyer, "Intertextuality in the Later Thirteenth Century: Wigamur, Gauriel, Lohengrin and the Fragments of Arthurian Romances," in W.H. and Silvia Ranawake (eds.), *The Arthur of the Germans. The Arthurian Legend in Medieval German and Dutch Literature* (Cardiff: University of Wales Press, 2000), 98–116, p. 111.
56 Volker Mertens, "Die Wiederentdeckung Wolframs und die Anfänge der Forschung," in Joachim Heinzle (ed.), *Wolfram von Eschenbach. Ein Handbuch. Bd. 1 Autor, Werk, Wirkung* (Berlin: de Gruyter, 2011), 705–741, p. 705; see also Jan Hallmann, *Studien zum mittelhochdeutschen Wartburgkrieg. Literaturgeschichtliche Stellung—Überliefereung—Rezeptionsgeschichte. Mit einer Edition der Wartburgkrieg-Texte* (Berlin: de Gruyter, 2015), pp. 300–320.
57 Hallmann, *Studien zum mittelhochdeutschen Wartburgkrieg*, p. 152.
58 Mertens distinguishes between the productive treatment of the Arthurian material, represented by Fuetrer, and the reproductive treatment that we see in the compilation of the Ambraser Heldenbuch. Both, however, end by the early sixteenth century. See Volker Mertens, *Der deutsche Artusroman* (Reclam: Stuttgart, 1998), p. 341.
59 Ehrismann, *Epoche*, p. 170.
60 Füssli considered Siegfried a "better Achilles." See Wolfgang Storch (ed.), *Die Nibelungen. Bilder von Liebe, Verrat und Untergang* (Munich: Prestel, 1987), p. 125. In the museum guide for the Nibelung Museum, the fictitious poet says that Füssli made his characters "look like heroes of antiquity" (*Book of the Anonymous Poet*, p. 61).
61 Francis G. Gentry and Ulrich Müller, "The Reception of the Middle Ages in Germany: An Overview," *Studies in Medievalism III*. 4 (Spring 1991): 399–422, p. 404.
62 Ehrismann, *Epoche*, p. 169.
63 Anderson asserts that the "energetic activities of these professional intellectuals were central the shaping of nineteenth-century European nationalisms." Benedict Anderson, *Imagined Communities: Reflections on the Origin and Spread of Nationalism*, Revised ed. (London, New York: Verso, 2006), p. 71.
64 Groebner, *Das Mittelalter hört nicht auf*, p. 58.
65 Ibid., p. 65.
66 Ehrismann, *Epoche*, p. 183ff.
67 Gerd-H. Zuchold, "The Prussian Royal House and Pictorial Representation of the Nibelung Saga," *Studies in Medievalism* V (1993): pp. 23–37.

68 David E. Barclay, "Medievalism and Nationalism in Nineteenth-Century Germany," *Studies in Medievalism* V (1993): 5–22, p. 5.
69 Ulrich Müller and Werner Wunderlich, "The Modern Reception of the Arthurian Legend," in W.H. and Silvia Ranawake (eds.), *The Arthur of the Germans. The Arthurian Legend in Medieval German and Dutch Literature* (Cardiff: University of Wales Press, 2000), 303–324, p. 304.
70 Richard Utz, "Academic Medievalism and Nationalism," in Louise D'Arcens (ed.), *The Cambridge Compansion to Medievalism* (Cambridge: Cambridge University Press, 2016), p. 123.
71 Helen Young, "Whiteness and Time: The Once, Present, and Future Race in Karl Fugelso," in Vincent Ferré and Alicia C. Montoya (eds.), *Studies in Medievalism XXIV Medievalism on the Margins Book* (Cambridge: D.S. Brewer, 2015), 39–49, pp. 42 and 45.
72 Barry Millington, *The Sorceror of Bayreuth. Richard Wagner, His Work and His World* (Oxford University Press, 2012), p. 87.
73 Stewart Spencer, "The 'Romantic Operas' and the Turn to Myth," in Thomas S. Grey (ed.), *Cambridge Companion to Wagner* (Cambridge: Cambridge University Press, 2008), pp. 67–74.
74 Ibid., p. 73.
75 Ulrich Müller, "Wolfram, Wagner and the Germans," in Will Hasty (ed.), *A Companion to Wolfram's Parzival* (Rochester: Camden House, 1999), 245–258, p. 255.
76 Müller and Wunderlich, "Modern Reception," pp. 303–304. Wagner's works are a reflection of his own time and his own age, not just a false perception of the Middle Ages, a fact which (for Mertens) should inspire us to question further. Mertens suggests that when we can follow Wagner "at a certain critical distance," Wagner and his work can productively "act as a mediator in our understanding of the Middle Ages." Volker Mertens, "Wagner's Middle Ages," in Ulrich Müller and Peter Wapnewski (eds.), *Wagner Handbook*, John Deathridge (trans.) (Boston: Harvard University Press, 1992), p. 268.
77 Klaus von See, "Die politische Rezeption der Siegfriedfigur im 19. und 20. Jahrhundert," in Volker Gallé (ed.), *Siegfried. Schmied und Drachentöter* (Worms: Worms-Verlag, 2005), 138–155, p. 153. See also Otfrid Ehrismann "Die literarische Rezeption der Siegfriedfigur von 1200 bis heute" in the same volume, p. 132.
78 Müller comments that this popularity of the *Nibelungenlied* would have puzzled medieval readers or listeners. (Wolfram, "Wagner, and the Germans," p. 245). As we will see in Chapter 4, it is this amazement that the poet-figure of the museum guide seeks to convey, as he responds to the way the "Mythenmaschine" has changed, adapted, and at times distorted his story unexpectedly.
79 Ehrismann, *Epoche*, pp. 180–181.

80 David J. Levin, *Richard Wagner, Fritz Lang, and the Nibelungen: The Dramaturgy of Disavowal* (Princeton, NJ: Princeton University Press, 1998), p. 120.
81 Bettina Bildhauer, *Filming the Middle Ages* (London: Reaktion, 2011), p. 174. Hebbel moves myth into history in his dramatic version of the Nibelung legend, while Wagner does the opposite to create myth out of history. Mary Cicora. *Wagner's* Ring *and German Drama. Comparative Studies in Mythology and History in Drama* (Westport, CT: Greenwood Press, 1999), p. 78.
82 Joachim Heinzle, "Einleitung: Der deutscheste aller deutschen Stoffe," in Joachim Heinzle and Anneliese Waldschmidt (eds.), *Die Nibelungen. Ein deutscher Wahn, ein deutscher Alptraum. Studien und Dokumente zur Rezpetion des Nibelungenstoffs im 19. und 20. Jahrhundert* (Frankfurt: Suhrkamp, 1991), 8–18, p. 15.
83 Heinz-B. Heller, "… nur dann überzeugend und eindringlich, wenn es sich mit dem Wesen der Zeit deckt … Fritz Langs *Nibelungen*-Film als 'Zeitbild'" in Joachim Heinzle, Klaus Klein und Ute Obhof (eds.), *Die Nibelungen. Sage—Epos—Mythos* (Reichert: Wiesbaden, 2003), 497–509, p. 500.
84 This is cited in Patrick McGilligan, *Fritz Lang: The Nature of the Beast* (University of Minnesota Press, 2013), p. 102.
85 Gene Phillips, "Fritz Lang Remembers," in Barry Keith Grant (ed.), *Fritz Lang Interviews* (Jackson, MS: University Press of Mississippi, 2000), 175–187, p. 179.
86 Heller, "… nur dann überzeugend und eindringlich," 499.
87 Heller, here p. 507, quotes Lang.
88 Ibid., p. 498.
89 Ibid., p. 506. Patterns, architecture, ornaments serve to highlight the "impression of Fate's irresistible power," as Kracauer puts it. Siegfried Kracauer, *From Caligari to Hitler. A Psychological History of the German Film* (Princeton, NJ: Princeton University Press, 1947), p. 94.
90 Astrid Lembke, "Umstrittene Souveränität. Herrschaft, Geschlecht und Stand im *Nibelungenlied* sowie in Thea von Harbous *Nibelungenbuch* und in Fritz Langs Film *Die Nibelungen*," in Nastaša Bedeković, Andreas Kraß, Astrid Lembke (eds.), *Durchkreuzte Helden. Das Nibelungenlied und Fritz Langs Film Die Nibelungen im Licht der Intersektionalitätsforschung* (Bielefeld: transcript Verlag, 2014), 51–75, pp. 72–73.
91 Paul Jensen, *The Cinema of Fritz Lang*. International Film Guide Series (New York: Barnes and Co., 1969), p. 57.
92 Laurie Finke and Martin Shichtman, *King Arthur and the Myth of History* (Tallahassee: University Press of Florida, 2004). They discuss the image of the flag bearer on p. 188.
93 Ibid., p. 190.
94 Martin Shichtman and Laurie Finke, "Exegetical history: Nazis at the Round Table," *Postmedieval* 5.3 (2014): 278–294, p. 284.

95 Ibid., p. 289, n. 7.
96 Joachim Heinzle, "Einleitung: Mythos Nibelungen," in Joachim Heinzle (ed.), *Mythos Nibelungen* (Stuttgart: Reclam), p. 60.
97 Shichtman and Finke, "Exegetical history," p. 278.
98 Ibid., p. 290.
99 Bernhard Martin, "Der deutsche Nationalstaat und das Nibelungenlied. Über die gesellschaftspolitische Funktion des Mythos," in Werner Wunderlich, Ulrich Müller, Detlef Scholz (eds.), "*Waz sider da geschach*": *American-German Studies on the Nibelungenlied: Text and Reception: With Bibliography 1980–1990/91* (Göppingen: Kümmerle, 1992), 179–188. Hohlbein (http://www.hohlbein.de/neu/aktuelles.php) and Lodemann (https://www.jürgen-lodemann.de/) have remained prolific novelists to the present, writing on a variety of topics in addition to the Nibelung legend (accessed January 20, 2019).
100 Müller and Wunderlich, "Modern Reception," p. 306.
101 Werner Wunderlich, "Arthurian Legend in German Literature of the Nineteen-Eighties," *Studies in Medievalism III*. 4 (1991): 423–442, p. 424.
102 Ibid., p. 426.
103 Müller and Wunderlich, "Modern Reception," 313.
104 Heinzle "Einleitung," *Deutscher Wahn* 8.
105 Ehrismann, *Epoche*, p. 166.
106 Heinzle, *Einführung*, p. 107.
107 Remensnyder, *Remembering*, p. 4.
108 Max Siller, "König Artus in Tirol," in *Artus auf Runkelstein. Der Traum vom guten Herrscher*. Stiftung Bozener Schlösser. Runkelsteiner Schriften zur Kulturgeschichte. Bd. 6 (Athesia, AG: Bozen, 2014), 103–136, p. 135.

Chapter 3

1 "Forests become lances!" Oskar Geidner, Hartmut Beck, Karl Bertau, and Dietmar Peschel-Rentsch (eds.), *Museum Wolfram von Eschenbach* (Wolframs-Eschenbach, 1994), p. 25. All translations from the museum guide are mine, as there is no English version available.
2 This flying image is far too fleet for fools. They can't think it through, for it knows how to dart from side to side before them, just like a startled hare. Wolfram von Eschenbach, *Parzival*, Karl Lachmann (ed.) (Berlin: de Gruyter, 1964). The English translation is from Wolfram von Eschenbach, *Parzival with Titurel and Love Lyrics*, Cyril Edwards (trans.) (Woodbridge and Rochester: D.S. Brewer, 2004), p. 3. All further translations from *Parzival* will be from Edwards and noted in the text.

3   Munich designer Michael Hoffer was responsible for the artistic layout of the museum; medieval scholar Karl Bertau worked closely with the creative team. Others on the team included Oskar Geidner (current museum director), Hartmut Beck, and Dietmar Peschel-Rentsch.
4   Work for this chapter was originally published previously in my article "Performing Medieval Literature and/as History: The Museum of Wolframs-Eschenbach," in Karl Fugelso (ed.), *Defining Neo Medievalisms (II). Studies in Medievalism XX* (Cambridge: D.S. Brewer, 2011), pp. 147–170.
5   Lange-Greve describes these challenges to display (*Nichtausstellbarkeit*) as a result of the relative immateriality of literature (*Ungegenständlichkeit*) and an inability to translate literature into concrete visualizations; literature and visualization seemed unreconcilable (*Unvereinbarkeit von Literatur und Visualisierung*). Susanne Lange-Greve, *Die kulturelle Bedeutung von Literaturausstellungen: Konzepte, Analysen und Wirkungen literturmusealer Präsentation: mit einem Anhang zum wissenschaftlichen Wert von Literaturmuseen* (Olms-Weidmann: Hildesheim, Zürich, 1995), pp. 91–92. Both Lange-Greve and Wehnert see new museums in the 1990s emerging despite Barthel's claim about literature's *Unausstellbarkeit*—that the idea of literature was too abstract for display. They see the task of the literature museum as critical and interpretive, engaging in dialogue and facilitating communication. See Stefanie Wehnert, *Literaturmuseen im Zeitalter der neuen Medien: Leseumfeld-Aufgaben-didaktische Konzepte* (Ludwig: Kiel, 2002), p. 188.
6   Geidner et al., *Museum Wolfram von Eschenbach*, p. 1.
7   Gottfried von Strassburg, *Tristan*, vol. 1 (Stuttgart: Reclam, 1984), v. 4638–4641 and 4665–4666.
8   Kugler, "Lokale und regionale Wolfram-Verehrung," 818–834, p. 827.
9   https://www.wolframs-eschenbach.de/Home.html (accessed January 29, 2019).
10 The Nibelung Museum in Worms functions similarly. As we shall see in Chapter 4, because of the nature of the narratives it puts on display, the Nibelung Museum dedicates more of its exhibits to the reception of the *Nibelungenlied* and the Nibelung myth, rather than the *Nibelungenlied* or the legend itself in the way that we see the Museum Wolfram von Eschenbach offer detailed analyses of Wolfram's individual works.
11 Geidner et al., *Museum Wolfram von Eschenbach*, 1. Kugler finds open explanations alongside hidden answers to questions that visitors will seek (Kugler, p. 828).
12 Geidner et al., *Museum Wolfram von Eschenbach*, p. 5.
13 Reviewers also comment on the blue color as the blue of a night sky, highlighting the metaphor of the new "world" of Wolfram von Eschenbach or the medieval "cosmos." The blue also evokes for some an atmosphere of mystery, since not much is known about Wolfram the person. The cobalt blue in this room also enhances the cathedral-like atmosphere, recalling the vivid blue typical of medieval stained glass. Blue may also serve here as a symbol of the medieval; the twelfth and thirteenth

centuries see the color become much more prominent in painting, clothing, and heraldry. See Michel Pastourneau, *Blue. The History of a Color* (Princeton and Oxford: Princeton University Press, 2001), p. 49. Also see Victoria Finlay, *The Brilliant History of Color in Art* (Los Angeles: The J. Paul Getty Museum, 2014).

14 Geidner et al., *Museum Wolfram von Eshenbach*, p. 1.
15 Ibid., p. 25.
16 It is worth quoting the German original here to show how the museum highlights the word "I" in all capital letters, making Wolfram's statement all the more emphatic: "Jede edle Dame von Verstand und Ehre—ICH bin mir sicher!—die dies als Buch geschrieben sieht, wird mir zugeben: mehr Gutes weiß ICH von Damen zu sagen, als ICH boshaft von einer im Lied einmal sang (Geidner et al., *Museum Wolfram von Eschenbach*, p. 8).
17 Ibid., p. 8.
18 Ibid., p. 6.
19 Want had brought hunger's need upon them. They had no cheese, meat, nor bread. They had no truck with toothpicks, nor did they grease the wind with their lips when they drank. Their bellies were sunken, their hips high and thin; the skin about their ribs was shriveled like a Hungarian's leather (*Parzival*, 184, 7–19; Edwards, p. 79).
20 Rarely did the tankard or the jug spill over with mean there; a Trühendingen frying pan seldom shrieked with doughnuts—for them that note was out of key! (*Parzival*, 184, 22–26; Edwards, p. 79). The words in this passage, the Count of Wertheim, a possible patron of Wolfram's, as well as the regional doughnuts (the castle of Hohentrühendingen is not far from Eschenbach), are often cited as evidence of Wolfram's origin.
21 da heime in mîn selbes hûs
  dâ wirt gefreut vil selten mûs.
  wan diu müese ir spîse steln:
  die dörfte niemen vor mir heln:
  ine vinde ir offenlîche niht.
  alze dicke daz geschiht
  mir Wolfram von Eschenbach,
  daz ich dulte alsolch gemach. (*Parzival*, 185, 1–8)
22 As the museum guide states, Wolfram explicitly says four times ("mit unbescheidenem Ich," p. 12) that he hails from a place called Eschenbach: *Parzival*, 114, 12; 185, 7; 827, 13; and Wolfram von Eschenbach, *Willehalm. Nach der Handschrift 857 der Stiftsbibliothek St. Gallen* Joachim Heinzle (ed.) (Tubingen: Max Niemeyer, 1994), p. 4, 19.
23 A small "note" on the map that explains the image on it—the map. There is a very short history of the town, observing that most of the places Wolfram mentions in his texts can be found in a radius of about fifty kilometers (as the crow flies) around the

town formerly known as Obereschenbach—this is the town that was, in 1917, renamed Wolframs-Eschenbach (Geidner et al., *Museum Wolfram von Eschenbach*, p. 13).

24 As mayor Anton Seitz notes: "Hier ist kein Detail dem Zufall überlassen." (*Schwäbische Donauzeitung*, January 7, 1995).

25 Geidner et al., *Museum Wolfram von Eschenbach*, p. 1.

26 The heading for this section is "The whole world told tales of Arthur." In a description of the Round Table, we find the joy of spring: "At the Round Table great joy reigns, wherever Arthur is there is splendid Pentecost weather, spring, fertility" (Geidner et al., *Museum Wolfram von Eschenbach*, p. 20).

27 "Sag mir doch, wer die Ritter erschafft?" "Das tut König Artus aus eigener Kraft." These are the knights that Parzival first mistook for God as they rode through the isolated waste land of Soltane, where Parzival's mother had raised him following the death of his father, far from the perils of court (*Parzival*, 123, 6–7).

28 Geidner et al., *Museum Wolfram von Eschenbach*, p. 25. *Parzival*, 379, 3–8:
Waz mag ich nu sprechen mêr?
Wan Poydiconjunz was hêr:
der reit dar zuo mit solher kraft,
wær Swarzwalt ieslich stûde ein schaft,
man dorft dâ niht mêr waldes sehn,
swer sîne schar wolde spehn.

29 The museum guide quotes the three sections from *Parzival* (379, 3–8), *Titurel* (31, 1–4), and *Willehalm* (389, 20–390, 8) that contain this phrase and this image (Geidner et al., *Museum Wolfram von Eschenbach*, p. 25). The citation from Parzival refers to a battle scene from book VII, in which Wolfram describes the approach of the knight Poydiconjunz.

30 On the "snowy" ground, the tracks are also an oblique reference to the three drops of blood from book VI of *Parzival* that mesmerize the hero by reminding him of his absent beloved (282, 20–283, 19).

31 This is Wolfram's message in the prologue to *Parzival*, 1, 15–19. This is also the substance, once again, of Gottfried's critique of Wolfram. For Gottfried, Wolfram is the inventor of wild haphazard tales; for Wolfram, the tale most worth telling is the one that takes a circuitous route, or at least not straight.

32 Geidner et al., *Museum Wolfram von Eschenbach*, p. 1.

33 Ibid., p. 26.

34 After Parzival defeats Segramors at the beginning of book VI, although Parzival remains captivated by the drops of blood in the snow, Segramors attempts to justify his loss by suggesting that one cannot always win at this game: "You have heard much of how chivalry is dice-play, and if a man falls by the joust—well…." (er sprach, ir habt des vreischet vil,/ritterschaft ist tolpelspil,/unt daz ein man von tjoste viel … *Parzival*, 289, 23–25; Edwards, 92). Other examples of the "game" metaphor abound.

35 On each wall, the designers have chosen to represent thematic clusters of what they consider the most important concepts of Parzival's life and story. The cluster "you and I" highlights Parzival's reunion with his brother in book XVI, but actually shows a trio—Parzival, Feirefiz, Condwiramurs—as husband, brother, and wife represent family past and present and future). There is the theme of murder, notably referring to Parzival's unchivalrous murder of his relative, the red knight Ither, when he comes to Arthur's court the first time; Red and White (Blood and Snow) demonstrate the love that Parzival has for his wife, the beautiful Condwiramurs, whose likeness he recalls when he sees drops of blood in the winter snow; when he is lost in thought, he defeats two opponents without coming out of his trance. Simplicity refers to the way in which Parzival has acted out of false understanding. The cluster that includes clan, (maternal) uncle and nephew reminds us of how we are all related. Finally, Black and White (Hell and Heaven) recalls the image of the magpie from *Parzival*'s prologue. The museum asks: "where would there be people, who are entirely black or entirely white?" (Geidner et al., *Museum Wolfram von Eschenbach*, p. 27).

36 Herzeloyde was sent out from Munsalvaesche into the courtly world to marry King Castis. Her brothers are the Grail king Anfortas and the hermit Trevrizent; her sisters are Schoysiane, the mother of Parzival's cousin Sigune (whose story is told in both *Parzival* and *Titurel*), and the Grail keeper Repanse de Schoye.

37 Geidner et al., *Museum Wolfram von Eschenbach*, p. 31.

38 The boldface print is part of the presentation in the museum guide (Geidner et al., *Museum Wolfram von Eschenbach*, pp. 31–32).

39 He came that evening to a lake. There huntsmen had moored—to them those waters were subject. When they saw him riding up, they were so close to the shore that they could clearly hear all he said. There was one man he saw in the boat who wore such clothing that even if all lands served him, it could be no better. His hat was trimmed with peacock feathers. This same fisherman he asked for information—that he might advise him, by God's favor and his courtesy's command, where he might find lodging (Wolfram von Eschenbach, *Parzival*, 225, 2-19; Edwards, p. 72).

40 "Go and take the sun's hatred with you!" said the squire. "You are a goose! If only you'd opened your gob and questioned the host! It has cost you much fame." (Wolfram von Eschenbach, *Parzival*, 247, 26-30; Edwards, p. 79).

41 Geidner et al., *Museum Wolfram von Eschenbach*, p. 33.

42 One or two examples from each will serve to illustrate. The symbol (stone, Grail, king) is repeated with each statement about it or its significance for the narrative: The stone is also called a thing (Ding); the stone calls its servants when they are children. The Grail castle is called Munsalvaesche; knights of the Grail carry the dove into battle; knights of the Grail are a brotherhood. The king of the Grail is called Anfortas; the king of the Grail suffers from a wound that cannot be healed;

the wound turns to ice when Saturn is at its zenith; the king of the Grail was disappointed by the one who came and did not ask the question (Geidner et al., *Museum Wolfram von Eschenbach*, p. 33).

43 Geidner et al., *Museum Wolfram von Eschenbach*, p. 1.
44 As noted earlier, the museum guide adds a more liberal translation: "Stellt euch vor: Der Schwarzwald! Jeder Baum eine Lanze für Dich, schönes Kind!" (Geidner et al., *Museum Wolfram von Eschenbach*, p. 25).
45 Wolfram von Eschenbach, *Parzival: With Titurel and Love Lyrics*, Cyril Edwards (trans.) (Suffolk, UK and Rochester: D.S. Brewer, 2004), pp. 292–293.
46 Geidner et al., *Museum Wolfram von Eschenbach*, p. 41. The voice in the recording brings the Middle High German original into a somber present: sîne klawen/durh die wolken sint geslagen, er stîget ûf mit grôzer kraft. (Edwards, *Love Lyrics*, p. 289).
47 Geidner et al., *Museum Wolfram von Eschenbach*, p. 1.
48 There is a way in which this room is perhaps the least successful of all of them. It is the least complex in terms of design and structure, dealing with texts that are also not as complex in scope or in language as *Parzival*. The connection of Wolfram's lyrics to modern readers and interpreters is also not quite as compelling.
49 The shields give information about the text: transmission, main themes, structure, historical background, precedents, a few quotations (that quite possibly gave the designers some ideas on how to structure the display); the museum guide offers a translation with the references to *Willehalm*: Over the earth a day of great loss appeared and the sky was alight with a special glow (*Willehalm* 14, 8–10); such knightly deeds were done that, if one were to name them properly, one would have to call them murder (*Willehalm* 10, 18–20).
50 Geidner et al., *Museum Wolfram von Eschenbach*, p. 1.
51 Geidner spoke with me about this for my essay on the Museum Wolfram von Eschenbach. Alexandra Sterling-Hellenbrand, "Performing Medieval Literature and/as History: The Museum of Wolframs-Eschenbach," in Karl Fugelso (ed.), *Defining Neo Medievalisms (II). Studies in Medievalism XX* (Cambridge: D.S. Brewer, 2011), 147–170, p. 163.
52 Such generosity could be seen among the noble heathens who served as carpet for the horses, even as their cudgels wreaked havoc on the other side (Geidner et al., *Museum Wolfram von Eschenbach*, p. 45). Wolfram says: "des under der getouften diet/vil maneger von dem leben schiet." Many of those among the baptized departed this life (*Willehalm* 20, 29–30).
53 "Die Zungen vieler Sprachen hatten dort viel Klagenswertes zu beklagen und zu Hause Unglück zu berichten Ist es Sünde, wenn man sie wie Vieh erschlägt, die nie von der Taufe gehört haben? Ich sage euch, es ist große Sünde. Es ist alles Gottes Schöpfung, alle zweiund siebzig Völker, die ER erhält." The museum guide cites *Willehalm* here (450, 12–20); Geidner et al., *Museum Wolfram von Eschenbach*, p. 47.
54 Geidner et al., *Museum Wolfram von Eschenbach*, p. 25. *Willehalm* 389.20–390.8.

55 Kugler, "Lokale und regionale Wolfram-Verehrung," p. 828 ("halbidentisch mit einem Türquerbalken").

56 Wolfram's works were adapted, continued, and imitated for centuries. Wolfram himself became the object of works of art as well. Because his works were so demanding, he remained fascinating for all areas of research (Geidner et al., *Museum Wolfram von Eschenbach*, p. 1).

57 Poet Ulrich von Liechtenstein mentions one such tournament in a poem from 1240, in which the narrator and his opponents play King Arthur and the knights of the Round Table.

58 Geidner et al., *Museum Wolfram von Eschenbach*, p. 1.

59 Holger Noltze, "Wolfram hinterlies keine Spur," *Frankfurter Allgemeine Zeitung*, 15.10.1994, Nr. 240, S. 35.

60 In a 2008 conversation, director Geidner said they took much from American concepts of interactive display in the 1990s when they were discussing the plans for the museum. The designers needed and wanted to make a museum that anyone could take something away from, even if they only have an interest in perhaps finding out more about the Middle Ages or the poet Wolfram. All the texts in the museum should take only about two hours to read in total, as that is about as much time as any average visitor will take for the museum. See Sterling-Hellenbrand, "Performing Literature and/as History."

61 Diepeveen and Van Laar contend that "art-making is social action," which implies "the connectedness of artworks and artists to other things," and they argue that this interconnectedness is "essential to understanding art and its conflicts." See Timothy Van Laar and Leonard Diepeveen, *Active Sights. Art as Social Interaction* (Mountain View, CA: Mayfield Publishing, 1998), p. 109.

62 Ibid., p. 110.

63 Noltze, "Wolfram hinterließ keine Spur."

64 Kugler, "Lokale und regionale Wolfram-Verehrung," p. 828.

65 Hans Robert Jauß, *Alterität und Modernität der mittelalterlichen Literatur. Gesammelte Aufsätze 1956–1976* (München: Wilhelm Fink Verlag, 1977), p. 11. We will revisit this sentiment in Chapter 6, as both the Museum Wolfram von Eschenbach and the Nibelung Museum participate in this process of active understanding—this is integral to their practice of medievalism through display.

66 Müller and Wunderlich, "The Modern Reception of the Arthurian Legend," 303–324, p. 303.

67 One still cannot escape the influence of Wagner in the concept of *Gesamtkunstwerk* frequently applied to the museum; however, the museum deftly manages to free its subject matter (Wolfram's texts) from that long shadow.

68 One will notice on the comment board comments like "Einfach fantastisch" (simply fantastic), "Danke für Esprit und große Mühe" (Thank you for wit and great effort), and "Weitermachen!" ("Keep it up!").

69　The regional edition of the *Süddeutsche Zeitung* (SZ) comments on the fact that Wolframs-Eschenbach has been overshadowed by other more popular and more well-known tourist sites in the area ("Längst ist Wolframs-Eschenbach nicht mehr so bedeutend. Wie viele andere Orte im westlichen Mittelfranken liegt es touristisch eher im Schatten bekannterer Ziele." Visitors are mainly hikers or cyclists or vacationers in the nearby lake district. ("Wanderer kommen hier vorbei, Radlfahrer und die Gäste, die im Fränkischen Seenland Urlaub machen.") Katja Auer, SZ Regionalausgabe, 29.09.2015, Ausgabe München West.

70　"Bunte Erlebniswelt statt dröger Texttafeln," *Nürnberger Nachrichten*, 27.05.2011, S. 27/ TIPPS ZUM WOCHENENDE, https://www.genios.de/document/NN__0C5C D863E1C13E4DC125789D0009E949 (accessed January 18, 2016).

71　Daniel Staffen-Quandt, Literatur in kleinen Häppchen serviert, *Mittelbayerische Zeitung*, 20.01.2015, https://www.genios.de/document/MIB__C8FFE42F 685D66375BB7FF2725792F9C-SCHWANDORF (accessed January 18, 2016).

72　*Nürnberger Nachrichten*, "Der Welt ist ein weiteres Heimatmuseum mit vergilbten Urkunden und alten Feuerwehreimern erspart geblieben."

73　Staffen-Quandt, "Auch knapp 20 Jahre nach der Eröffnung wirkt das Museum noch immer konzeptionell modern - auch wenn es keine Touch-Screens oder andere technischen Spielereien gibt."

74　Staffen-Quandt comments that everything is "bite-sized" pieces ("Alles ist in kleine Häppchen aufgeteilt, kein Text hat mehr als fünf Sätze").

75　I remain very grateful to a vigorous discussion about this aspect of the museum that occurred at the International Arthurian Studies conference at the University of Bristol (Bristol UK) in July 2011.

76　The report in the *Nürnberger Nachrichten* (2011) compares the Museum Wolfram von Eschenbach favorably with other museums where the emphasis would clearly be on more text that would perhaps be perceived as too much effort. The operative word is "experience" ("erleben"). The report continues by saying that the museum welcomes guests with all senses. The answer to the museums' question "Kann man Literatur ausstellen?" is, for this reporter, "please come in" ("Bitte eintreten") and we can see for ourselves.

77　Museum director Geidner also tells Staffen-Quandt that the museum's goals will have been achieved if visitors leave the museum admitting that Wolfram certainly was interesting even if the visitors did not understand everything in the museum. "Die Dauerausstellung holt die Besucher bei null ab, bietet aber auch Fachkundigen noch Interessantes" (Staffen-Quandt).

78　Katja Auer, "Wissenswertes," *SZ Regionalausgabe*, 11.08.2015, Ausgabe München West.

79　As Muschg puts it, Wolfram does not really need Wolframs-Eschenbach for validation of his importance for the history of German language and literature;

similarly, those who make use of his narrative and his work are not necessarily located in Wolframs-Eschenbach. Thus, Muschg chooses an apt description of the place (the museum and the town) as the "Abdruck einer Spur, die hier nicht gefunden, sondern geschaffen wurde" (the outline of a trace, that wasn't found but rather created here). See Muschg, "Abdruck einer Spur," pp. 2–5.
80 Biddick, *The Shock of Medievalism*, p. 84.
81 Kugler, "Lokale und regionale Wolfram-Verehrung," p. 828.

Chapter 4

1 *Das Nibelungenlied*. The translation is by Edwards: The most perfect thing that lay among the treasures was a little rod of gold. A man who had learned its secrets might easily be master over every man in the world. Many of Albrich's kinsfolk left along with Gernot. *The Nibelungenlied: The Lay of the Nibelungs*, Cyril Edwards (trans. and ed.) (Oxford: Oxford University Press, 2010), p. 105.
2 *Das Buch des anonymen Dichters. Museumsführer* (Worms: A+H/ Nibelungenmuseum, 2001), p. 29.
3 One could argue that Wolfram is similarly anonymous, since we have no trace of him except his writings (regardless of how fervently we wish to believe who he was and where he lived). Wolfram, however, bursts out of his narratives with a strong personality that seems to define itself despite the absence of biographical documentation. The Nibelung Museum decides to create such a persona for its poet.
4 The *Nibelungenlied* remains anonymous, despite numerous attempts to identify the poet.
5 Ulrike Schäfer, Rhein-Main Presse, *Allgemeine Zeitung*, 22.07.2011, https://www.genios.de:443/document/MAZ__36544480001311285600 (accessed November 22, 2015) ("weil das der Vorstellung der Menschen von Mittelalter am ehesten entspreche"). It was also a part of the city in need of revitalization.
6 *The Book of the Anonymous Poet*, 7.
7 In the first place, manuscripts are expensive and rare. Furthermore, not far down the Rhine in Karlsruhe, the state museum of Baden-Wuerttemberg had recently acquired the *Nibelungenlied* manuscript known as C.
8 Eckhart Kauntz, "An der Wormser Stadtmauer ein Platz für die Nibelungen?" *Frankfurter Allgemeine Zeitung* (06.03.1998, Nr. 55, S. 13), https://www.genios.de:443/document/FAZ__F19980306WORMS--100 (accessed November 22, 2015).
9 Heiland made two further arguments in favor of the literary museum at the city wall in 1998. The architectural foundations of the wall would not be affected by the new construction, and finally the project was planned for an area of the city

slated for renovation/renewal and therefore the financing of the project would be much easier to manage. The state would assume 70 percent of the costs, where the remainder would likely come from income as a result of the sale of previously renovated buildings. See Eckhart Kauntz, "An der Wormser Stadtmauer ein Platz für die Nibelungen?" *Frankfurter Allgemeine Zeitung*, 06.03.1998, Nr. 55, S. 13. See also Gottfried Knapp, "Gute Minne zum virtuellen Spiel. Das 'Nibelungen-Museum' in Worms lässt ein deutsches Stück Weltliteratur wieder aufleben," *Süddeutsche Zeitung*, 20.08.2001.

10 It was called an ambitious project ("ein ehrgeiziges Projekt," "Mit Siegfried in virtuellen Welten," 02.04.1998) or an expensive ditch ("Millionen-Grab," *Wormser Zeitung*, 10.12.1998). A referendum was held with local elections in June 1999 ("Bürgerentscheid") and almost stopped the process; however, though a majority of the votes were against the museum, a quorum of voters was not reached and therefore the resistance could not halt the project (*Wormser Zeitung*, 13.09.1999; *Frankfurter Rundschau*, 21.08.2011). Ground was officially broken for construction in 1999.

11 Ulrike Schäfer, *Wormser Zeitung*, 22.07.2011, http://www.wormser-zeitung.de/region/worms/meldungen/print_10972914.htm. Another summary of the controversy in August 2011 was entitled "Zehn Jahre Nibelungenmuseum in Worms—Rückblick auf eine Kontroverse" (Johannes Götzen, *Wormser Zeitung*, 17.08.2011, http://www.wormser-zeitung.de/region/worms/kultur/11063015.htm.)

12 Sharon Macdonald. "Museum Europe," 47–65, p. 60.

13 *Book of the Anonymous Poet*, 8.

14 Ibid.

15 Given the potentially problematic nature of the material, the design team was well chosen particularly because it was a French design firm that won the competition. As a result, they could offer fresh perspectives on the material, and they would not perhaps have been as burdened by history as a German team might have been.

16 The treasure is the motor of the story, the scepter is the motor of the treasure and its power, to continue accumulating images, hopes and desires. *Das Buch des anonymen Dichters. Museumsführer* (Worms: A+H/Nibelungenmuseum, 2001), p. 79.

17 *Book of the Anonymous Poet*, p. 8.

18 *Stuttgarter Zeitung*, 20.08.2001.

19 The *Süddeutsche Zeitung* puns on the museum's ability to deal with this lack of material and the subject of it: it has not a single object on display but it makes an opportunity out of its need ("Not")—indeed out of the Nibelungs sorrow ("Der Nibelungen Nôt")—and places the literary work in the middle of its museal project.

20 *Stuttgarter Zeitung*, 20.08.2001.

21 Thomas Wolff, "Siegfried, verzweifelt gesucht," *Frankfurter Rundschau Magazin-Reisen*, 11.08.2001.

22 Peter Iden, "Was sind und sagen und die Nibelungen? Worms präsentiert in der ausgebauten Stadtmauer eine erstaunliche Einlassung auf das Epos des 12. Jahrhunderts." *Frankfurter Rundschau*, 21.08.2001.
23 *Book of the Anonymous Poet*, p. 9.
24 The reviewer for the *Süddeutsche Zeitung* imagines the congestion that would result from school field trips.
25 Need update on equipment—new audio guides on iPods, with two tracks: one for kids and one for adults.
26 The poet is voiced by German actor Mario Adorf, who, voices the poet in the audio guide, was slated to play the role of Hagen in the 2002 Nibelungen Festspiele in Worms. The narrative of the guide is based on a text by German medievalist Joachim Heinzle, whose extensive scholarship on the Nibelung myth is evident in the museum as well.
27 The use of modern media for the presentation is the common thread running through the installation. Various languages available in the audioguide; in addition, the museum guide/book is available in English and German and French. The book reproduces the script of the audio guide.
28 Some of the critics mention glitches with the guides and the sensors, which in 2001 could not be controlled by the listener. The sensors and the tape were automatic. The issues that were originally noted are now less of a problem because the iPod technology is no longer dependent on a sensor that can be finicky and unreliable. The basic script has not changed, however. And the constraints of the space remain, so there is not much else one can tinker with in terms of improving the museum. This is a very confined and restricted permanent exhibit, leaving little room for special or rotating exhibitions.
29 For NZZ (*Neue Zürcher Zeitung*) reviewer Seifert, this strategy had the effect of a school amateur ("Schulfunk-Gestus"). Heribert Seifert, "Hörturm und Schatzkammer. In Worms wurde ein Nibelungenmuseum eröffnet," 19.09.2001, *Neue Zürcher Zeitung*, S.62.
30 Wolff, "Siegfried, verzweifelt gesucht."
31 *The Book of the Anonymous Poet*, p. 31.
32 Ibid., p. 31.
33 From Cologne, this is the story of friendly little gnomes who take care of tasks for the city's laborers (butchers, carpenters, bakers, cobblers, tailors) unseen while all are asleep. All is well until a tailor's wife becomes curious and tries to catch them at work one night. They never come back.
34 Volker Gallé (ed.), *Siegfried. Schmied und Drachentöter* (Worms: Worms-Verlag, 2005), p. 5.
35 *The Book of the Anonymous Poet*, p. 44. This is the translation in the guide. The term "appropriation" might be a better translation of "Vereinnahmung" in the original.

36 This element recalls the work of memory in medieval texts, as discussed in Chapter 1. The simultaneity of images and the need to discern among them on multiple planes would have been entirely acceptable and "normal" for a medieval audience: the act of memory facilitated by images that encourage the words to be "en-acted." The design of the museum wants the images to become physical, to become somatic, to become action. This offers another mechanism for past presencing; it is how the "join" functions.
37 *Book of the Anonymous Poet*, p. 10.
38 The reviewer in the *Frankfurter Rundschau* commented on the contrasts evident in the combination of the material from the old saga with cutting-edge new technology. The contrast is not always productive, leading to an irritating distance rather then proximity.
39 Wolff, "Siegfried verzweifelt gesucht," calls the Sehturm, and by extension the museum, a puzzle of fragments ("ein Puzzle aus Fragmenten"). The reviewer praises the way in which the museum encourages visitors to put the legend together for themselves in a way that is highly entertaining ("höchst unterhaltsam").
40 *Book of the Anonymous Poet*, p. 11.
41 Ibid., pp. 30 and 42.
42 Ibid., p. 33.
43 Ibid., p. 38.
44 Ibid., p. 47. Of course, the museum designers are themselves also creating a new fiction as they attempt to lay out the fictions of the Nibelung reception for the viewer/listener.
45 *Book of the Anonymous Poet*, p. 10.
46 Ibid., p. 10.
47 *Book of the Anonymous Poet*, p. 81.
48 In 2015, the museum renumbered the stations in the *Hörturm* in order to make the order more user-friendly. In the original version, which is still evident in the guidebook, the stations followed a strictly chronological and unidirectional format. Once one reached the map in the room at the top of the tower, the stations were at an end and visitors were directed to the last installation in the lowest level. One can see, though, how difficult it is to make even such small changes. In 2015, the plaques still had the original numbering on them; the guidebook has the same order as well, while the audio guide could more easily be reorganized because it was electronic. And they could attach different numbers to the displays. But not much more can be changed without distorting the display. There is very little room, if at all, for the museum to grow and change like a living museum should do.
49 Modern audiences will lack the immediate recognition they experience when looking at a visual quote from Disney's *Sleeping Beauty* or the image of Luke Skywalker.
50 *Book of the Anonymous Poet*, p. 81.

51 *Book of the Anonymous Poet*, pp. 81–82.
52 The fictive poet of the Nibelung Museum relates the story behind the image of Gunnar in the pit of snakes playing the harp with his feet. "The sculptor, who was alive whilst I was writing the *Nibelungenlied*, also illustrated the story of Siegfried and the Burgundians on a series of medallions. You could say they are reminiscent of modern cartoons, like *Mickey Mouse* and *Asterix* (yes, I did quite a bit of research about the modern world before speaking to you.) Only the balloons are missing" (*Book of the Anonymous Poet*, p. 69).
53 Again, the physical need to move vertically from one "plane" of the story to another is quite thoughtprovoking, offering a moment for reflection and distance from the subject material.
54 *The Mythenlabor* is the next generation of the treasure chamber, demonstrating the ways in which the museum has adapted to audience feedback over the first ten years of its existence.
55 *Book of the Anonymous Poet*, p. 12.
56 This is in the Boston Digital Industry May 2001 edition. An electronic copy of the article is available at http://km2.net/aplush/nibelungenmuseum/presse/bdi.jpg (accessed January 29, 2019).
57 Shirin Sojitrawalla, "Nebelheim," *Die Zeit*, 35/2001, http://www.zeit.de/2001/35/Nebelheim (accessed January 31, 2019).
58 Peter Thomas, "Der virtuelle Schatz von Worms. Nibelungenmuseum: Multimediale Momentaufnahmen eines Mythos," *Darmstädter Echo*, 20.08.2001.
59 Christine Dirigo, "Den Museumsbesuch zum Erlebnis machen—Ulrike Standke vom Nibelungenmuseum ist Mittlerin zwischen Wissenschaft und Gästen/Pläne für das 'Mythenlabor'," *Bürstädter Zeitung*, 01.11.2008/Lokales, https://www.genios.de:443/document/BUER__1987282170001225494000 (accessed November 22, 2015).
60 Johannes Götzen, "Die richtige Richtung," *Wormser Zeitung*, 01.10.2008/Lokales, https://www.genios.de:443/document/WORZ__1972141210001222812000 (accessed November 22, 2015).
61 From the beginning, the Nibelung Museum was planned as a multimedia museum and this concept would be realized with the new "Mythenlabor." Johannes Götzen, "Wandlungsfähiger, moderner Klassiker—Mythenlabor als Ersatz für die Schatzkammer unter dem Nibelungenmuseum eröffnet," *Wormser Zeitung*, 11.10.2008/Lokales, https://www.genios.de:443/document/WORZ__1976800170001223676000 (accessed November 22, 2015).
62 Museum director Olaf Mückain spoke of the museum as a "classic" capable of change, one that would fit well in the contemporary museum landscape of Worms. Johannes Götzen, "Wandlungsfähiger, moderner Klassiker."
63 Johannes Götzen, "Bürgerforum: Museum ist Kostengrab," *Wormser Zeitung*, 04.10.2008/Lokales, https://www.genios.de:443/document/WORZ__1973388810001223071200 (accessed November 22, 2015).

64 Johannes Götzen, "Europäische Mythen statt Schätze—Nibelungenmuseum weiht neuen Raum ein/Besucher können dort Erlebtes vertiefen," *Wormser Zeitung*, 01.10.2008/Lokales, https://www.genios.de:443/document/WORZ__1972141050001222812000 (accessed November 22, 2015).
65 Müller, Susanne, "Ausstellungsstücke zum Anfassen—Wie Geschichte buchstäblich begreifbar wird," *Wormser Zeitung*, 31.01.2009/Lokales, https://www.genios.de:443/document/WORZ__2026669850001233356400 (accessed November 22, 2015).
66 Ulrike Schäfer, "Statt Videoschau ein Mythenlabor. Neues im Nibelungenmuseum," Ein Artikel zum Vortrag, *Wormser Zeitung*, 30.07.2007, http://www.nibelungenlied-gesellschaft.de/03_beitrag/eichfelder/fs07_eichf.html (accessed May 29, 2018).
67 Ibid., p. 38.
68 This is opposed to tangible heritage, which "considers the locality as a dimension without it being subject to it in a definitive or durable way." Ahmed Skounti, "The Authentic Illusion Humanity's Intangible Cultural Heritage, the Moroccan Experience," in Laurajane Smith and Natsuko Akagawa (eds.), *Intangible Heritage* (New York and London: Routledge, 2008), 74–92, p. 75.
69 Barbara Kirshenblatt-Gimblett, "Intangible Heritage as Metacultural Production," *Museum international* 56.1–2 (2004): 52–65.

Chapter 5

1 "Wissenschaftlich streng und doch verspielt, aktualisierungs- und anspielungslustig, didaktisch, pathetisch, voll tiefem Witz … ein Mini-Gesamtkunstwerk … ein Literaturmuseum eigener Art." Tobias Gohlis, "Der Ritter mit der Leier," *Die Zeit*, July 1996. Translation mine, https://www.genios.de/document/ZEIT__02960914986NX%7CZEIA__02960914986NX (accessed January 28, 2019).
2 Elizabeth Crooke, *Museums and Community. Ideas, Issues and Challenges* (London and New York: Routledge, 2007), p. 13. Crooke sees museums as integral to a community's sense of identity; museum and heritage become "a means of communication and governance," p. 137.
3 Keith Basso, *Wisdom Sits in Places. Landscape and Language among the Western Apache* (Albuquerque: University of New Mexico Press, 1996), p. 107.
4 Adolf Muschg, "Abdruck einer Spur," 2–5, p. 3. Translation mine.
5 Gohlis, "Der Ritter mit der Leier." Translation mine.
6 I am rather freely adapting Jeffrey Jerome Cohen's comment on the nature of things (objects) in time and over in his short afterword on "Intertemporality" to *Cultural Studies of the Modern Middle Ages*. Cohen says: "Every object is therefore a temporal archive, a repository for multiple parts and a trigger for unanticipated

futures." The museums become objects themselves as archives of intertexts that have accumulated over time. Jeffrey Jerome Cohen, "Intertemporality," in Eileen A. Joy, Myra J. Seaman, Kimberly Bell, and Mary K. Ramsey (eds.), *Cultural Studies of the Modern Middle Ages* (New York and Basingstoke: Palgrave Macmillan, 2007), 295–300, p. 297.

7 Francis G. Gentry and Ulrich Müller suggest four following models of medieval reception:

"(1) the productive, i.e., creative reception of the Middle Ages; (2) the reproductive reception of the Middle Ages: the original form of medieval works is reconstructed in a manner viewed as 'authentic,' as in musical productions or renovations (for example, paintings and monuments) (3) the academic reception of the Middle Ages; (4) the political-ideological reception of the Middle Ages: medieval works, themes, 'ideas' or persons are used and 'reworked' for political purposes." I have to thank one of the anonymous reviewers for commenting that I might perhaps suggest a new category. The museums in *Medieval Literature on Display* certainly demonstrate characteristics of each type of reception here. In that regard, for purposes of this study, we might call it adaptive reception. Gentry and Müller, "The Reception of the Middle Ages in Germany," p. 401.

8 Horst Brunner, *Wolfram von Eschenbach. Auf den Spuren der Dichter und Denker durch Franken* (Gunzenhausen: Schrenk-Verlag, 2010), p. 55.

9 Volker Gallé (ed.), *Siegfried. Schmied und Drachentöter* (Worms: Worms-Verlag, 2005), p. 5.

10 This would be an aspect of what Andrew Elliott calls "banal medievalism." Andrew B.R. Elliott, *Medievalism, Politics, and Mass Media: Appropriating the Middle Ages in the Twenty-First Century* (Cambridge: D.S. Brewer, 2017), p. 36.

11 Lisa Lampert, "Race, Periodicity, and the (Neo-) Middle Ages," *Modern Language Quarterly* 65.3 (September 2004): 391–421, p. 392.

12 Muschg, "Abdruck einer Spur," p. 4.

13 Macdonald, *Memorylands*, p. 140.

14 In that respect I would have to agree with Horst Brunner when he suggests that the museum in Wolframs-Eschenbach is much more innovative in its interpretations than the Nibelung Museum. The Nibelung Museum has a different task, however; Wolfram's reception was never as politically laden as that of the Nibelung material.

15 This offers an even more provocative frame for the question that the Museum Wolfram von Eschenbach raises: Can one display literature? (Kann man Literatur ausstellen?). And furthermore, what does "Mittelalterrezeption" have to do with it?

16 Alon Confino, *The Nation as a Local Metaphor: Württemberg, Imperial Germany, and National Memory, 1871–1918* (Chapel Hill, NC: University of North Carolina Press, 1997), p. 134.

17 Confino, p. 153.

18 Steven Hoelscher, "Heritage," in Sharon Macdonald (ed.), *A Companion to Museum Studies* (Oxford: Blackwell, 2006), 198–218, p. 202.
19 The museum proudly touts its 301 square meters of space where one can take a peek into the earlier life of a small farm town ("Einblick in das frühere Leben, Wohnen und Arbeiten in einer kleinen Ackerbürgerstadt"), https://www.merkendorf.de/Tourismus-Freizeit/Sehenswertes/Museen.html (accessed January 30, 2019).
20 There are over sixty museums listed on the website for the association of museums in western central Franconia (Museumsland Westmittelfranken), http://www.museumsland.de/ (accessed January 30, 2019).
21 Macdonald, *Memorylands*, pp. 136–149.
22 There are other public displays in Wolframs-Eschenbach. A literary path leads around the pond just outside the city walls; this path, with several stations, showcases various regional poets with biographical information and passages from texts. A marker in front of the museum honors displaced persons from the Second World War and a memorial on the path around the city commemorates veterans of both world wars. These memorials are relatively recent additions to the memorial landscape in Wolframs-Eschenbach, as though the town wanted to show it was not only interested in medieval fictions. The town has layers of its own history that it needed and wanted to display.
23 John von Düffel sees traces of the myth still visible in Worms through the Nibelung festival and the museum that allow the memory of older times and stories to live again consciously and critically. John von Düffel, "Halbstarke Helden— NIBELUNGENSAGE Das Epos ist auch eine Geschichte, über die man sich herrlich amüsieren kann," *Allgemeine Zeitung. Rhein Main Presse*, 07.11.2015/Report, https://www.genios.de:443/document/MAZ__135185220001446850800 (accessed January 28, 2018).
24 http://www.nibelungen-siegfriedstrasse.de/ (accessed January 28, 2018).
25 https://www.worms.de/de/kultur/nibelungen/?navid=277231315609 (accessed January 28, 2018).
26 Basso, *Wisdom Sits in Places*, p. 107.
27 Basso stresses the importance of place-making and of constructing what he calls place-worlds. The latter provide a means of not only reviving former times but also *revising* them. Basso, p. 6.
28 Edward W. Said, "Invention, Memory, and Place," *Critical Inquiry* 26.2 (Winter, 2000): 175–192, p. 179.
29 Macdonald, *Memorylands*, p. 138.
30 Ibid., p. 139.
31 Peter M. McIsaac and Gabriele Mueller (eds.), "Introduction," in *Exhibiting the German Past: Museums, Film, and Musealization* (Toronto: University of Toronto Press, 2015), p. 9.

32 Mark Rectanus, "Refracted Memory: Museums, Film, and Visual Culture in Urban Space," in Peter M. McIsaac and Gabriele Mueller (eds.), *Exhibiting the German Past* (Toronto: University of Toronto Press, 2015), 42–62, p. 52.
33 McIsaac and Mueller, "Introduction," p. 12.
34 Heritage becomes "an instrument of modernization and mark of modernity, particularly in the form of a museum." Barbara Kirshenblatt-Gimblett, "Intangible Heritage as Metacultural Production," *Museum International* 56.1–2 (2014): 163–174, p. 172.
35 Leonard Diepveen and Timothy Van Laar, *Art with a Difference. Looking at Difficult and Unfamiliar Art* (New York: McGraw-Hill, 2001), p. 11.
36 Crooke, *Museums and Community*, p. 13.
37 Diepeveen and Van Laar. From chapter 1 "Art Museums: Organizers of Culture" in Art with a Difference, p. 21.
38 Museums continue to examine their future in a time when the "storyline of national identity" is being rewritten in the twenty-first century, in the age of globalization. This examination is not new, having begun with the study of museums in the 1970s as social institutions. See Flora Edouwaye S. Kaplan, "Making and Remaking National Identities," in Sharon Macdonald (ed.), *A Companion to Museum Studies* (Oxford: Blackwell, 2006), 152–169, p. 168. See Steven Conn, *Do Museums Still Need Objects?* (Philadelphia: University of Pennsylvania Press, 2010). Conn sees the disappearance of objects in museums corresponding "with the rise of other kinds of activities inside the museum and might prompt some questions about the relationship between those activities—education, recreational, commercial—the objects themselves, and how those relationships have changed over time" (Conn, p. 26).
39 Lara Schöffel, "Nibelungenmuseum als Streitpunkt—BÜRGERHAUSHALT Kontroverse Debatte im Internet über Ausstellungsstätte/Zahlreiche Interessengruppen gebildet," *Wormser Zeitung*, 21.06.2011/Lokales, 26.07.2011, https://www.genios.de:443/document/WORZ__34911390001308607200 (accessed November 22, 2015).
40 See Michaela Weber, "Das begehbare Hörbuch—VERNISSAGE 40 Tablets bringen dem Besucher das Nibelungen-Drama und Richard Wagner nahe," *Allgemeine Zeitung*, 10.11.2015, https://www.genios.de:443/document/MAZ__135382150001447110000 (accessed December 14, 2015).
41 One of the anonymous reviewers remarked that the Nibelung Museum does not itself refer to the Jewish community in Worms, commenting further that exclusion reflects the narrative of "Germania" that the Nibelung museum constructs. I would have to agree. On the other hand, the museums of the city of Worms are all administered by the same unit of the city's cultural affairs office. The Nibelung Museum and the Jewish Museum collaborate often on programming.

42 Julie Sanders, *Adaptation and Appropriation*, 2nd ed. (London and New York: Routledge, 2016), p. 34.
43 Hutcheon, with Siobhan O'Flynn. *A Theory of Adaptation*, p. 173.
44 Erll, *Memory in Culture,* p. 146.
45 Sanders, *Adaptation and Appropriation*, p. 35.
46 Trigg, "Medievalism and Theories of Temporality," pp. 196–210.

Chapter 6

1   Helen Dell, "Nostalgia and Medievalism," 115–126, p. 124.
2   Hans Robert Jauß, *Alterität und Modernität der mittelalterlichen Literatur*, p. 11. (Bedeutsamkeit … ist kein zeitloser, immer schon gegebener Grundbestand, sondern das prozeßhafte, nie abgeschlossene Ergebnis fortschreitender und anreichernder Auslegung, die das textimmanente Sinnpotential im Horizontwandel historischer Lebenswelten immer wieder neu und anders konkretisiert.) Translation from Hans Robert Jauß, "The Alterity and Modernity of Medieval Literature," Timothy Bahti (trans.), *New Literary History* 10.2, *Medieval Literature and Contemporary Theory* (Winter, 1979): 181–229, p. 183.
3   Dinshaw, *How Soon Is Now?*, p. 24.
4   Hutcheon with Siobhan O'Flynn, *A Theory of Adaptation*, p. 139. This is Hutcheon's term on p. 139, which also describes the work of the audience, as "it is the audience who must experience the adaptation *as an adaptation*" (Hutcheon's emphasis, 172).
5   Ibid., p. 15.
6   Ibid., p. 173.
7   Erll, *Memory in Culture*, p. 171.
8   Ibid., p. 147.
9   Ibid., p. 141.
10 Sharon Macdonald, *Difficult Heritage: Negotiating the Nazi Past in Nuremberg and Beyond* (London and New York: Routledge, 2009), p. 7.
11 Tison Pugh and Susan Aronstein (eds.), *The Disney Middle Ages: A Fairy-Tale and Fantasy Past* (New York: Palgrave Macmillan, 2012), p. 16.
12 Kline and Ashton suggest that we "continually create a Middle Ages that we cannot ever retrieve or fully know" but it is more than simply a "palimpsest in the present." See Gail Ashton and Daniel T. Kline (eds.), *Medieval Afterlives in Popular Culture* (New York and Basingstoke: Palgrave Macmillan, 2012), p. 5.
13 Angela Jane Weisl, *The Persistence of Medievalism: Narrative Adventures in Contemporary Culture* (New York and Basingstoke: Palgrave Macmillan, 2003), p. 31.
14 Pugh and Weisel, *Medievalisms*, p. 1.

15 Gustafson believes that museums must provoke: "The more the story is loaded with differences—conflict, dilemma and drama—the more it will open up new perspectives, alternative questions and new imaginings." Brigitte Gustafson, "A Meaning of Places through Stories," *Museum International* 63.1–2 (2012): 63–69, p. 67.
16 Bildhauer, *Filming the Middle Ages*, p. 219.
17 Biddick's "dream-frame" describes this process of reception, which is performative and engaged. Biddick, *The Shock of Medievalism*, p. 84.
18 Kirshenblatt-Gimblett, *Destination Culture*, pp. 7–8.
19 Svetlana Boym, *The Future of Nostalgia* (New York: Basic Books, 2001), p. 15.
20 Ibid., p. 17.
21 Louise D'Arcens, "Laughing in the Face of the Past: Satire and Nostalgia in Medieval Heritage Tourism," *Postmedieval: A Journal of Medieval Cultural Studies* 2 (2011): 155–170, p. 156.
22 Stephanie Trigg, "Walking through Cathedrals: Scholars, Pilgrims, and Medieval Tourists," *New Medieval Literatures* 7 (2005): 9–33.
23 D'Arcens, "Laughing," p. 156.
24 Gundolf Graml, "(Re)mapping the Nation: Sound of Music Tourism and National Identity in Austria, ca. 2000 CE," *Tourist Studies* 4.2 (2004): 137–159, p. 154.
25 Gundolf Graml, "'The Hills Are Alive …:' Sound of Music Tourism and the Performative Construction of Places," *Women in German Yearbook* (2005): 192–214, p. 207.
26 Dinshaw, *How Soon Is Now?*, pp. 4–5.
27 Sharon Macdonald, "Is 'Difficult Heritage' Still 'Difficult'? Why Public Knowledge of Past Perpetration May No Longer Be so Unsettling to Collective Identities," *Museum International* (2015): 6–22, p. 7.
28 Macdonald, *Memorylands*, p. 139.
29 Hoelscher views Nora's sites of memory as "essentially … displays of heritage." See Hoelscher, "Heritage," note 1, pp. 216–217.
30 Macdonald, *Memorylands*, p. 18.
31 Ibid., p. 138.
32 Macdonald, "Museum Europe," p. 61.
33 Gustafson, "A Meaning of Places through Stories," p. 68.
34 *The Book of the Anonymous Poet*, p. 47.
35 Geidner et al. (eds.), *Museum Wolfram von Eschenbach*, p. 27.
36 Macdonald, "Is 'Difficult Heritage' Still 'Difficult'? Why Public Knowledge of Past Perpetration May No Longer Be so Unsettling to Collective Identities," 6–22, p. 14.
37 Ibid., p. 15.
38 Ibid., p. 15.
39 Ibid., p. 7. Macdonald sees "evidence of a fundamental—though far from universal—change underway in how national identity is performed in relation

to troubling pasts" (p. 7). She cites Austria as a significant example of shifting a perception of victim (the occupied) to a more nuanced exploration of complicity.
40 Hoelscher, "Heritage," p. 200.
41 The language of heritage is often old, focusing on preservation and restoration. But concerns are often new/contemporary, as the concerns for preservation reflect the needs of the present generation (Hoelscher, p. 206). Heritage may look old but it is really something new, a mode of cultural production in the present that has recourse to the past. See Kirshenblatt-Gimblett, *Destination Culture*, p. 7.
42 Hoelscher, "Heritage," p. 201.
43 Michaela Fenske, "Making the New by Rebuilding the Old: Histourism in Werben, Germany," *Anthropological Journal of European Cultures* 22.1, THEMATIC FOCUS: History, Heritage and Place-Making (2013): 7–25.
44 Ibid., p. 11. Fenske says further: "By using history as a cultural resource, the people in Werben try to find answers for other small cities that, like them, are situated at the rural peripheries while facing the demands of a globally aware and connected planet" (p. 11).
45 Ibid., p. 13.
46 Ibid., pp. 9–10.
47 Barbara Krug-Richter, "Abenteuer Mittelalter? Zur populären Mittelalter-Rezeption in der Gegenwart," OZV LXIII/112, 2009, Heft 2, 53–75, p. 63.
48 Ibid., p. 73.
49 Krug-Richter sees an arc both back and forward: the Middle Ages ends up in the early twenty-first century where some of the audience had experienced it in the 1980s. It serves as a pool for ideas, myths, and stories, for facts and fictions that widen the horizon for individual experiences while leaving space for individual interpretations (p. 73).
50 Rectanus, "Refracted Memory," 42–62, p. 52.
51 The museums fulfill at least three of Czaplicka's criteria for authenticity: they each have a structural material presence and a specificity of site (the Rathaus in Wolframs-Eschenbach, the Bürgerturm in Worms), as well as a way to engage the imagination. Their "factual augmentation" does not consist of photos or documents in the traditional sense; we find videoclips, images, interpretive, and (to a lesser degree) interactive display. John Czaplicka, "History, Aesthetics, and Contemporary Commemorative Practice in Berlin," *New German Critique Cultural History/Cultural Studies* 65 (Spring/Summer 1995): 155–187, p. 186.
52 Erll, *Memory in Culture*, p. 131.
53 Louise D'Arcens, "Introduction. Medievalism: Scope and Complexity," in *Cambridge Companion to Medievalism* (Cambridge: Cambridge University Press, 2016), p. 6.
54 Macdonald, "Museum Europe," p. 61.
55 Ibid., p. 57.

Bibliography

Primary Texts and Translations

Arthurian Romances, Tales and Lyric Poetry. The Complete Works of Hartmann von Aue, (trans.) Frank Tobin, Kim Vivian, and Richard Lawson (University Park, PA: The Pennsylvania University Press, 2001).

Augustine and Vernon J. Bourke, *Confessions* (Washington: Catholic University of America Press, 1966).

Das Buch des anonymen Dichters. Museumsführer (Worms: A+H/Nibelungenmuseum, 2001).

Das Nibelungenlied. Mittelhochdeutsch. Neuhochdeutsch, (ed.) Ursula Schulze, (trans.) Siegfried Grosse (Stuttgart: Reclam, 2010).

Geidner, Oskar, Hartmut Beck, Karl Bertau, and Dietmar Peschel-Rentsch (eds.), *Museum Wolfram von Eschenbach* (Wolframs-Eschenbach, 1994).

Hartmann von Aue. *Iwein. Text und Übersetzung.* Text der siebenten Ausgabe von G.F. Benecke, K. Lachmann und L. Wolff. Übersetzung und Nachwort von Thomas Cramer (Berlin: De Gruyter, 2001).

Morrison, Toni, *Beloved* (New York: Penguin, 1987).

The Book of the Anonymous Poet. Guide of the Nibelungen Museum (Worms: A+H/Nibelungenmuseum, 2001).

The Nibelungenlied: The Lay of the Nibelungs (trans. and ed.) Cyril Edwards (Oxford: Oxford University Press, 2010).

Wolfram von Eschenbach, *Parzival*, (eds.) Karl Lachmann (Berlin: de Gruyter, 1964).

Wolfram von Eschenbach, *Willehalm. Nach der Handschrift 857 der Stiftsbibliothek St. Gallen*, (ed.) Joachim Heinzle (Tubingen: Max Niemeyer, 1994).

Wolfram von Eschenbach, *Parzival with Titurel and Love Lyrics*, (trans.) Cyril Edwards (Woodbridge and Rochester: D.S. Brewer, 2004).

Wolfram von Eschenbach, *Parzival and Titurel*, (trans.) Cyril Edwards (Oxford: Oxford University Press, 2006).

Secondary Texts

Allaire, Gloria and Regina Psaki (eds), *The Arthur of the Italians. The Arthurian Legend in Medieval Italian Literature and Culture* (Cardiff: University of Wales Press, 2014).

Anderson, Benedict, *Imagined Communities. Reflections on the Origin and Spread of Nationalism*, Revised ed. (London, New York: Verso, 2006).
Andersson, Theodore, *A Preface to the Nibelungenlied* (Stanford: Stanford University Press, 1987).
Ashton, Gail and Daniel T. Kline (eds.), *Medieval Afterlives in Popular Culture* (New York and Basingstoke: Palgrave Macmillan, 2012).
Assmann, Aleida, *Der lange Schatten der Vergangenheit. Erinnerungskultur und Geschichtspolitik*, 2nd ed. (Munich: C.H. Beck, 2014).
Assmann, Aleida and Sebastian Conrad (ed.), *Memory in a Global Age. Discourses, Practices and Trajectories* (New York and Basingstoke: Palgrave Macmillan, 2010).
Assmann, Jan, *Religion and Cultural Memory*, (trans.) Rodney Livingstone (Stanford: Stanford University Press, 2006).
Assmann, Jan and John Czaplicka, "Collective Memory and Cultural Identity," *New German Critique. Cultural History/Cultural Studies* 65 (Spring/Summer 1995), pp. 125–133.
Bakhtin, M.M., *The Dialogic Imagination, Four Essays*, (ed.) Michael Holquist, (trans.) Caryl Emerson and Michael Holquist (Austin and London: University of Texas Press, 1981).
Barclay, David E., "Medievalism and Nationalism in Nineteenth-Century Germany," *Medievalism in Europe. Studies in Medievalism* V (1993), pp. 5–22.
Basso, Keith, *Wisdom Sits in Places. Landscape and Language among the Western Apache* (Albuquerque: University of New Mexico Press, 1996).
Bennewitz, Ingrid, "Das *Nibelungenlied* als Weltkulturerbe," in Andrea Schindler and Andrea Stieldorf (eds.), *WeltkulturerbeN. Formen, Funktionen und Objekte kulturellen Erinnerns im und an das Mittelalter* (Bamberg: University of Bamberg Press, 2015), pp. 35–51.
Berdahl, Daphne, *Where the World Ended: Re-Unification and Identity in the German Borderland* (Berkeley and Los Angeles: University of California Press, 1999).
Bertau, Karl, *Deutsche Literatur im europäischen Mittelalter*, vol. 2, 1195–1220 (München: C.H. Beck, 1973).
Bhabha, Homi, "The World and the Home," *Social Text* (1992), pp. 141–153.
Bhabha, Homi, *Location of Culture* (London and New York: Routledge, 1994).
Biddick, Kathleen, *The Shock of Medievalism* (Durham: Duke University Press, 1998).
Bildhauer, Bettina, *Filming the Middle Ages* (London: Reaktion, 2011).
Bernau, Anke and Bettina Bildhauer (eds.), *Medieval Film* (Manchester: Manchester University Press, 2012).
Bonnet, Anne-Marie, *Rodenegg und Schmalkalden. Untersuchungen zur Illustration einer ritterlich-höfischen Erzählung und zur Entstehung profaner Epenillustration in den ersten Jahrzehnten des 13. Jahrhunderts* (München: tuduv-Verlagsgesellschaft, 1986).
de Boor, Helmut, *Die höfische Literatur: Vorbereitung, Blüte, Ausklang 1170–1250* (Munich: C.H. Beck, 1974).
Boym, Svetlana, *The Future of Nostalgia* (New York: Basic Books, 2008).

Brenner, Elma, Meredith Cohen and Mary Franklin-Brown (eds.), *Memory and Commemoration in Medieval Culture* (Surrey and Burlington, VT: Ashgate, 2013).

Brunner, Horst, *Wolfram von Eschenbach. Auf den Spuren der Dichter und Denker durch Franken* (Gunzenhausen: Schrenk-Verlag, 2010).

Bulang, Tobias, "Intertextualität und Interfiguralität des 'Wartburgkriegs,'" in Gert Hübner and Dorothea Klein (eds.), *Sangspruchdichtung um 1300. Akten der Tagung in Basel vom 7. Bis 9. November 2013* (Hildesheim: Weidmann, 2015), pp. 127–146.

Bumke, Joachim, *Die Wolfram von Eschenbach Forschung seit 1945. Bericht und Bibliographie* (Munich: Wilhelm Fink, 1970).

Bumke, Joachim, *Höfische Kultur: Literatur und Gesellschaft im hohen Mittelalter* (Munich: Deutscher Taschenbuch Verlag, 1990).

Bumke, Joachim, *Wolfram von Eschenbach*, 8th ed. (Stuttgart: Metzler, 2004).

Camille, Michael, *Gothic Art: Glorious Visions* (New York: Harry N. Abrams, 1996).

Carruthers, Mary, *The Book of Memory: A Study of Memory in Medieval Culture* (Cambridge: Cambridge University Press, 1990).

Carruthers, Mary, *The Craft of Thought: Meditation, Rhetoric, and the Making of Images: 400–1200* (New York: Cambridge University Press, 1998).

Cicora, Mary A., *From History to Myth: Wagner's Tannhäuser and Its Literary Sources*, Germanic Studies in America, No. 63 (New York, Bern: Peter Lang, 1992).

Cohen, Jeffrey Jerome, "Intertemporality. Afterword," in Eileen A. Joy, Myra J. Seaman, Kimberly Bell, and Mary K. Ramsey (eds.), *Cultural Studies of the Modern Middle Ages* (New York and Basingstoke: Palgrave Macmillan, 2007), pp. 295–300.

Cohen, Jeffrey Jerome, "Time out of Memory," in Elizabeth Scala and Sylvia Federico (eds.), *The Post-Historical Middle Ages* (New York and Basingstoke: Palgrave MacMillan, 2009), pp. 37–61.

Confino, Alon, *The Nation as a Local Metaphor: Württemberg, Imperial Germany, and National Memory, 1871–1918* (Chapel Hill, NC: University of North Carolina Press, 1997).

Conn, Steven, *Do Museums Still Need Objects?* (Philadelphia: University of Pennsylvania Press, 2010).

Crane, Susan A. (ed.), *Museums and Memory* (Stanford: Stanford University Press, 2000).

Crooke, Elizabeth, *Museums and Community. Ideas, Issues and Challenges* (London and New York: Routledge, 2007).

Curschmann, Michael, "Pictura laicorum litteratura? Überlegungen zum Verhältnis von Bild und volkssprachlicher Schriftlichkeit im Hoch- und Spätmittelalter bis zum Codex Manesse," in Hagen Keller, Klaus Grubmüller, and Nikolaus Staubach, (eds.), *Pragmatische Schriftlichkeit im Mittelalter. Erscheinungsformen und Entwicklungsstufen* (Munich: Wilhelm Fink, 1992), pp. 211–229.

Curschmann, Michael, *Vom Wandel im bildlichen Umgang mit literarischen Gegenständen: Rodenegg, Wildenstein und das Flaarsche Haus in Stein am Rhein* (Freiburg Schweiz: Universitätsverlag, 1997).

Curschmann, Michael, *Wort, Bild, Text. Studien zur Medialität des Literarischen im Hochmittelalter und früher Neuzeit* (Baden-Baden: Valentin Koerner, 2007).

Czaplicka, John, "History, Aesthetics, and Contemporary Commemorative Practice in Berlin," *New German Critique Cultural History/Cultural Studies* 65 (Spring/Summer 1995), pp. 155–187.

D'Arcens, Louise, "Laughing in the Face of the Past: Satire and Nostalgia in Medieval Heritage Tourism," *Postmedieval: A Journal of Medieval Cultural Studies* 2 (2011), pp. 155–170.

D'Arcens, Louise, *Comic Medievalism* (Cambridge: D.S. Brewer, 2014).

D'Arcens, Louise, "Presentism," in Elizabeth Emery and Richard Utz (eds.), *Medievalism: Key Critical Terms* (Cambridge: DS Brewer, 2014), pp. 181–189.

D'Arcens, Louise (ed.), *Cambridge Companion to Medievalism* (Cambridge: Cambridge University Press, 2016).

Van D'Elden, Stephanie Cain, "Specific and Generic Scenes: A Model for Analyzing Medieval Illustrated Texts Based on the Example of *Ywain/Iwein*," *Bibliographical Bulletin of the International Arthurian* Sciety 44 (1992), pp. 255–269.

Van D'Elden, Stephanie Cain, "Discursive Illustrations in Three Tristan Manuscripts," in Keith Busby (ed.), *Word and Image in Arthurian Literature* (London: Garland, 1996), pp. 284–319.

Van D'Elden, Stephanie Cain, "Specific and Generic Scenes in Verse *Tristan* Illustrations," in Jutta Eming, Ann Marie Rasmussen and Kathryn Starkey (eds.), *Visuality and Materiality in the Story of Tristan and Isolde* (Notre Dame, IN: University of Notre Dame Press, 2012), pp. 269–298.

Dell, Helen, "Nostalgia and Medievalism: Conversations, Contradictions, Impasses," *postmedieval: a journal of medieval cultural studies* 2 (2011), pp. 115–126.

Diepeveen, Leonard and Timothy Van Laar, *Art with a Difference. Looking at Difficult and Unfamiliar Art* (New York: McGraw-Hill, 2001).

Dinshaw, Carolyn, *How Soon Is Now? Medieval Texts, Amateur Readers, and the Queerness of Time* (Durham and London: Duke University Press, 2012).

Dunlop, Anne, *Painted Palaces. The Rise of Secular Art in Early Renaissance Italy* (University Park, PA: The Penn State Press, 2009).

Eco, Umberto, *Travels in Hyperreality* (New York, Orlando: Harcourt Brace [Harvest Books], 1986).

Erll, Astrid, *Memory in Culture*, (trans.) Sara B. Young (New York and Basingstoke: Palgrave Macmillan, 2011).

Ehrismann, Otfried, *Nibelungenlied. Epoche-Werk-Wirkung*, 2nd ed. (Munich: C.H. Beck, 2002).

Ehrismann, Otfried, "Die literarische Rezeption der Siegfriedfigur von 1200 bis heute," in Volker Gallé (ed.), *Siegfried. Schmied und Drachentöter* (Worms: Worms-Verlag, 2005), pp. 124–137.

Elliott, Andrew B.R., *Remaking the Middle Ages. The Methods of Cinema and History in Portraying the Medieval World* (Jefferson, NC: McFarland Publishing, 2011).

Elliott, Andrew B.R., *Medievalism, Politics, and Mass Media: Appropriating the Middle Ages in the Twenty-First Century* (Cambridge: D.S. Brewer, 2017).

Emery, Elizabeth, "Medievalism and the Middle Ages," *Studies in Medievalism* 17 (2009), pp. 77–85.

Emery, Elizabeth and Richard Utz (eds.), *Medievalism: Key Critical Terms* (Cambridge: D.S. Brewer, 2014).

Eming, Jutta, Ingrid Kasten, Elke Koch, and Andrea Sieber, "Emotionalität und Performativität in narrativen Texten des Mittelalters," *Theorien des Performativen. Paragrana* Band 10 Heft 1 (2010), pp. 215–233.

Eming, Jutta, Ann Marie Rasmussen and Kathryn Starkey (eds.), *Visuality and Materiality in the Story of Tristan and Isolde* (Notre Dame, IN: University of Notre Dame Press, 2012).

Fetz, Bernhard, "Ein Museum für österreichische Literatur," in Bernard Fetz (ed.), *Das Literaturmuseum. 101 Objekte und Geschichten* (Salzburg and Vienna: Jung, 2015), pp. 14–22.

Finke, Laurie and Martin Shichtman, *King Arthur and the Myth of History* (Tallahassee: University Press of Florida, 2004).

Finlay, Victoria, *The Brilliant History of Color in Art* (Los Angeles: The J. Paul Getty Museum, 2014).

Frühmorgen-Voss, Hella. *Text und Illustration im Mittelalter. Aufsätze zu den Wechselbeziehungen zwischen Literatur und bildender Kunst*, vol. 50 (Munich: C.H. Beck, 1975).

Gallé, Volker (ed.), *Siegfried: Schmied und Drachentöter. Band 1 der Nibelungentraditionen* (Worms: Worms Verlag, 2005).

Gallé, Volker, "Wenn Städte sich erzählen," in Jörg Koch (ed.), *Wormser Nibelungen-Lexikon* (Worms: Worms Verlag 2014), pp. 4–6.

Gentry, Francis G. and Ulrich Müller, "The Reception of the Middle Ages in Germany: An Overview," *Studies in Medievalism* III.4 (Spring 1991), pp. 399–422.

Gentry, Francis G., Winder McConnell, Ulrich Müller, Werner Wunderlich (eds.), *The Nibelungen Tradition. An Encyclopedia* (New York: Routledge, 2002).

Gibbs, Marion, "Fragment and Expansion: Wolfram von Eschenbach, *Titurel*, and Albrecht, *Jüngerer Titurel*," in W.H. Jackson, W.H., and Silvia Ranawake (eds.), *The Arthur of the Germans. The Arthurian Legend in Medieval* German *and Dutch Literature* (Cardiff: University of Wales Press, 2000), pp. 69–80.

Goebel, Stefan, *The Great War and Medieval Memory. War, Remembrance and Medievalism in Britain and Germany, 1914–1940* (Cambridge: Cambridge University Press, 2007).

Groebner, Valentin, *Das Mittelalter hört nicht auf. Über historisches Erzählen* (Munich: C.H. Beck, 2008).

Gunning, Tom, *The Films of Fritz Lang. Allegories of Vision and Modernity* (London: bfi Publishing, 2000).

Gustafson, Brigitte, "A Meaning of Places through Stories," *Museum International* 63.1–2 (2012), pp. 63–69.

Hafner, Susanne, "Erzählen im Raum. Der Schmalkaldener *Iwein*," in Horst Wenzel and C. Stephen Jaeger (eds.), *Visualisierungsstrategien in mittelalterlichen Bildern und Texten* (Berlin: Erich Schmidt, 2006), pp. 90–98.

Hallmann, Jan, *Studien zum mittelhochdeutschen Wartburgkrieg. Literaturgeschichtliche Stellung—Überliefereung—Rezeptionsgeschichte. Mit einer Edition der Wartburgkrieg-Texte* (Berlin: de Gruyter, 2015).

Hansen, Eric, *Die Nibelungenreise. Mit dem VW Bus durchs Mittelalter. Aus dem Amerikanischen übersetzt von Astrid Ule und Cornelia Stoll. Deutsche Bearbeitung von Astrid Ule* (Munich: Piper, 2004).

Haug, Walter, *Vernacular Literary Theory in the Middle Ages. The German Tradition, 800-1300, in Its European Context*, (trans.) Joanna M. Catling (Cambridge: Cambridge University Press, 1997).

Hayden, Dolores, *The Power of Place. Urban Landscapes as Public History* (Cambridge, MA: MIT Press, 1995).

Heinzle, Joachim, "Einleitung: Der deutscheste aller deutschen Stoffe," in Joachim Heinzle and Anneliese Waldschmidt (eds.), *Die Nibelungen. Ein deutscher Wahn, ein deutscher Alptraum. Studien und Dokumente zur Rezpetion des Nibelungenstoffs im 19. und 20. Jahrhundert* (Frankfurt: Suhrkamp, 1991), pp. 8–18.

Heinzle, Joachim, *Das Nibelungenlied. Eine Einführung* (Frankfurt a. M.: Fischer Taschenbuch, 1994).

Heinzle, Joachim (ed.), *Wolfram von Eschenbach. Ein Handbuch. Bd. 1-2 Autor, Werk, Wirkung* (Berlin: de Gruyter, 2011).

Heinzle, Joachim (ed.), *Mythos Nibelungen* (Stuttgart: Reclam, 2013).

Heinzle, Joachim, Klaus Klein, and Ute Obhof (eds.), *Die Nibelungen. Sage—Epos—Mythos* (Wiesbaden: Reichert, 2003).

Haymes, Edward, *The Nibelungenlied. History and Interpretation* (Urbana and Chicago: University of Illinois Press, 1986).

Heller, Heinz-B., "'Man stellt Denkmäler nicht auf den flachen Asphalt.' Fritz Langs Nibelungen-Film Die Nibelungen," in Joachim Heinzle and Anneliese Waldschmidt (eds.), *Ein deutscher Wahn, ein deutscher Alptraum. Studien und Dokumente zur Rezpetion des Nibelungenstoffs im 19. und 20. Jahrhundert* (Frankfurt: Suhrkamp, 1991), pp. 351–369.

Heller, Heinz-B., "… nur dann überzeugend und eindringlich, wenn es sich mit dem Wesen der Zeit deckt …" Fritz Langs *Nibelungen*-Film als "Zeitbild," in Joachim Heinzle, Klaus Klein, und Ute Obhof (eds.), *Die Nibelungen. Sage—Epos—Mythos* (Wiesbaden: Reichert, 2003), pp. 497–509.

Herweg, Mathias and Stefan Keppler-Tasaki (eds.), *Rezeptionskulturen. Fünfhundert Jahre literarischer Mittelalterrezeption zwischen Kanon und Populärkultur* (Berlin: de Gruyter, 2012).

Herweg, Mathias, *Das Mittelalter des Historismus. Formen und Funktionen in Literatur und Kunst, Film und Technik* (Würzburg: Königshausen und Neumann, 2015).

Heusler, Andreas, *Nibelungensage und Nibelungenlied. Die Stoffgeschichte des deutschen Heldenepos* (Darmstadt: Wissenschaftliche Buchgesellschaft, 1973).

Hoelscher, Steven, "Heritage," in Sharon Macdonald (ed.), *A Companion to Museum Studies* (Oxford: Blackwell, 2006), pp. 198–218.

Hogenbirk, Marjolein "Intertextuality," in Leah Tether and Johnny McFadyen (eds.), *Handbook of Arthurian Romance. King Arthur's Court in Medieval European Literature* (Berlin: de Gruyter, 2017), pp. 183–198.

Holsinger, Bruce W., "Analytical Survey 6: Medieval Literature and Cultures of Performance," *New Medieval Literatures* 6 (2003), pp. 271–311.

Hürlimann, Anneliese and Nicola Lepp, "Zur Ausstellungskonzeption von Ärschlein bis Zettel," in Anneliese Hürlimann and Nicola Lepp (eds.) with the city of Kassel, *Die Grimmwelt. Von Ärschlein bis Zettel Taschenbuch* (Kassel: Sieveking, 2015), pp. 22–26.

Hutcheon, Linda with Siobhan O'Flynn. *A Theory of Adaptation*, 2nd ed. (London and New York: Routledge, 2012).

Huyssen, Andreas, *Twilight Memories. Marking Time in a Culture of Amnesia* (New York and London: Routledge, 1995).

Jackson, William H. and Silvia Ranawake (eds.), *The Arthur of the Germans. The Arthurian Legend in Medieval German and Dutch Literature* (Cardiff: University of Wales Press, 2000).

Jauß, Hans Robert, *Alterität und Modernität der mittelalterlichen Literatur. Gesammelte Aufsätze 1956–1976* (Munich: Wilhelm Fink, 1977).

Joy, Eileen and Craig Dionne, "Before the Trains of Thought Have Been Laid Down so Firmly: The Premodern Post/Human," *postmedieval: a journal of medieval cultural studies* 1.2 (2010), pp. 1–9.

Kaplan, Flora Edouwaye S., "Making and Remaking National Identities", in Sharon Macdonald (ed.), *A Companion to Museum Studies* (Oxford: Blackwell, 2006), pp. 152–169.

Kirshenblatt-Gimblett, Barbara, *Destination Culture: Tourism, Museums, and Heritage* (Berkeley: University of California Press, 1998).

Kirshenblatt-Gimblett, Barbara, "Intangible Heritage as Metacultural Production," *Museum International* 56.1–2 (2014), pp. 163–174.

Kracauer, Siegfried, *From Caligari to Hitler. A Psychological History of the German Film* (Princeton, NJ: Princeton University Press, 1947).

Kreps, Christina, *Liberating Culture: Cross-Cultural Perspectives on Museums, Curation, and Heritage Preservation* (London and New York: Routledge, 2003).

Kugler, Hartmut, "Lokale und regionale Wolfram-Verehrung," in Joachim Heinzle (ed.), *Wolfram von Eschenbach: ein Handbuch* (Berlin: de Gruyter, 2011), pp. 818–834.

Kühebacher, Egon, *Literatur und bildende Kunst im Tiroler Mittelalter: die Iwein-Fresken von Rodenegg und andere Zeugnisse der Wechselwirkung von Literatur und bildender Kunst* (Innsbruck: Institut für Germanistik der Universität Innsbruck, 1982).

Kurz, Johann Baptist, *Heimat und Geschlecht Wolframs von Eschenbach* (Ansbach: C. Brügel und Sohn, 1916).

Kurz, Johann Baptist, *Wolfram von Eschenbach. Ein Buch vom größten Dichter des deutschen Mittelalters* (Ansbach: C. Brügel und Sohn, 1929).

Lampert, Lisa, "Race, Periodicity, and the (Neo-) Middle Ages," *Modern Language Quarterly* 65.3 (September 2004), pp. 391–421.

Lange-Greve, Susanne, *Die kulturelle Bedeutung von Literaturausstellungen: Konzepte, Analysen und Wirkungen literaturmusealer Präsentation: mit einem Anhang zum wissenschaftlichen Wert von Literaturmuseen* (Olms-Weidmann: Hildesheim, Zürich, 1995).

Lembke, Astrid, "Umstrittene Souveränität. Herrschaft, Geschlecht und Stand im *Nibelungenlied* sowie in Thea von Harbous *Nibelungenbuch* und in Fritz Langs Film *Die Nibelungen*," in Nastaša Bedeković, Andreas Kraß, and Astrid Lembke (eds.), *Durchkreuzte Helden. Das Nibelungenlied und Fritz Langs Film Die Nibelungen im Licht der Intersektionalitätsforschung* (Bielefeld: transcript Verlag, 2014), pp. 51–75.

Macdonald, Sharon, "Museum Europe: Negotiating Heritage," *Anthropological Journal of European Cultures* 17.2 (2008), pp. 47–65.

Macdonald, Sharon, *Difficult Heritage: Negotiating the Nazi Past in Nuremberg and Beyond* (London and New York: Routledge, 2009).

Macdonald, Sharon (ed.), *A Companion to Museum Studies* (London: Wiley-Blackwell, 2010).

Macdonald, Sharon, "Presencing Europe's Pasts," in Ullrich Kockel, Máiréad Nic Craith, and Jonas Frykman (eds.), *A Companion to the Anthology of Europe* (Oxford: Wiley-Blackwell, 2012), pp. 233–253.

Macdonald, Sharon, *Memorylands. Heritage and Identity in Europe Today* (London and New York: Routledge, 2013).

Macdonald, Sharon, "Is 'Difficult Heritage' Still 'Difficult'? Why Public Knowledge of Past Perpetration May No Longer Be so Unsettling to Collective Identities," *Museum International* (2015), pp. 6–22.

Macdonald, Sharon, "New Constellations of Difference in Europe's 21st Century Museumscape," *Museum Anthropology* 39.1 (2016), pp. 4–19.

MacGregor, Neil, *Germany: Memories of a Nation* (London: Penguin UK, 2014).

Madsen, Axel, "Interview with Fritz Lang," in Barry Keith Grant (ed.), *Fritz Lang Interviews* (Jackson, MS: University Press of Mississippi, 2000), pp. 81–91.

Martin, Bernhard, "Der deutsche Nationalstaat und das Nibelungenlied. Über die gesellschaftspolitische Funktion des Mythos," in Werner Wunderlich, Ulrich Müller, Detlef Scholz (eds.), *"Waz sider da geschac": American-German Studies on the Nibelungenlied: Text and Reception: with Bibliography 1980–1990/91* (Göppingen: Kümmerle, 1992), pp. 179–188.

Matthews, David, *Medievalism: A Critical History* (Cambridge: D.S. Brewer, 2015).

McConnell, Winder (ed.), *A Companion to the Nibelungenlied* (Columbia, SC: Camden House, 1998).

McGilligan, Patrick, *Fritz Lang: The Nature of the Beast* (Minneapolis: University of Minnesota Press, 2013).

McIsaac, Peter and Gabriele Mueller (eds.), *Exhibiting the German Past. Museums, Film, and Musealization* (Toronto: University of Toronto Press, 2015).

Mertens, Volker, "Imitatio Arthuri. Zum Prolog von Hartmanns 'Iwein'," *Zeitschrift für deutsches Altertum und deutsche Literatur* 106. Bd., H. 4 (1977), pp. 350–358.

Mertens, Volker, "Wagner's Middle Ages," in Ulrich Müller and Peter Wapnewski (eds.), *Wagner Handbook*, (trans.) John Deathridge (Boston: Harvard University Press, 1992).

Mertens, Volker, *Der deutsche Artusroman* (Stuttgart: Reclam, 1998).

Meyer, Matthias, "Intertextuality in the Later Thirteenth Century: Wigamur, Gauriel, Lohengrin and the Fragments of Arthurian Romances," in W.H. Jackson and Silvia Ranawake (eds.), *The Arthur of the Germans. The Arthurian Legend in Medieval German and Dutch Literature* (Cardiff: University of Wales Press, 2000), pp. 98–116.

Morsch, Carsten, "Bewegte Betrachter. Kinästhetische Erfahrung im Schauraum mittelalterlicher Texte," in Carsten Morsch and Christina Lechtermann (eds.), *Kunst der Bewegung. Kinästhetische Wahrnehmung und Probehandeln in virtuellen Welten* (Bern, Berlin: Peter Lang, 2004), pp. 45–72.

Müller, Jan-Dirk, *Rules for the Endgame. The World of the Nibelungenlied*, (trans.) William T. Whobrey (Baltimore: Johns Hopkins University Press, 2007).

Müller, Jan-Dirk, *Episches Erzählen. Erzählformen früher volkssprachliger Schriftlichkeit* (Berlin: Erich Schmidt, 2017).

Müller, Ulrich, "Wolfram, Wagner and the Germans," in Will Hasty (ed.), *A Companion to Wolfram's Parzival* (Rochester: Camden House, 1999), pp. 245–258.

Müller, Ulrich and Werner Wunderlich, "The Modern Reception of the Arthurian Legend," in W.H. Jackson and Silvia Ranawake (eds.), *The Arthur of the Germans. The Arthurian Legend in Medieval German and Dutch Literature* (Cardiff: University of Wales Press, 2000), pp. 303–324.

Muschg, Adolf, "Abdruck einer Spur. Rede für Wolframs-Eschenbach," *Literatur in Bayern* 39 (1995), pp. 2–5.

Nora, Pierre, "Between Memory and History: Les Lieux de Mémoire," *Representations*. No. 26 *Special Issue: Memory and Counter-Memory* (Spring 1989), pp. 7–24.

Norberg, Jakob, "German Literary Studies and the Nation," *The German Quarterly* 91.1 (2018), pp. 1–17.

Oergel, Maike, *The Return of King Arthur and the Nibelungen: National Myth in Nineteenth-Century English and German Literature* (Berlin and New York: de Gruyter, 1998).

Ott, Norbert H. and Wolfgang Wallicek, "Bildprogramm und Textstruktur. Anmerkungen zu den Iwein-Zyklen auf Rodeneck und in Schmalkalden," in Christoph Cormeau (ed.), *Deutsche Literatur im Mittelalter. Kontakte und Perspektiven. H. Kuhn zum Gedächtnis* (Stuttgart: Metzler, 1979), pp. 473–500.

Pastourneau, Michel, *Blue. The History of a Color* (Princeton and Oxford: Princeton University Press, 2001).

Phillips, Gene, "Fritz Lang Remembers," in Barry Keith Grant (ed.), *Fritz Lang Interviews* (Jackson, MS: University Press of Mississippi, 2000), pp. 175–187.

Puff, Helmut, "Ein Rezeptionszeugnis zu Wolfram von Eschenbach vom Ausgang des Mittelalters," *Zeitschrift für deutsches Altertum und deutsche Literatur* 129.1 (2000), pp. 70–83.

Pugh, Tison and Angela Jane Weisl, *Medievalisms: Making the Past in the Present* (New York and London: Routledge, 2012).

Pugh, Tison and Susan Aronstein (eds.), *The Disney Middle Ages: A Fairy-Tale and Fantasy Past* (New York: Palgrave Macmillan, 2012).

Rectanus, Mark, "Globalization: Incorporating the Museum," in Sharon Macdonald (ed.), *A Companion to Museum Studies* (Oxford: Blackwell, 2006), pp. 381–397.

Rectanus, Mark, "Refracted Memory: Museums, Film, and Visual Culture in Urban Space," in Peter M. McIsaac and Gabriele Mueller (eds.), *Exhibiting the German Past* (Toronto: University of Toronto Press, 2015), pp. 42–62.

Reijnders, Stijn, *Places of the Imagination. Media, Tourism, Culture* (Surrey, UK and Burlington, VT: Ashgate, 2011).

Remensnyder, Amy G., *Remembering Kings Past. Monastic Foundation Legends in Medieval Southern France* (Ithaca and London: Cornell University Press, 1995).

Remensnyder, Amy G., "Topographies of Memory," in Gerd Althoff, Johannes Fried, and Patrick Geary (eds.), *Medieval Concepts of the Past: Ritual, Memory, Historiography* (Washington, DC: Cambridge University Press, 2002), pp. 193–215.

Ruf, Oliver, "Literaturvermittlung, Literaturausstellung, 'ästhetische Erziehung'. Das Literaturmuseum der Moderne," in Katerina Kroucheva and Barbara Schaff (eds.), *Kafkas Gabel. Überlegungen zum Ausstellen von Literatur* (Bielefeld: transcript, 2013), pp. 95–141.

Rushing, James A., *Images of Adventure. Ywain in the Visual Arts* (Princeton, NJ: Princeton University Press, 1995).

Rushing, James A., "The Medieval German Pictorial Evidence," in W.H. Jackson and S.A. Ranawake (eds.), *The Arthur of the Germans. The Arthurian Legend in Medieval German and Dutch Literature* (Cardiff: University of Wales Press, 2000), pp. 257–280.

Sager, Alexander, *Minne von maeren: on Wolfram's "Titurel"* (Göttingen: V&R Unipress, 2006).

Said, Edward, "Invention, Memory and Place," *Critical Inquiry* 26.2 (Winter 2000), pp. 175–192.

Sanders, Julie, *Adaptation and Appropriation*, 2nd ed. (New York, London: Routledge, 2016).

Schäfer, Ulrike, *Worms zu Fuß* (Ingelheim: Leinpfad Verlag, 2012).

Schirok, Bernd, "Die Bilderhandschriften und Bildzeugnisse," in Joachim Heinzle (ed.), *Wolfram von Eschenbach. Ein Handbuch. Bd. 1 Autor, Werk, Wirkung* (Berlin: de Gruyter, 2011), pp. 335–365.

Schloss Neuenbürg, *Ein Führer durch das Nordschwarzwaldmuseum. Zweigmuseum des Badischen Landesmuseums* (Karlsruhe: Badisches Landesmusem, 2011).

Schupp, Volker, "Die Ywain-Erzählung von Schloss Rodenegg," in Egon Kühebacher (ed.), *Literatur und Bildende Kunst im Tiroler Mittelalter. Die Iwein-Fresken von Rodenegg und andere Zeugnisse der Wechselwirkung von Literatur und bildender Kunst. Im Auftrag des Südtiroler Kulturinstitutes* (Innsbruck: Institut für Germanistik, 1982.), pp. 1–29.

von See, Klaus, "Das *Nibelungenlied*—ein Nationalepos?" in Joachim Heinzle and Anneliese Waldschmidt (eds.), *Die Nibelungen. Ein deutscher Wahn, ein deutscher Alptraum. Studien und Dokumente zur Rezpetion des Nibelungenstoffs im 19. und 20. Jahrhundert* (Frankfurt: Suhrkamp, 1991), pp. 43–110.

von See, Klaus. "Die politische Rezeption der Siegfriedfigur im 19. und 20. Jahrhundert," in Volker Gallé (ed.), *Siegfried. Schmied und Drachentöter* (Worms: Worms-Verlag, 2005), pp. 138–155.

Seitz, Erwin and Oskar Geidner, *Wolframs-Eschenbach. Der Deutsche Orden baut eine Stadt* (Verlagsdruckerei Schmidt Gmbh: Neustadt an der Aisch, 1997).

Shichtman, Martin and Laurie Finke, "Exegetical History: Nazis at the Round Table," *postmedieval: a journal of medieval cultural studies* 5.3 (2014), pp. 278–294.

Shippey, Tom, "Medievalisms and Why They Matter," *Studies in Medievalism* 17 (2009), pp. 45–54.

Skounti, Ahmed, "The Authentic Illusion Humanity's Intangible Cultural Heritage, the Moroccan Experience," in Laurajane Smith and Natsuko Akagawa (eds.), *Intangible Heritage* (London: Routledge, 2008), pp. 74–92.

Siller, Max, "König Artus in Tirol," in Mark Mersiowsky and LeoAndergassen, et al. (eds.), *Artus auf Runkelstein. Der Traum vom guten Herrscher*. Stiftung Bozener Schlösser. Runkelsteiner Schriften zur Kulturgeschichte. Bd. 6 (Bozen: Athesia, 2014), pp. 103–136.

Stampfer, Helmut, *Schloß Rodenegg. Geschichte und Kunst* (Bozen: Pluristamp, 1988).

Starkey, Kathryn, *Reading the Medieval Book. Word, Image, and Performance in Wolfram von Eschenbach's Willehalm* (Notre Dame, IN: University of Notre Dame Press, 2004).

Starkey, Kathryn and Horst Wenzel (eds.), *Visual Culture and the German Middle Ages* (New York: Palgrave Macmillan, 2005).

Sterling-Hellenbrand, Alexandra, "Performing Medieval Literature and/as History: The Museum of Wolframs-Eschenbach," in Karl Fugelso (ed.), *Defining Neo Medievalisms (II). Studies in Medievalism XX* (Cambridge: D.S. Brewer, 2011), pp. 147–170.

Sterling-Hellenbrand, Alexandra, "The Nibelungenlied and Its Interfigures: Old Texts on the Museal Stage. The Machinery of Myth at the Nibelungen Museum in Worms," in Sibylle Jefferis (ed.), *Studies and New Texts of the Nibelungenlied, Walther, Neidhart, and Other Works in Medieval German Literature: In Memory of Ulrich Müller* II *(Kalamazoo Papers 2014)*. Göppinger Arbeiten zur Germanistik 780 (Göppingen: Kümmerle, 2015), pp. 249–267.

Sterling-Hellenbrand, Alexandra, "Siegfried, Dornröschen und Luke Skywalker: Die Inszenierung eines deutschen Mittelalters für ein globales Publikum im Wormser Nibelungenmuseum," in Nathaniel Busch et al. (eds.), *Jahrbuch für internationale Germanistik. Abhandlungen zum Rahmenthema "Die Auslandsgermanisten und ihr Mittelalter,"* Jahrgang L-Heft 2 (Bern: Peter Lang, 2018), pp. 195–208.

Storch, Wolfgang (ed.), *Die Nibelungen. Bilder von Liebe, Verrat und Untergang* (Munich: Prestel, 1987).

Trigg, Stephanie, "Walking through Cathedrals: Scholars, Pilgrims, and Medieval Tourists," *New Medieval Literatures* 7 (2005), pp. 9–33.

Trigg, Stephanie, "Medievalism and Theories of Temporality," in Louise D'Arcens (ed.), *Cambridge Companion to Medievalism* (Cambridge: Cambridge University Press, 2016), pp. 196–209.

Trost, Ralph, *Vom Umgang mit Helden. Das Museum Nibelungen(h)ort Xanten* (Frankfurt: Peter Lang, 2012).

Utz, Richard, "A Panel Discussion," in Roger Dahoud (ed.), *The Future of the Middle Ages and the Renaissance. Problems, Trends, and Opportunities for Research* (Turnhout: Brepols, 1998), pp. 3–19.

Utz, Richard, "Resistance to (The New) Medievalism? Comparative Deliberations on (National) Philology, Mediävalismus, and Mittelalter-Rezeption in Germany and North America," in Roger Dahood (ed.), *The Future of the Middle Ages and the Renaissance: Problems, Trends, and Opportunities in Research* (Turnhout: Brepols, 1998), pp. 151–170.

Utz, Richard, "Speaking of Medievalism: An Interview with Leslie Workman," in Richard Utz and Tom Shippey (eds.), *Medievalism in the Modern* World. *Essays in Honor of Leslie Workman* (Amsterdam: Brepols, 1998), pp. 480–499.

Utz, Richard, "The Chameleon Principle: Reflections on the Status of Arthurian Studies in the Academy," *Arthuriana* 17.4 (2007), pp. 111–114.

Utz, Richard, *Medievalism: A Manifesto* (Leeds, UK: Arc Humanities Press, 2017).

Vitz, Evelyn Birge, *Orality and Performance in Early French Romance* (Cambridge: D.S. Brewer, 1999).

Vitz, Evelyn Birge, "Tales with Guts: A 'Rasic' Aesthetic in Medieval French Storytelling," *TDR: The Drama Review* 52.4 [T 200] (Winter 2008), pp. 145–173.

Wandhoff, Haiko, "Jenseits der Gutenberg-Galaxis. Das Mittelalter und die Medientheorie," in Volker Mertens and Carmen Stange (eds.), *Bilder vom Mittelalter. Eine Berliner Ringvorlesung* (Göttingen: V&R unipress, 2007), pp. 13–34.

Wehnert, Stefanie, *Literaturmuseen im Zeitalter der neuen Medien: Leseumfeld-Aufgaben-didaktische Konzepte* (Ludwig: Kiel, 2002).

Weisl, Angela Jane, *The Persistence of Medievalism: Narrative Adventures in Contemporary Culture* (New York and Basingstoke: Palgrave Macmillan, 2003).

Weisl, Angela Jane, "Spectacle," in Elizabeth Emery and Richard Utz (eds.), *Medievalism: Key Critical Terms* (Cambridge: D.S. Brewer, 2014), pp. 231–238.

Wenzel, Horst, *Hören und Sehen, Schrift und Bild: Kultur und Gedächtnis im Mittelalter* (Munich: C.H. Beck, 1995).

Wenzel, Horst, "Repräsentation und Wahrnehmung. Zur Inszenierung höfisch-ritterlicher Imagination im 'Welschen Gast' des Thomas von Zerclaere," in Gerd Althoff (ed.), *Zeichen-Rituale-Werte. Internationales Kolloquium des Sonderforschungsbereichs 496 an der Westfälischen Wilhelms-Universität Münster* (Münster: Rhema, 2004), pp. 303–325.

Wenzel, Horst, *Mediengeschichte vor und nach Gutenberg* (Darmstadt: Wissenschaftliche Buchgesellschft, 2007).

Wenzel, Horst, *Spiegelungen. Zur Kultur der Visualität im Mittelalter* (Berlin: Erich Schmidt, 2009).

Wenzel, Horst and Christina Lechtermann, "Repräsentation und Kinästhetik," *Theorien des Performativen. Paragrana*. Bd. 10. Heft 1 (2001), pp. 191–214.

Whitaker, Muriel, *The Legends of King Arthur in Art* (Woodbridge, Suffolk/ Rochester, NY: D.S. Brewer, 1990).

Wollenberg, Daniel, *Medieval Imagery in Today's Politics*. Past Imperfect Series (Leeds, UK: Arc Humanities Press, 2018).

Workman, Leslie and Kathleen Verduin (eds.), *Medievalism in Europe II. Studies in Medievalism VIII* (Cambridge: D.S. Brewer, 1996).

Wunderlich, Werner, "Arthurian Legend in German Literature of the Nineteen-Eighties," *Studies in Medievalism III.4* (1991), pp. 423–442.

Wunderlich, Werner, Ulrich Müller and Detlef Scholz (eds.), *"Waz sider da geschach": American-German Studies on the Nibelungenlied: Text and Reception: with Bibliography 1980–1990/91* (Göppingen: Kümmerle, 1992).

Yates, Frances, *The Art of Memory* (Chicago: University of Chicago Press, 1966).

Young, Helen, "Whiteness and Time: The Once, Present, and Future Race," in Karl Fugelso, Vincent Ferré, Alicia C. Montoya (eds.), *Studies in Medievalism XXIV Medievalism on the Margins Book* (Cambridge: D.S. Brewer, 2015), pp. 39–49.

Zuchold, Gerd-H, "The Prussian Royal House and Pictorial Representation of the Nibelung Saga," *Studies in Medievalism* V (1993), pp. 23–37.

Newspaper articles (print and web)

Auer, Katja, "Ja, so warn's," SZ Regionalausgabe, 29.09.2015, Ausgabe München West, https://www.genios.de:443/document/SZRE__A61432680 (accessed December 14, 2015).

Auer, Katja. "Wissenswertes" *Suddeutsche Zeitung* SZ Regionalausgabe, 11.08.2015, Ausgabe Munchen West, https://www.genios.de:443/document/SZRE__A60979766.

"Bunte Erlebniswelt statt dröger Texttafeln," Nürnberger Nachrichten, 27.05.2011, S. 27 / TIPPS ZUM WOCHENENDE, https://www.genios.de/document/NN__0C5CD 863E1C13E4DC125789D0009E949 (accessed January 18, 2016).

Das Ärschlein, Verbrechen und ein "C," *Frankfurter Allgemeine Zeitung*, 21.08.2013, Nr. 193, S. 46, https://www.genios.de/document/RMO__FDA201308213981726 (accessed January 18, 2016).

"Das Literaturmuseum Strauhof wird fortgeführt," *Neue Zürcher Zeitung*, 30.11.2017, https://www.nzz.ch/feuilleton/das-literaturmuseum-strauhof-wird-fortgefuehrt-ld.1334227 (accessed September 6, 2019).

Dirigo, Christine, "Den Museumsbesuch zum Erlebnis machen - Ulrike Standke vom Nibelungenmuseum ist Mittlerin zwischen Wissenschaft und Gästen / Pläne für das

'Mythenlabor,'" Bürstädter Zeitung, 01.11.2008 / Lokales, https://www.genios.de:443/document/BUER__198728217000I225494000 (accessed November 22, 2015).

von Düffel, John, "Halbstarke Helden—NIBELUNGENSAGE Das Epos ist auch eine Geschichte, über die man sich herrlich amüsieren kann," *Allgemeine Zeitung. Rhein Main Presse*, 07.11.2015 / Report, https://www.genios.de:443/document/MAZ__135185220001446850800 (accessed December 14, 2015).

Gaede, Peter-Matthias, "Heilige Hallen," SZ-Magazin Nr. 9 vom 3. März 2017, https://www.genios.de/document/SZDE__A70154276 (accessed January 12, 2018).

"Gäste kommen von überall her" *Frankfurter Allegmeine Zeitung*, 29.12.2015. Nr. 301, S. 41, https://www.genios.de/document/RMO__FDA201512294749141 (accessed January 18, 2016).

Gohlis, Tobias, "Der Ritter mit der Leier," *Die Zeit,* July 1996, http://www.zeit.de/1996/07/Der_Ritter_mit_der_Leier (accessed September 7, 2019).

Götzen, Johannes, "Wandlungsfähiger, moderner Klassiker—Mythenlabor als Ersatz für die Schatzkammer unter dem Nibelungenmuseum eröffnet," *Wormser Zeitung*, 11.10.2008/Lokales, https://www.genios.de:443/document/WORZ__197680017000I223676000 (accessed November 22, 2015).

Götzen, Johannes. "Zehn Jahre Nibelungenmuseum in Worms—Rückblick auf eine Kontroverse," *Wormser Zeitung*, 17.08.2011, http://www.wormser-zeitung.de/region/worms/kultur/11063015.htm (accessed July 28, 2014).

Iden, Peter, Was sind und sagen uns die Nibelungen? *Frankfurter Rundschau*, 21.08.2001, S.18.

Kauntz, Eckhart, "An der Wormser Stadtmauer ein Platz für die Nibelungen?" *Frankfurter Allgemeine Zeitung*, 06.03.1998, Nr. 55, S. 13, https://www.genios.de:443/document/WORZ__197680017000I223676000 (accessed November 22, 2015).

Knapp, Gottfried, "Gute Minne zum virtuellen Spiel. Das "Nibelungen-Museum," in Worms lässt ein deutsches Stück Weltliteratur wieder aufleben," *Süddeutsche Zeitung*, Montag 20. August 2001. München Seite 13, Bayern Seite, 13.

Müller, Susanne, "Ausstellungsstücke zum Anfassen - Wie Geschichte buchstäblich begreifbar wird," *Wormser Zeitung*, 31.01.2009/Lokales, https://www.genios.de:443/document/WORZ__202666985000I233356400 (accessed November 22, 2015).

Noltze, Holger, "Wolfram hinterließ keine Spur," *Frankfurter Allgemeine Zeitung*, 15.10.1994, Nr. 240, S. 35, https://www.genios.de/document/FAZ__F19941015WOLFRAM100 (accessed January 18, 2016).

Parade, Heidi, "Worms ladt zum virtuellen Blick auf Hagen und Brunnhilde," *Stuttgarter Zeitung*, 20.08.2001, S. 17, https://www.genios.de:443/document/STZ__STZ-20010820-17-8 (accessed November 22, 2015).

Renöckl, Georg, "Glücksfall und Wurf," *Neue Zürcher Zeitung*, 06.05.2015, https://www.nzz.ch/feuilleton/buecher/gluecksfall-und-wurf-1.18536078 (accessed September 6, 2019).

Schäfer, Ulrike, "Statt Videoschau ein Mythenlabor. Neues im Nibelungenmuseum," Ein Artikel zum Vortrag, *Wormser Zeitung*, 30.07.2007, http://www.nibelungenlied-gesellschaft.de/03_beitrag/eichfelder/fs07_eichf.html (accessed January 29, 2019).

Schäfer, Ulrike, "Umstrittenes Geburtstagskind—JUBILÄUM Im August feiert Worms das zehnjährige Bestehen des Nibelungenmuseums," *Allgemeine Zeitung*, 22.07.2011 / Region, https://www.genios.de/document/MAZ__36544480001311285600 (accessed November 22, 2015).

Schöffel, Lara, "Nibelungenmuseum als Streitpunkt—BÜRGERHAUSHALT Kontroverse Debatte im Internet über Ausstellungsstätte / Zahlreiche Interessengruppen gebildet," *Wormser Zeitung*, 21.06.2011 / Lokales, 26.07.2011, https://www.genios.de:443/document/WORZ__34911390001308607200 (accessed November 22, 2015).

"Schon 200 000 Besucher in der Grimm-Welt," *Darmstädter Echo*, 25.02.2017, Seite 6 / Region, https://www.genios.de/document/DECH__177980670001487977200 (accessed January 12, 2018).

Seifert, Heribert, "Hörturm und Schatzkammer. In Worms wurde ein Nibelungenmuseum eröffnet," 19.09.2001, *Neue Zürcher Zeitung*, S.62 / fe Feuilleton, https://www.genios.de/document/NZZ__7N8H2 (accessed January 31, 2019).

Senne, Thomas, "Für Mäuse kein Grund zum Feiern. Museum für Wolfram von Eschenbach, der einst den 'Parzival' schrieb," *Süddeutsche Zeitung*, SZ, 13.02.1995, SEITE: 37 / Ressort: Bayern, https://www.genios.de/document/SZH__A59896BC69213BA4EEED1AA6ABA7A040 (accessed January 18, 2016).

Sojitrawalla, Shirin, "Nebelheim," *DIE ZEIT*, 35/2001, http://www.zeit.de/2001/35/Nebelheim (accessed January 31, 2019).

Staffen-Quandt, Daniel, "Literatur in kleinen Häppchen serviert," *Mittelbayerische Zeitung*, 20.01.2015/ Bayerische Nachrichten | Schwandorf, https://www.genios.de/document/MIB__C8FFE42F685D66375BB7FF2725792F9C-SCHWANDORF (accessed January 18, 2016).

Stankiewitz, Karl, "Gralsburg hinter Fachwerk. Ein neues zum Mittelalterdichter Museum Wolfram von Eschenbach," *Frankfurter Rundschau*, 11.11.1995, S. 4 / MRE, https://www.genios.de/document/FR__0BFABAA9EDA68FD2F04DC48A33961ECD (accessed January 18, 2016).

Thiede, Veit-Mario, "Dem Volk aufs Maul geschaut. Kassel präsentiert die Ausstellung 'Luther und Grimm wortwörtlich,'" *Frankfurt Neue Presse*, 12.07.2016, Seite KuS 1 / Kultur und Service, https://www.genios.de/document/FNP__75271D34F7ABA4233000 (accessed September 7, 2019).

Thomas, Peter, "Der virtuelle Schatz von Worms. Nibelungenmuseum: Multimediale Momentaufnahmen eines Mythos," *Darmstädter Echo*, 20.08.2001.

Weber, Michaela, "Das begehbare Hörbuch—VERNISSAGE 40 Tablets bringen dem Besucher das Nibelungen-Drama und Richard Wagner nahe," *Allgemeine Zeitung*, 10.11.2015, https://www.genios.de:443/document/MAZ__135382150001447110000 (accessed December 14, 2015).

Wolff, Thomas, "Siegfried, verzweifelt gesucht," *Frankfurter Rundschau Magazin-Reisen*, 11.08.2001.

"Wolframs Überdruß an der ritterlichen Schlachten-Welt ist verdinglicht in Baum—Modellen, deren Stämme sich in einem Wald von Lanzen auflösen," *Schwäbische Donauzeitung*, 07.01.1995.

Index

adaptation xxiii, xxv, xxx–xxxii, 9, 13, 15, 64, 71, 73–4, 101, 105
    after 1750 in text and image 55–65
    Hutcheon's concept 41, 136, 155, 159
    medieval narratives 33, 35–40
    memory and 159–60
    Nibelungenlied (Lay of the Nibelungs) 43, 52–3, 128–9, 132, 139, 155
    palimpsests 40–2, 111, 119
    Wolfram von Eschenbach 53–4, 137, 140, 150, 155–6
Adorf, Mario 134
Albrecht von Scharfenberg
    Jüngerer Titurel 53–4
Andreasstift (Stadtmuseum Worms) 146, 152
Aronstein, Susan 160
Arthur (King)/Arthurian 10, 33–4, 37, 48, 60, 64, 79–80, 85
    romance xxx, 33–5, 54, 62, 73, 79
    tales 62–3
    modern receptions 61–2
Assmann, Aleida xxxiii, 168
Asterix 128
Augustine
    Confessions 1
    on time and memory 2
Austrian national library 22–3

Badisches Landesmuseum (state museum of Baden-Württemberg) 24
Bakhtin, Mikhail xxiii
    on textual narratives 41, 133, 174–5 n.21
Bhabha, Homi 42, xxviii
    the join, concept of 29–30, 64–5
    on the power of literature 156
Book of the Anonymous Poet 53, 106, 112, 183 n.31, 185 n.60
Bond, James 116, 118, 120, 123, 132
Boston CyberArts festival 130
Boym, Svetlana
    Future of Nostalgia 18
    on heritage 162
    nostalgia, categories 18
Brentano, Clemens 117–18
Brunner, Horst 136–7, 202 n.8, 202 n.14

Carruthers, Mary, *The Book of Memory* 8, 176 n.5
Chretien de Troyes 80
    Perceval 35, 48, 54
Cold War 21, 149, 180 n.65
collective memory 2, 21, 78, 145, 169
Crooke, Elizabeth 135, 150, 201 n.2
cultural memory 17–18, 105, 140, 156, 160, 170–1

D'Arcens, Louise 162, 178 n.40
    Cambridge Companion to Medievalism 13
    on medieval tourism 162
Dell, Helen 157–8
Dietrich von Bern 4
Dinshaw, Carolyn 18, 158
    How Soon is Now 13, 163, 178 n.30
Dionne, Craig 180 n.57
    Postmedieval 19
Disney, Walt 26, 113, 116–20, 125
    Sleeping Beauty 113, 118–19, 125
Dorst, Tankred 62

Eco, Umberto 12, 180 n.59
    Travels in Hyperreality 1, 176 n.2
Elliott, Andrew 202 n.10
    Medievalism, Politics, and Mass Media: Appropriating the Middle Ages in the Twenty-first Century 14
Erll, Astrid 7, 14
    on cultural memory 159

Fenske, Michaela 168–9, 207 n.43
Finke, Laurie, *King Arthur and the Myth of History* 60, 187 n.92
First World War 3, 59, 117, 147, 154

Fouqué, Friedrich de la Motte, *Der Krieg der Sänger auf der Wartburg* xxiii
Freyer, Achim, *Ring* 154

Gallé, Volker xxvi–xxvii, 107, 120, 175 n.30
Geidner, Oskar xxii, 93, 99
　Wolframs-Eschenbach. Der Deutsche Orden baut eine Stadt xx
Gentry, Francis xiii, 55, 136
Geoffrey of Monmouth xxx
German/Germany. *See also Mittelalterrezeption*
　collective memory 21
　literary archives 22
　medievalism 15
　Middle Ages 16, 55, 57, 140, 152, 160
　Nazi period 3, 15, 21, 60–1, 107, 117–19, 132, 167
　postmodern culture.16
　reunification ix, xi, 21, 167–9
　theoretical perspectives.16
Gesamtkunstwerk 135, 152, 194 n.67, 201 n.1
Goethe Institutes (Paris and Boston) 130
Gottfried von Strassburg
　Dichterexkurs of *Tristan* 47, 70
　Tristan 47
Graml, Gundolf, on display of identity 163, 206 n.24
　Sound of Music 163
Grimm brothers (Jacob and Wilhelm Grimm) 3, 22, 56
　Jacob Grimm 3, 56
　Kinder- und Hausmärchen (*Children's and Household Tales*) 25
　Wilhelm Grimm 25, 56
Grimmwelt museum (Kassel) xxx, 22, 25–6
Groebner, Valentin 16, 55–6, 160, 179 n.45
Gunzenhausen city museum 144–6
Gustafson, Brigitte 165, 206 n.15

Hagen von Tronje 4, 116–19, 130
　Hagenstrasse 147
　Monument 147
Handke, Peter 23, 62
Hansen, Eric xix, xvii, 96
　Die Nibelungenreise xv, 173 n.3
Harbou, Thea von 58–9, 116, 118, 187 n.90

Hartmann von Aue vii, 9–11, 33–4, 38, 40, 47, 53
　Erec 33
　Iwein 9–10, 35–7, 39, 64, 164, xxx
　on process of memory 11–12
Hauff, Wilhelm, *Das kalte Herz* (The Cold Heart) 24
Heiland, Gunter 108, 196 n.9
Heimatmuseum viii, xvii, xxxiii, 98, 136, 144, 151
Hein, Christoph, *Ritter der Tafelrunde* 62
Heine, Heinrich 118
heritage xviii, xx, xxv, xxvii–xxxiv, 6, 12–13, 17, 28, 55, 59, 67, 107, 133–6, 140, 143–4, 149–51, 155–6, 158–9
　medievalism and 162–4
　musealization 164–8
　role in nostalgia 19–20
　role of place 19–21
Herweg, Mathias 16, 179 n.43
Heyl, Cornelius 147
Hoffmann, E.T.A. *Der Krieg der Sänger* xxiii
Hölderlin, Friedrich 118
Hutcheon, Linda
　adaptations, definition 41
　"palimpsestic intertextuality" concept 104–5
　A Theory of Adaptation 155, 159

Iwein xxx, 9–12, 17, 35–7, 39, 64, 164
　process of memory 36–7
　visualization of medieval spaces 37–40

Jauß, Hans Robert 157
　Alterität and Modernität der mittelalterlichen Literatur 170
　Rezeptionsgeschichte 15
Jewish Museum (Worms) 146, 204 n.41
Joy, Eileen, *Postmedieval* 19
Jud Süss (film) 153

Kenobi, Obi-Wan 120
Keppler-Tasaki, Stefan 16, 179 n.43
Kirshenblatt-Gimblett, Barbara 134, 176 n.38, 204 n.34
　concept of display 162

Die Klage or the Lament 42, 52
Koshar, Rudy 7, 21, 61, 176 n.37, 180 n.65
Kriemhild xxvii, 4, 27, 43–4, 52
   as princess 116, 118
   quarreling queens (Nettlich) 157
Kummer, Eberhard 4, 12

Lachmann, Karl xxiv, 55, 95
Lang, Fritz 36, 57, 112, 116, 118, 122
   Die Nibelungen (films) 58–9, 154
   Kriemhild's Revenge 42, 58–9
   Siegfried (film) 42, 58–9, 114
   storytelling 116
literary museums. *See also* specific museums
   categories 22
   contexts and comparisons 21–8
literary reception and adaptation 42, 159. *See also* medieval literature
literature archives (*Deutsches Literaturarchiv*) 22
Literaturmuseum der Moderne (Marbach) xxx, 22
Literaturmuseum der österreichischen Nationalbibliothek 22
   Grillparzer house (central Vienna) 22
Literaturmuseum Nibelungen(h)ort. *See* Siegfried Museum in Xanten
Literaturmuseum Strauhof 23
Luther, Martin 107, 143

Macdonald, Sharon
   on heritage 20–1, 159–60, 165, 167–8, 171
   on memorylands of Europe xv, xxv, 7, 144, 175 n.33
   on musealization of everyday life xxvi, 145, 149
   presencing the past 11, 13, 17, 105, 147, 177 n.21
   role of place in nostalgia 19–20
Markgrafen Museum in Ansbach 144–5
Matthews, David
   Medievalism: A Critical History 13
   working model of medievalism 14
Maximilian I xxix
Maximilian II xx–xxii
medievalism xvii–xviii, xx, xxix–xxxii, xxxiv, 41–2, 56–8, 60–1, 64, 70–1, 100–1, 114, 136, 139, 154–8, 160–4, 170–2. *See also* German/Germany
   Anglo-American context 15–16, 63
   cycle of regeneration 12
   definitions 13–15
   heritage and 162–4
   Mittelalterrezeption 15–17
   and memory 1–2, 160–2
   Nazis 3, 15, 21, 60–1, 107, 117–19, 132, 167
   nostalgia 6, 17–21, 57, 60, 63, 158, 162, 168
   presencing the medieval past 2, 6–8, 11–13, 17, 19–20, 28, 135, 147, 151, 156, 161–2, 164, 170
   Workman's definition 13–15
medieval literature
   adaptations after 1750 in text and image 55–65
   adaptations until around 1600 52–4
   Nazi misappropriation of German 15
   source material and themes 42–3
medieval narratives xxviii, xxx, xxxii, 20
   adaptation 35, 64
   modern visitors 71, 170
   museum interpretations 136
   presencing the past 33–6, 155
medieval past xxiii, xxix. *See also* medieval literature
   contemporary present 6
   global audience 160–3, 167
   nostalgia 17–18, 20–1
   process of presencing 2, 12–13, 15, 17
memory xviii, xxii–xxiii, xxv–xxvi, xxviii–xxxiv
   adaptation and 156, 158–9
   collective 2, 21, 78, 145, 169
   cultural 17–18, 105, 140, 156, 160, 170–1
   heritage 6, 12–13, 17, 19–21, 28
   medievalism and 160–2
   past presencing 6, 8–9, 11–21, 25
   performative process 164
memorylands xxv, xxxiii–xxxiv, 7–8, 134, 163, 167
Merkendorf museum 144–6
Mertens, Volker 54

Middle Ages
    medievalisms 13–15
    time travel phenomenon 124, 169
Mittelalterrezeption viii
    medievalisms 15–16
    reception history
        (Rezeptionsgeschichte) 15, 96, 101,
        119
    monument xvi–xx, xxii–xxix, 9, 17, 28,
        41, 54–5, 69, 71, 74, 107, 110, 119,
        140, 143, 147, 150
Moore, Roger 120, 132
Morrison, Toni, Beloved 30, 65
Müller, Ulrich 55, 61, 62, 97, 136
    The Arthur of the Germans 97,
    186 n.69
Muschg, Adolf 100, 135
    Der rote Ritter (The Red Knight) xxv
    Rede für Wolframs Eschenbach xv
musealization xxvi, xxxiv, 7, 20, 145, 149,
    158, 164–5
museums. See also adaptation; memory;
    specific museums
    historical roots 19–21
    literary 21–8
    role in nostalgia 19
Museum Strauhof 22
Museum Wolfram von Eschenbach
    adaptation process 71, 74, 101, 136–7
    architecture 69, 88
    chivalry's dangerous games 138–40
    contemporary audiences/visitors 161,
        170
    creative designs 68–70, 140
    exterior-entrance 68
    guide book 70
    interactions of place and memory
        170–1
    interior, room organization 71–96
    literary interpretation and reception
        68–70, 75, 135–7, 140–1, 164–8
    major issues 154
    organization of Rooms 71–3
        Room I 71
        Room II 71, 76–9
        Room III-V 71, 73, 79–87, 98
        Room VI 71, 87–90
        Room VII 71, 90–1
        Room VIII 71, 92–4, 98

        Rooms IX 71, 95–6
        Room X 71, 95–6
    past presencing 71, 136–7
    source texts
        dawn-song (Tagelied) 47, 90–1
        Parzival 42, 47–8, 70–1, 73, 76–8
        Titurel 42, 47, 49–50, 73
        Willehalm 47–51, 73, 77, 92–4
    Wolfram's texts, interpretation 68–71

national literatures 23–4
national museums 22, 162
National Socialism 20, 57, 59, 111–23,
    139, 150, 154–5
    Goebbels and propaganda 122, 123
Nazi medievalism 3, 15, 21, 60–1, 107,
    117–19, 132, 167
Nibelungenlied (Lay of the Nibelungs).
    See also Lang, Fritz; Wagner,
    Richard
    audience, thirteenth and twentieth
        centuries 5, 27
    cultural context 43
    first stanza of the C version 2–3, 5, 12,
        52 Friedrich von der Hagen 3, 43
    as German Iliad 3, 55
    later versions 44
    Middle High German 3–4, 59, 129,
        133, 140
    modern German 4, 30, 55, 104, 121, 125
    myriad forms 5–6
    national sentiment 59–60
    older sources 35
    past and present 9
    performance by Eberhard Kummer
        4, 12
    reception history 27–8, 52
    summary of plots/story's evolution
        43–6, 119–20, 122
    Verhoeven film Das schreckliche
        Mädchen 3
Nibelung Festival (Nibelungen Festspiele)
    119, 203 n.23
Nibelung Museum
    adaptation process 105, 111, 119–20,
        128, 136–9
    chivalry's dangerous games 138–40
    contemporary audiences/visitors 161,
        170

criticisms 108
display of narrative 109
exterior 106
Harry Potter 131
Hörturm 5, 28, 110, 124–9
interactions of place and memory 170–1
interior 111
literary interpretation and reception 135–7, 164–8
Lord of the Rings 131
major issues 152–3
medieval city wall 105–8
Mythenlabor 110, 129–33
Mythenmaschine (machinery of myth) 104–5, 110–11, 133–4, 154
palimpsests of older narratives 59–63
past presencing 28, 105, 137, 162
Schatzkammer installation 130–1
Sehturm 110–23, 125, 127–30, 132, 141–2, 153, 166
source texts 42–3
    Book of the Anonymous Poet 53, 106, 112
    Die Klage, or the *Lament* 42, 52
    Prose Edda 42, 45
    Rose Garden (*Rosengarten*) 42, 52–3
    Tale of Siegfried and the Skin of Horn (*Der Hurnen Seyfrit*) 52–3
textual interpretation 141–2
use of technology 110, 138
Wehrgang (Time travel) 124
Wolfram von Eschenbach museum comparison with 103–4, 109
nostalgia xxiii xxix, xxxiv, 6, 17–21, 57, 60, 63, 158, 162, 168
    definition 18
    medieval past 17–19
    role of place 19–21

palimpsest xviii, xxiii–xxv, xxix, 4, 6–7, 19, 29, 33, 40–2, 57, 74, 127, 136, 138, 159
    definition of adaptations 40–1
    intertextual 150, 160
Parzival xix, xvii, xx, xxiii, xxiv, xxv, xxxi, xxxiii, 33–6, 42–4, 47–51, 53–5, 57, 62, 67, 70–1, 73, 76–80, 82–90, 92, 94–5, 97, 127–8, 137–8, 143, 150
    adaptations after 1750 55
    story 48–9
past presencing xxv–xxvi, xxviii–xxix, xxxi–xxxii
    memory 6, 8–9, 11–21, 25, 28, 64, 71, 105, 137, 147, 149, 162, 170
    Nibelung Museum 28, 105, 137, 162
    Wolfram von Eschenbach museum 71, 136–7
presence of the past 2–6
    memory 7–12
Prose Edda 42, 45
Pugh, Tison 12, 14, 16, 177 n.22
    on magic of the Middle Ages 160

reception 22, 27, 28, 34, 36, 40, 42, 45, 55, 62, 97, 109, 149 *See also Mittelalterrezeption*
    and adaptation 150, 159
    models of 136
    museum comparison 137, 141, 142
Reformation, the 107, 155
regional museums 22
Remensnyder, Amy 8, 183 n.21
Riedel, Eduard von xix
Rodenegg murals vi, xxx, 9, 35, 37–40, 64, 164
romance *See* Arthur (King)/Arthurian
Romanesque architecture 4, 107
Romanticism 56–7, 114, 117, 150, 154
Rose Garden (*Rosengarten*) 42, 52–3

Said, Edward 148
Sanders, Julie 155, 205 n.42
Schiller, Friedrich xxii, 22
    Schiller National-Museum 22
Schirok, Bernd 47, 184 nn.36–8
Schloss Neuenbürg museum 24
Schmalkalden murals xxx, 35, 37, 39–40, 64
Schneider, Romy 113, 117, 132
Second World War 7, 15, 21, 60, 63, 65, 92, 123, 125, 154, 203 n.22
Seitz, Anton xx
Seitz, Erwin xx–xxi
shared experience 2, 150, 156

Shichtman, Martin, *King Arthur and the Myth of History* 60, 187 n.92
Simrock, Karl xxiv, 55
Skywalker, Luke 113, 116, 120, 123, 125, 199 n.49

Tale of Siegfried and the Skin of Horn (*Der Hurnen Seyfrit*) 52–3
Teutonic Order xx–xxi, 87, 99
Titurel xxxi, 34, 36, 42, 53–4, 70–1, 73, 81, 87–91, 95, 137
  story 47–50
Trigg, Stephanie 156, 162–3
  on medieval tourism 162

UNESCO 25, 164
Utz, Richard 14
  Medievalism: A Manifesto 13

Verhoeven, Michael, *Das schreckliche Mädchen* (film) 3
visualization 96, 100
Völker, Susanne (*See also* Grimmwelt) 26

Wagner, Richard
  Der Ring des Nibelungen 58
  Nibelungenlied's reception history 56–8
  operas xxiv, xxxi, 36, 57, 119, 122
  Ring 57–8, 118, 154
  Tannhäuser xxiii, 57
  visions of Middle Ages 16
Wandhoff, Haiko 40, 182 n.12
Wartburg xix, xxiii, xxix, 21, 47, 54, 57, 67, 107
Weisl, Angela Jane 12, 14, 16, 18
  magic of the Middle Ages 160
  on medievalist performance 18
Werben (town), Colonial Williamsburg 168
Willehalm xxxi, 36, 42, 44, 47–8, 53, 70–1, 73, 76–8, 81–2, 92–4, 137–8, 150
  adaptations after 1750 55
  story 50–1

Wolfram Monument xvi, xviii, xxii–xxiii, xxix, xxv–xxvi, 9, 28, 41, 54–5, 71, 140, 147, 150
Wolframs-Eschenbach (town)
  change of name 67, 71, 143
  comparison with Worms (town) 154–6
  land and cityscape 143–6, 171
  monuments and heritage 149–52
  tourist office 99
Wolfram von Eschenbach (poet). *See also specific works*
  biography 46
  creative period 47
  major works 47
  popularity in the Middle Ages 53–4
  tomb xxvii
Wolfram von Eschenbach (museum). *See* Museum Wolfram von Eschenbach
Wollenberg, Daniel, *Medieval Imagery in Today's Politics* 14
Workman, Leslie, *Studies in Medievalism* 13
Worms City Museum (Stadtmuseum Worms) 144, 146, 154
Worms (town). *See also* Nibelung Museum
  comparison with Wolframs Eschenbach 154–6
  land and cityscape 146–9, 171
  medieval stories and histories 106–9
  monuments and heritage 149–52
Wunderlich, Werner, *The Arthur of the Germans* 97, 186 n.69

Xanten xxx, 22, 26, 27
  actual narrative of the *Nibelungenlied* 137
  Siegfried Museum (Xanten) 22, 26–8

Young, Helen 56

Zentrum für Kunst und Medientechnologie (ZKM) 131